THE VERY, VERY RICH*

AND HOW THEY GOT THAT WAY

MAX GUNTHER

> *YOU'RE NOT VERY, VERY RICH UNTIL YOU HAVE MADE YOUR FIRST ONE HUNDRED MILLION DOLLARS

PLAYBOY PRESS PAPERBACKS

S0-BRE-460

THE VERY, VERY RICH AND HOW THEY GOT THAT WAY

Copyright © 1972 by Max Gunther. All rights reserved. No part of this book may be reproduced, stored in a retrieval system or transmitted in any form by an electronic, mechanical, photocopying, recording means or otherwise without prior written permission of the author.

Published simultaneously in the United States and Canada by Playboy Press Paperbacks, New York, New York. Printed in the United States of America. Playboy Press hardcover edition published 1972.

Books are available at quantity discounts for promotional and industrial use. For further information, write our sales promotion agency: Ventura Associates, 40 East 49th Street, New York, New York 10017.

ISBN: 0-872-16645-7

First printing January 1973.
Third printing November 1979.

Also by Max Gunther

The Split-Level Trap (with Dr. Richard Gordon)
The Weekenders
Writing the Modern Magazine Article
Casebook of a Crime Psychiatrist (with Dr. James Brussel)
Wall Street and Witchcraft

Contents

1

The Golden Gallery

Come with me now, ye seekers, and stand before this great gilded door. In a while we will turn the jeweled key and go in. Step softly. Speak in whispers. You in the back, there, get rid of that damned beer can. We are about to enter the presence of Wealth.

Did I pronounce it with an awestruck capital *W?* I intended to. This is not ordinary wealth we are about to study, not the mere upper crust, not even the tribe of mere millionaires. No, we are about to see Wealth in its most exaggerated—some would say gorgeous, some would say disgusting—manifestations. The very poorest individuals we'll meet will have net assets of $100 million or not far below, and some will have more than a billion.

What is the purpose of our visit to this golden gallery? Why, you ask, should we study these, the immoderately rich?

It is a sharp question, and we must acknowledge from the start that some will say there is no sensible answer. Our quest, we will be told, is foolish. A historical record stretching back some 2500 years reveals that wealth and seekers after wealth and seekers after the seekers (in which final category we now find ourselves) have all been steadfastly jeered at in every clime and culture. Wealth, the 2500-year-old platitude goes, is only an ephemeral thing and may not even be real at all. A man is better advised to spend his life in quest of something else: truth, perhaps, or beauty, but not money. Money isn't worth the seeking.

Nobody knows who first noted that you can't take it with you—probably a Cro-Magnon man bellyaching about his neighbor's flashy new leopard skin. The Greek philosopher Theognis was one of the first to put the sour old cliché in writing. "No one goes to heaven with all his immense wealth," Theognis grumped in the Fifth or Sixth Century B.C. Very probably not a single year has since gone by in which some man of intellectual stature has not reiterated the thought in hopes of cooling off whatever rat race was then afoot. Cicero said it in materialistic Rome. Shakespeare said it to the earthy Elizabethans, while, across the English Channel, Rembrandt, himself a moderately rich man, was saying it to the boom-maddened Dutch. Shelley said it in reference to a departed king named Ozymandias. Thoreau said it at Walden. It would probably be a safe bet that at least 100,000 novels published in the 20th Century have said it in one way or another. The Bible says it not once but many times.

Every so often, however, a refreshing new intellect comes around and unsays it. One such was Jesse Livermore, a famous stock-market speculator who flourished on Wall Street in the first half of this century. "It's true you can't take it with you," said Livermore one day, contemplating a large capital gain he had just scored, "but you can sure as hell use it until you go."

Right on, dear old Jesse. It will be assumed that all visitors to this gallery share Livermore's view or at least are willing to suspend judgment about it. Those who think Livermore wrong are, of course, welcome to come in and browse, but they will find nobody here willing to debate with them. The argument for and against wealth is a proper subject for other times and places, but not now and not here.

With that prickly subject neatly sidestepped, let's now consider what we stand to gain from our visit. For one thing, we stand to be entertained. The very, very rich are an un-usual and fascinating group—obviously different from you and me, as F. Scott Fitzgerald pointed out, yet not so very different that we can't see our own humanity reflected in their faces. Their stories are stories of ordinary human beings raised to stunning magnitude by forces from within and without. Each is a man who took his material environment as he found it and not only figured out how to survive in it, not only rose above it, but conquered it absolutely.

In a sense these are fairy tales. Each starts with a ragged hero pursuing some risky course, going out alone to fight giants. Each ends with the hero sitting on a bag of gold, grinning. But there is one notable difference: The reader of a fairy tale cannot hope any such adventure will ever happen to him. The reader of these rich men's tales may nurture this hope—in fact, is cordially invited to do so.

Which brings up the second good reason for our visit to the gallery: The lives of the rich men gathered here are highly instructive.

With a few exceptions, which will be justified when the time comes, all the venturers you'll meet here started from the bottom. We have categorically excluded all holders of great inherited wealth: Rockefellers, Mellons, Fords. Each of our men started as nobody in particular: an ordinary man like you or me, drifting on the great economic tides of our times with millions of other ordinary men. Some were plain middle-class salary earners; some started even lower, in conditions of actual poverty. Each, by using his own brain and backbone, rose to become one of the mighty.

By watching how they did it, you can (if you wish) think about how you will do it. The gallery is organized by the various routes these men took to the top. One man played the stock market, another developed a technological innovation, and so on. One or more of the routes may attract you by reason of temperament or past experience. Pick your route, study the man who took it to its end, and then . . . well, the rest will be up to you.

You'll note that no route is easy, especially in the beginning. The first few steps are always highly risky. Every one of these rich men—*every* one—had to start by turning his back on safety and security. It is patently impossible to get rich by sticking with a salaried job. You can hope for slightly more wealth by selling a professional skill on a free-lance basis—by becoming a famous actor, surgeon, novelist—but even then your chances of becoming a hundred-millionaire or even a ten-millionaire are so close to zero that the difference isn't worth considering. To make the big money you must take the big risks. Every one of the very, very rich, as you'll see, had to be willing at some early stage to put himself in a highly vulnerable position—a position from which he could go either straight up to wealth or swiftly down to bankruptcy.

It should be pointed out that these high-stakes games produce losers as well as winners. We have collected only the winners here. Nobody knows the losers' names. It is interesting to speculate about the reasons for winning and losing, why one man goes up while another man, starting out on the same route in substantially the same way, goes down. Character has something to do with it, and so does plain luck. We will study both these phenomena in the course of our visit.

It should also be pointed out that the size of the pot raked in by each winner is partly a matter of conjecture—even, sometimes, to the winner himself. J. Paul Getty, one of the very richest of the rich, has said several times in response to reporters' questions that he honestly doesn't know just how much he is worth. If you own a million shares of stock, the value of your holding can rise or fall by a million dollars in a single day. This makes an exact assessment difficult even in cases where the stock has a known market value. If the stock isn't publicly traded, the difficulty is multiplied.

Howard Hughes, to take just one example, is sole owner of the very profitable Hughes Tool Company. There is no public market for the stock of this company, and therefore it is impossible to say with precision what Hughes's holding is worth. The only way to arrive at a guess is to look at the company's sales, earnings and assets—but these are also matters of conjecture, for a privately owned company isn't required to publish such figures, and Hughes Tool, in fact, doesn't. Thus, you must be satisfied with an estimate based on an estimate—a leaky piece of arithmetic at best. You estimate how the company performs in terms of profitability, and then you estimate how the stock market might evaluate that performance if the company's common shares were ever offered for public trading. The resulting rickety figure is your guess as to your rich man's pile.

The rich man himself could offer some enlightenment, but the chances are he won't—even if, unlike Getty, he knows the answer. Only a few of the very wealthy have publicly stated their net worth. For legal and tax reasons, and because of a highly developed sense of personal privacy that seems characteristic of the very, very rich, most tend to keep their mouths shut on this subject.

For more than a century the fortunes of the rich in America have been the focus of a national guessing game. Every so often somebody comes up with a new set of guesses, only to be shot down by somebody else.

Fortune magazine, for instance, occasionally collects what it believes to be a fairly complete list of the country's richest men and women. Back in 1957 the magazine said it could identify 155 Americans with piles of $50 million or more. In 1968, with fortunes swollen by continuing prosperity and inflation, *Fortune* raised the lower limit to $100 million and said it had found 153 people on or above that line. (*Fortune* called them "centimillionaires." Somehow the word makes me think of rich centipedes. Trusting *Fortune* won't mind, I'll find other words.)

In publishing both lists, *Fortune* frankly admitted the likelihood that some important names had been omitted. "Some forms of wealth," the magazine said, ". . . absolutely defy detection." *Fortune* also admitted it might be wrong in some of its estimates about people on the lists. Some might be far poorer than estimated, some far richer.

But it did the magazine no good to display such charming modesty. Ferdinand Lundberg, a lifelong student of the wealthy, sailed into *Fortune* with huge and predatory delight in his odd 1968 book, *The Rich and the Super-Rich*. Many of the magazine's 1957 wealth estimates, he said, were grossly wrong. He presented estimates of his own, the majority lower than *Fortune*'s. He also dredged up some new names that hadn't appeared on the magazine's list.

My own very rough calculations about some of the disputed piles suggest to me that *Fortune* was often closer to the mark than Lundberg. It seems worth recognizing that Lundberg is a lone scholar, while *Fortune* has a large staff of highly trained reporters and other financial diggers—people with the time and expense money to poke into probate records, proxy statements, company earnings reports, and the like. Moreover, Lundberg, brilliant scholar though he is, seems to labor sometimes under the weight of a heavy set of biases. He doesn't like the rich very much, says they manipulate the country and all that. His political viewpoint is decidedly not conservative. He spends many pages of his book enthusiastically roasting poor old William F. Buckley, Jr., and the *National Review*. As for *Fortune*, key spokesman of management and hence of the rich, Lundberg obviously doesn't keep that fat, square, money-loving journal on his bedside table to sweeten his night's dreams. In charging *Fortune* with error, he often seems motivated mainly by the sheer pleasure of quarreling with the magazine.

The wealth estimates presented here in our gallery cannot lay claim to being more accurate than *Fortune*'s, Lundberg's or anybody else's. They must be taken as simply one more set of estimates—with which the next estimator, as usual, is privileged to argue. Nor does our list lay any kind of claim to completeness. Omitted, of course, are all holders of large inherited wealth—who made up more than half of *Fortune*'s 1968 list. Others have been omitted for random reasons. In some cases, for instance, two or more men might have had substantially similar careers. The man among them whose career seemed the most instructive or dramatic or just plain interesting has been included; the rest must await other biographers.

It is possible, even likely, that some observers of the current business scene will quarrel with the cast of characters here assembled. "Why did you pick X instead of Y?" they'll ask. "X may have a hundred million but Y has *two* hundred million." The answer in all cases will be that sheer money hasn't been the only criterion for including or excluding any given fat cat. Money is the main criterion but not always the overriding one. Maybe X is more willing to talk to reporters than Y. Maybe X is simply a more likable fellow.

And, in any case, can it really make a difference whether a man has $100 million or $200 million? Either way, his wealth is so huge as nearly to surpass understanding. One hundred million dollars are more dollars than the mind can comfortably conceive. Laid end to end, they would stretch from here to—well, a hell of a long way. Piled up, they would surely topple over. If you had a salary of $200,000 a year, cheated on your income tax and managed to salt away half, it would take you 1000 years to accumulate $100 million. If you didn't cheat and managed to save half the after-tax take-home, it would take you at least 4000 years. (As we've noted, you can't get rich on a salary.) The sum of $100 million is so colossal that the income it would produce, if it were locked away in a savings bank at a modest five-percent annual interest, would be enough to support 100 ordinary men like you and me in a style most of us would consider quite comfortable. The income would be five million dollars. If 100 of us owned joint title to that $100 million in a savings bank, we could each draw 50 grand a year for all eternity, without ever touching a dime of the capital.

Yes, $100 million is a hard sum to visualize. But the fact remains that there are men alive today—not gods but plain men, made of bone and brain presumably no better in basic quality than yours or mine—who have each accumulated that much money in less than one adult lifetime.

Let's see how on earth they did it. Welcome to the gallery of the very, very rich.

2

From Croesus to Crassus to Cornfeld

The men in this gallery are all living. They are contemporaries of ours. They made their colossal fortunes in our own economic era or in recently phased-out eras that were not grossly different from our own. Each took the economic environment as it existed in his day, and instead of letting it walk on him as most of us do, he grabbed it by the neck and beat it into submission.

The supremely wealthy have always done that and always will. No matter what the environment was like, some men have figured out how to beat it. There is, it turns out, always a way.

This optimistic statement seems worth enlarging. In every era, including our own, people have tended to believe that the days of great wealth-gathering opportunity are over. The era just past has almost always looked better. Today people complain that high taxes, high prices, high labor costs and other problems prevent them from getting rich, and they look back sadly to the time when Andrew Carnegie could collect a personal income of $30 million a year without paying a dime of income tax, and they figure the good old days are finished and why try anymore? And yet we have before us the spectacle of such a man as Jean Paul Getty (chapter 9), who amassed a fortune of about a billion dollars in our own era, paying the full legal tax bite all the way. Getty tartly addressed himself to the point a few years ago. To say that the modern era is hopeless from the viewpoint of wealth gathering, wrote Getty, "is only an excuse for not trying."

It is quite probable that, when the first nomadic tribes settled down to cultivate farms at the dawn of human history, there were wandering hunters who went around grumping that the world was now all staked out and the hell with it. It is equally probable that people in the 21st Century will gloomily contemplate whatever economic problems beset them and will say, "Nope, you can't make it anymore today. If only we were back in the 1970s. . . ."

Let's see what kinds of environment men have beaten in the past. Later in the book (chapter 24) we'll speculate about possible environments of the future.

It must be admitted that through most of recorded history, up until the late-16th and the 17th centuries, the great mass of ordinary men apparently had small hope of becoming really rich. Each man worked alone on his farm or at his craft or trade. Since there was a physical limit to the amount of work one man could turn out, there was an absolute limit to his wealth. The modern corporation hadn't been invented, nor had machines that could dramatically speed up the work. There was no commonly available way to make a business grow cumulatively—that is, to set it up so that each year's profits could be used to expand the business and produce still bigger profits the year after. Until the 17th Century most men were in roughly the position of the modern wage or salary earner, who can't multiply himself cumulatively and is limited by the ironbound and immutable fact that there are only 24 hours in his day. The only thing between him and starvation is the work he personally can put out.

Despite these problems, some clever and aggressive families took power into their hands and became tribal chiefs, barons, kings and queens. They, like modern tycoons, were able to build fortunes through the use of other people's work and money. This was universally acknowledged to be the surest way to get rich. In fairy tales, myths and dramas written before 1600, if the plot calls for a rich man, he is almost invariably portrayed as a king or prince. Many of the Grimm brothers' mercenary tales end with the deadbeat hero marrying a princess—the ancient version of marrying the boss's daughter. The two most famous rich men of ancient times were Croesus and Midas, both kings. (Croesus was real; Midas was a mythological fiction.) Both their names are embedded in most of the Western world's languages as clichés describing great wealth.

There were some common men who got uncommonly

rich, of course. Generally this happened when, through some lucky series of circumstances, a commoner became friendly with the ruling powers and was granted certain business favors or outright cash gifts. Such a man was Marcus Licinius Crassus, who flourished in Rome during the First Century B.C. His name isn't the source of our word *crass*, but it might as well be. Crassus did some favors for the dictator Sulla and was rewarded by being given first option to buy certain confiscated lands at ridiculously low prices. Not only that, Sulla also loaned Crassus money from the Roman treasury with which to buy the lands. Crassus borrowed, bought the lands, sold them at high prices, paid off the loan, used the profits to buy more confiscated lands (some of which were confiscated especially for his benefit), repeated the process and thus became one of history's most famous and successful real-estate speculators. In Rome they called him "Dives"—"The Rich."

But men like Crassus were exceptions. The very fact that history has bothered to remember his name and accomplishments indicates how unusual he was. In terms of modern spending power (a highly unreliable and even ridiculous comparison, but it's the only comparison we've got) his wealth was probably in the general neighborhood of one to five million dollars. That isn't enough money to put a man in history books today. But it certainly was in Crassus's day, and it remained so for 1700 years longer.

Sometime in the 16th Century the first rudimentary bank-like enterprises began to appear, and a few lucky citizens got rich by this route. Notable among these was an energetic German family named Fugger. The founding father was a weaver, poor most of his life. His sons and grandsons stuck together as a family company, expanded into various kinds of merchandising and, by around 1500, had accumulated so much capital among them that they began to earn income by lending the money at interest to various governments and noble families. By the end of the 16th Century the Fuggers' banks were so wealthy and powerful that at least three nations gave them official permission to coin and issue money.

Like Crassus, the Fuggers were financial freaks in their day. It wasn't usual for ordinary men to rise to such wealth. But in the 17th Century the average man's chances abruptly began to look better.

The Industrial Revolution is generally pegged as having started in the 18th Century, but it was the 17th Century that saw the development of financial and corporate mechanisms without which the first industrial plants could never have been built or operated. Humble citizens who got in on the ground floor of these financial developments grew rich.

Following the lead of the Fuggers and a few others, money-men in the 17th Century expanded and refined the idea of banking. They invented corporate structures resembling the publicly owned companies we know today. They designed the first workable credit system. And they set up the first full-scale, broad-based stock and commodity exchanges. This financial revolution took place mainly in England, Germany, Italy and, most notably and brilliantly, in the Netherlands.

While nobody was looking, the Netherlands had risen to become the world's wealthiest and most powerful nation. (Actually, it was less a nation than a chummy fraternity of nearly autonomous states, of which the biggest and richest was Holland. Ever since, people have been calling the whole country Holland. The tolerant Dutch long ago gave up trying to correct the mistake.) The Dutch navy had put on so much muscle that it virtually ruled the oceans, regularly and easily defeating the navies of Spain and England and France, which had each been thought invincible. Dutch land armies attempted no forays into other European countries but were capable of repelling invaders without even trying. Sometime late in the 16th Century the more ambitious and conquest-minded of Europe's rulers, notably Philip of Spain and Elizabeth of England, woke up with a start and realized that the Netherlands simply could not be taken.

Where did all this muscle come from? Money. Without actually planning it in advance, the Dutch had set up an outrageously successful new economic system in which the common man, by enriching himself, enriched his nation.

Most of Europe's rulers felt the Dutch must be mad. These "heavy fellows" and "rude mechanicals," as Elizabeth sourly called them, were trying to run a thing called a re-public. They hadn't really wanted it that way. The problem was that they couldn't find a suitable king; so they were gamely struggling along without one—temporarily, they thought at first. Their state and city governments were run by merchants and other business-oriented burghers—what we would today call middle-class citizens—and the local laws were naturally favorable to private entrepreneurship. Taxes were light. Government revenues were spent on businesslike things such as dock improvements instead of going into kings' and nobles' private coffers. There were few class or religious barriers to prevent a man from going into business. Any ragged farmer's son, any Jew fleeing from Spain or Quaker from England or Lutheran from Germany was welcome to come around, dump his money into the local economy and lose his shirt in a business venture—or make his fortune if he could.

The Dutch had always been seamen. Around 1600 they were establishing colonies and looking into business opportunities in North and South America, Africa, India and other far-off places. The opportunities looked gorgeous, and to finance the needed ships they began to develop a rudimentary stock exchange at Amsterdam. (Similar exchanges were growing up at Hamburg, London and other cities, but for sundry reasons Amsterdam's succeeded best.) If you had a little extra cash, you could go to Amsterdam and, in effect, buy stock in a shipping venture. You might buy, for instance, a 100th or 1000th interest in the fortunes of a certain ship that was to be built for a trip to India. Thus you, a common citizen, helped finance the growth of your nation. If the ship sank or simply failed to return, you lost your investment. If it returned laden with silks and spices, you got your share of the possibly huge profits, which you could then plow into some other venture. Or perhaps, before the ship returned, you might have wanted to sell your share to somebody else. You did this simply by sauntering around Amsterdam and finding a buyer among the hundreds of speculators who were always milling about or drinking in the taverns.

From these simple beginnings the Amsterdam equity market expanded to great size and complexity. By 1625 it contained most of the elements we recognize today as belonging to a full-scale stock exchange. There were rules for fair and orderly trading, there were brokers, there were provisions for various sideline techniques such as short selling, and the variety of enterprises in which you could buy stock ranged all the way from shipping to tulip farming. (You could even buy stock in some profitable Amsterdam brothels.)

Since the brokers and speculators often needed large

amounts of money, private syndicates sprang up to provide pools of risk capital. Thus some rudimentary investment-banking outfits came into being. Since nobody wanted to walk the streets carrying sacks of guilders and florins, some bankers and brokers offered special cash-storage facilities, and a kind of checking-account system evolved.

As ever more shipping ventures were launched, money began to pour into the little nation at an astonishing rate. Amsterdam became the financial capital of Europe. Government agents of all nations went there to borrow war money, buy guns and make other big-scale deals requiring large financial resources. Private entrepreneurs from as far away as Russia went there to float stock in shipping or mining ventures or to borrow development money for the first crude laborsaving machines.

As a result, the Netherlands in the early 17th Century may have been the first nation on earth in which substantial numbers of ordinary citizens got rich—in which wealth was not a startling exception to the norm. The nation's initial wealth had come from trading and shipping, but as the century progressed, the wealth came more and more from the Netherlands' central position in the flow of European money.

Some three centuries later an American named Bernard Cornfeld (chapter 7) was to remark that the best way to make money is to deal directly with money itself, rather than approach it obliquely by dealing with goods and services. It may not be the best way for everybody, but it is certainly an excellent way for some. Large numbers of 17th Century Netherlanders became millionaires.

Fairly typical of the new breed was one Roemer Visscher, an Amsterdam shipping speculator, merchant and investment banker. Visscher's fortune appears to have amounted to something like one to two million guilders. As we've noted, any attempt to translate the currency and spending power of one era into those of an entirely different era is fraught with booby traps, but as a very rough comparison, a guilder back then had about the financial oomph of ten dollars today. Thus, Visscher was worth perhaps $10 to $20 million. The most interesting fact about him is that he was not particularly interesting to his fellow Dutchmen. Nobody said "ooh" and "ah" over his wealth. He seems to have been but one of many.

Elizabeth of England called the Dutch "heavy fellows," devoid of breeding or social grace, but it should be said in passing that Visscher and his fellow burghers provided the necessary financial support for what was later labeled the golden age of Dutch art and literature. The very wealthy have always been interested in art and still are today (see, for example, the story of stock speculator Joe Hirshhorn, chapter 6). Among those who hung around Visscher's palatial home and freeloaded at his table were Rembrandt, Jan van Goyen, sometimes Peter Paul Rubens from Antwerp and the scientist Constantijn Huygens, inventor of the pendulum clock.

The 17th Century Dutch explored and developed the money-handling route to wealth, the technique of putting yourself into some money pipeline so that you can control the flow and direct some of it into your own bank account. In the next century a whole new set of possibilities opened up. The financial revolution was succeeded by the Industrial Revolution. It now became possible for an ordinary citizen to get rich by putting his money behind various technological innovations.

For many and complicated reasons the Industrial Revolution didn't quickly bring on a golden age of prosperity such as the Dutch had enjoyed 100 years before. The masses of common citizens in most nations remained trapped without money and without much hope of getting any. But some of them did make it big, and from about 1750 onward the pages of history books glitter more and more often with the names of self-made rich men. Their number increased steadily through the 19th Century, particularly in America, the new economic colossus that had suddenly and quietly arisen across the Atlantic.

Among the best-known nonkingly names in 18th and 19th Century Europe was that of Rothschild. Mayer Rothschild started as a two-bit moneylender in Frankfurt around 1765 and expanded his business step by step until he became one of Europe's most important investment bankers. He helped finance some of the first textile mills and other industrial plants in England and some of the first heavy-machinery factories in Germany. He had five sons, each of whom went to a different city to set up his own banking and venture-capital operation.

The son generally conceded to be the most brilliant of the lot was Nathan, who hung out his shingle in London. He made fortunes in the London stock market and also, later, in the young but lusty New York market. One of his secrets, in this age before telephones, was to make sure he received news of international developments before anybody else did. He had agents hanging around the fringes of the Battle of Waterloo, for instance. They brought him the news of Napoleon's defeat some six hours before the rest of London knew about it. Those six hours were enough for Nathan Rothschild. He bought up depressed currencies, government bonds and industrial shares, gleefully watched them rise in a post-Waterloo bull market and walked away with a killing. Like his father, he helped finance early industrial corporations and technical innovations, among them railroads. He was just starting to put his money into the first American railroads when he died, in 1836. The House of Rothschild stayed in business, however, and lived to help finance the adventures of such 20th Century buccaneers as Bernard Cornfeld.

It was in America, starting around 1850, that the possibilities of self-made wealth reached their gaudiest and finest flowering. Never before in all history, not even in the 17th Century Netherlands, had the average man been offered such stunning opportunities to strike it rich. All kinds of routes were opening up as the huge, empty nation expanded and matured. And all kinds of men suddenly shot from obscurity to dazzling prominence.

Jay Cooke specialized in brokerage. He came from nowhere in particular, set up a small Wall Street brokerage house in the mid-19th Century, watched it grow as the New York stock market grew. He made his big pile when President Lincoln's administration asked him to sell Civil War bonds to the public. He sent agents out to sell door-to-door, and he cheerfully and shamelessly paid newspaper editors all over the country to tout the bonds' financial and patriotic glories. He sold about two and a half billion dollars' worth. His commissions, fees and other payoffs on this one stupendous sale totaled nearly $100 million, tax-free.

Jay Gould showed up on Wall Street around 1860 with a couple hundred dollars in his pocket and rapidly parlayed the sum into a fortune. His favorite gambit was to construct phantom companies, particularly in the railroad industry. Railroad fever had seized the country, and too many railroads were being built too fast. Many small operations, poorly capitalized and badly managed, were going bankrupt. Gould would buy up a few of them for nickels and dimes, put them together to form a new railroad company with some grand-sounding name, publicize the new company, drive up its stock price and sell out, after which the rickety structure would collapse. Gould became so famous for doing this that when he went to London to propose a European railroad deal to the House of Rothschild, the Rothschilds dismissed him with a curt note: "Dear Mr. Gould: Europe is not for sale."

Junius Spencer Morgan and his son and grandson, both named John Pierpont, were investment bankers who specialized in building monopolies. Old Junius had started as a Connecticut dry-goods merchant and had put his money into banking just as the Industrial Revolution was creeping into America. Under his son and grandson the House of Morgan grew as powerful as the House of Rothschild or, centuries before, Fugger. The Morgans loved railroads. At one time they controlled the New York Central, the New Haven, the Lehigh Valley, the Erie, the Reading, the Chesapeake and Ohio, the Northern Pacific and a bundle of others—simultaneously. They organized U.S. Steel. They engineered trusts that came to own most of the anthracite and soft-coal production in the country. The story is told of John Pierpont, Jr., that when he attended a banquet in Europe around 1900, an aged countess came up to him and said in all seriousness, "I understand, Mr. Morgan, that you're the controlling stockholder of America."

The Astor family rose to prominence by a different route. John Jacob Astor was an immigrant from Germany by way of England. He landed in New York in 1784, broke and hungry. He sold musical instruments for a while, wandered around looking for a better business, ended as a fur trader in the Mohawk Valley. Business was good: He bought furs cheaply from Indian tribes, sold them at huge markups in Montreal, New York and later London. As his capital built up, he invested it in what must surely count as one of history's most glorious real-estate speculations. Even old Crassus would have been jealous. Astor bought large chunks of upper Manhattan Island, north of what were then the New York

City limits. His estate was valued at about $30 million when he died. His eldest son picked up the ball by building about 1000 houses on some of the uptown lots, and later generations of Astors cleverly traded still other uptown lots for downtown ones on which they built hotels and office buildings. The family fortune rose to the neighborhood of one billion dollars.

John D. Rockefeller got in on another kind of ground floor: that of the oil industry. He started his career as a 16-year-old clerk in a Cleveland mercantile company in the 1850s, was promoted to bookkeeper and cashier because he was good at figuring, quit the job in 1858 to go into business for himself as a kind of manufacturers' representative, selling goods on a commission basis. In the 1860s he met an expert oil refiner named Samuel Andrews who convinced him money could be made in the newborn petroleum business. (The first successful American oil well had been drilled at Titusville, Pennsylvania, in 1859.) Rockefeller's little company borrowed money and built a small refinery called the Standard Oil Works. It turned out to be highly profitable. The company then began a long and not altogether honorable career of absorbing competitors or price-squeezing them to death. When the courts dissolved Standard Oil's monopoly, in 1892, the former clerk had become, as far as is known, the world's first humbly born billionaire.

We could spend hours looking at the careers of early American tycoons. Never before in history, nowhere else in the world, had so many men of humble beginnings risen so high. Samuel Insull, Andrew Carnegie, Andrew Mellon, Joseph Kennedy—the list could go on and on. Each man found a way to wrestle his environment to the ground and end on top, riding it.

The economic environment has become a somewhat trickier opponent as the 20th Century has progressed. Corporate and personal taxes have increased enormously. Antitrust and other business laws have been tightened. The stock market's rules have been doctored so that manipulations and killings require considerably more thought, planning and patience. The country is generally less empty and open than it once was. There is less elbowroom. You can no longer buy an acre of Manhattan for a couple hundred bucks.

And yet there are still men making fortunes. How? Let's visit some of them and find out.

3

How to Get Rich Without Really Trying

It is not easy to become one of the very, very rich. We've noted and will note again that the process takes guts. It takes work. It takes self-assurance. It takes these and other attributes in almost superhuman measure. The ordinary unrich —you and I—may display such characteristics from time to time when we're feeling good, but that doesn't seem to be enough. What is required is that you step up the voltage and keep it stepped up all day, every day.

In our tour through this gallery we're going to meet men of such outrageously high voltage that we will wonder why their fuses don't blow. The average man's energy output, compared with theirs, is a mere dribble. They perform prodigious amounts of work. Their brains generate ideas in a seemingly endless stream. They leap into situations of enormous risk, unworried, supremely confident. They do things that other men wouldn't dare do or simply would never think of doing. They seem a little more than human sometimes, and this may trouble us if we harbor any hope of emulating them. We'll be tempted to think, *These are men of a special and superior breed. What they did can't be done by anybody else. Adventures like these aren't for just folks.*

William Benton:
One Hundred Fifty Million Dollars

In the light of this, it seems like a good idea to comfort ourselves right in the beginning by looking at a man who is (and we hope he will pardon the expression) just folks. He is William Benton, cofounder of the advertising agency Benton and Bowles, briefly a U.S. senator, today sole owner (with his family) of Encyclopaedia Britannica.

24

The *Saturday Review* once characterized Benton as a "smoothly whirring dynamo of a man." A dynamo, to be sure—a man of constant, high energy output. But he whirs smoothly, and that is what makes Benton a comfort to the unrich. Unlike other men we'll meet here, he doesn't quiver and crackle with frighteningly high voltage. His life has been generally calm, orderly, a smooth and patient progression from one step to the next. He took risks, certainly. He recognized early in his life that nobody ever gets rich on a salary, and he voluntarily left a secure job to step out into the scary world of the self-employed. Yet he kept his risks to a minimum. He was content to begin modestly and build slowly. Unlike other hundred-millionaires, he didn't make it by betting everything on some mad scheme that could either shoot him skyward or flatten him in an instant. He did nothing that could be called startling or unusual. He generally stayed within established patterns of business behavior, trod the trodden paths. Like a good mountain climber, he tested each new handhold before letting go of the one below.

Probably the main reason for the tranquility of Benton's climb was that he never really wanted to be one of the great rich. He was not driven by the compulsions that screeched and seethed inside most of the other men you'll meet here. He determined early in life that he would quit the business world when he reached a moderately comfortable level of wealth—and that is actually what he did, at age 35. Circumstances conspired against him, however, and he got rich after all, by accident.

He sometimes seems irritated by the fact. When *Fortune* included him without comment or qualification in its 1968 list of the nation's richest people, he howled in dismay. He argued that he *wasn't* rich. He pointed out that he lived modestly. Almost his entire worth was bound up in Britannica, he said, and since he had no intention of ever selling the company and converting his equity to spendable cash, he felt that to class him with the great rich was not only erroneous but impudent.

Fortune's editors found his argument puzzling. As one of them puts it: "You measure a man's worth by the property he owns today, not by what he intends to do with it tomorrow. Britannica is a tidy lump of wealth no matter how you look at it."

If you want to learn how to get rich, Benton may not be

the best man to emulate. Statistically, not much of a case can be made for his nonchalant, easygoing approach. When you've met all the glittering people in this gallery, you'll have to conclude that the majority are compulsives and mavericks. Some have been called mad. Some may even be clinically mad. They took hair-raising risks, did things that everybody was sure couldn't be done. When they were starting their careers, before they achieved the ultimate justification of $100 million or more, conventional businessmen labeled them unsound, unstable, unlikely to succeed. It is probable that most of them, if they were to apply today for responsible salaried jobs under assumed names, would be rejected as unfit. (One of them, in fact—Jeno Paulucci, whom you'll meet in chapter 20—once generated a little fun by applying incognito for a job in his own company. A psychological test showed him to be a miserable misfit. As he later reported in high glee, he was denied employment.)

Thus, if you hope to become a hundred-millionaire some day, it appears that you shouldn't invest too much hope in the calm, smooth, patient, conventional route of Bill Benton. Yet the fact that Benton did it this way indicates that, at least in some cases, it can be done.

Bill Benton was born in Minnesota on April 1, 1900, a child of the century. His father was a quiet, undistinguished college professor who, even if he had lived, would probably never have exerted much influence on the boy. The father died when young Bill was in his early teens. (You'll note as we go through the gallery that many of the very, very rich lost a parent at an early age. This fact gives rise to some odd psychiatric speculations, which we'll consider in a later chapter.) Bill and his younger brother, Dan, were brought up from then on by their schoolteacher mother, in conditions of genteel poverty.

The mother was quite equal to the task. She was a formidable woman of large intellect, strong will and unshakable opinions, a member of the Daughters of the American Revolution and the Women's Christian Temperance Union and other intimidating outfits. Bill Benton spent much of his time as boy and man trying to justify his thoughts and actions to her, never quite succeeding. He wrote letters to her almost daily from the time he left home to seek his fortune—and these illuminating pleas and protests, which she saved, crowd the 600 pages of Sydney Hyman's massive biography, *The Lives of William Benton*. Many of the letters, even from Benton as an adult, have the tone of a small boy trying to explain to a disapproving parent why he needs 50 cents to go to the movies.

Biographer Hyman seems baffled, as was Bill Benton himself, by the stark difference between the two brothers. Bill was a straight-A man in school. He wasn't tall or handsome or athletic, but he made up for these social drawbacks with a driving energy that pushed him to leadership in every school he attended. He was the class-president type, the kind of superbusy kid who organized fund drives and ran school dances. His mother demanded that he excel; it seemed to be as simple as that. Yet his brother, Dan, went in the opposite direction. The mother's expectations were so high that Dan apparently despaired of living up to them. He plodded through school without distinction, a classic underachiever. Sadly, he never had a chance to show what he could do as an adult, for he died of a viral infection in his teens. He might have turned out to be a late bloomer, as were some of the other men you'll meet here. But judging by the start he made, he seemed doomed as a loser.

Why does one man head for fame and fortune while his brother, reared in the same environment, goes nowhere? What spark lights so hot a fire in a man that he ends with $100 million, and where does the spark come from? Neither Benton nor his mother nor his biographer could answer those questions. We will be on the trail of this elusive spark from here to the other end of the gallery. Maybe we'll pin it down and maybe we won't. But the hunt promises to be most exhilarating.

Benton went to Yale University with scholarship aid and was graduated in 1921. This fact in itself makes him unusual, for three-fourths of the men in our gallery aren't college graduates, and half aren't even high-school graduates. But Benton was no maverick. He bought the standard advice given out to younger men by older men: If you want to succeed, get an education.

After college he sold cash registers in Utica, New York, for a while, then drifted to New York City. The advertising business attracted him in a vague way, and he landed a $25-a-week job with an agency called Lord and Thomas. He had been an aggressive kid in school, and he was an aggressive young man in business—not the kind who disrupts the established order and gets everybody mad at him, but the kind who works within the organizational structure and delicately, without damaging it, turns it to his own advantage. This technique had always carried him to the top of social structures in school, and now it sent him zigzagging upward through the ranks of Lord and Thomas. By 1925 he was in charge of a group of copywriters, some of them older than he.

He was now 25 years old, a man of medium height and slight build, with a square face and a thin, curved beak of a nose. Later in his life, when he became a U.S. senator, some who liked him called him Hawk and some who didn't called him Hook. The nose gave him a faintly predatory look.

Early in 1925 he hired a young assistant, a newly graduated Yale man named Chester Bowles. The two became close friends and within a couple of years were dreaming and talking about starting their own ad agency. The middle and late 1920s were bullish times, and there was a lot of money around and a lot of optimism in the air. Benton and Bowles probed here and there to see what clients, if any, the dreamed-of new agency could hope to capture. One possibility was General Foods, whose advertising chief had been impressed with the copywriting work both young men were doing at Lord and Thomas. The ad chief indicated that, if the new agency ever got itself born, it could count on getting at least some of General Foods' business.

The firm of Benton and Bowles got itself born on July 15, 1929, a few months short of the worst stock-market crash in history. The capitalization was a slender $18,000, with each man putting up half. Benton had managed to save only some $5000 during his salaried years at Lord and Thomas; so he couldn't immediately come up with his $9000 share of the capital. He borrowed the missing $4000 from Bowles, who was blessed with a moderately wealthy family.

General Foods, true to its promise, gave the new agency the job of advertising Hellman's mayonnaise and a jelly additive. Working out of a small, cramped New York office, the little outfit blundered bravely into the hurricane of the Great Depression. For a while it looked as though Benton and Bowles would sink from sight along with thousands of other small, leaky businesses that had been launched in the calm and friendly seas of the 1920s. But, by bailing furiously, the two men managed to keep their battered little craft afloat. They did it mainly by establishing a reputation as an agency that was ready to try novel ideas—among them the utterly goofy idea that radio was probably as good an advertising medium as magazines and newspapers.

Benton roamed around the country to convince potential clients that the sensible reaction to hard times was to buy more advertising, not less—and that, since conventional selling approaches obviously weren't prying customers loose from their money, novel approaches were the way to go. General Foods and some other companies gradually slid around to this point of view, and by the mid-1930s Benton and Bowles had about half of GF's colossal ad business, plus other lucrative accounts such as Colgate-Palmolive. For these clients Benton and Bowles launched radio shows that became famous in their day: shows such as Fred Allen's *Town Hall* and the *Maxwell House Show Boat*. It turned out, as Benton had predicted, that radio advertising had enormous power to move products. By 1935 the six-year-old agency of Benton and Bowles was rich. And the 35-year-old Bill Benton was ready to retire.

His net worth, including the estimated value of his equity in Benton and Bowles, was somewhere near one million dollars. He was a remarkably greedless man. He had no pressing desire to get any richer. Moreover, he now found himself fed up with the world of business. His youthful aggressiveness was cooling off markedly as he aged. He thought he might like to go into politics, perhaps, or education. He didn't really know what he wanted to do, but he did know he wanted to leave Madison Avenue.

And so he made a decision that is very unusual in the annals of the rich. He said, *I have enough*. And he quit.

He and the Benton and Bowles agency made a deal: The agency was to buy his stock from him in installments over a five-year period, and the price he received for each block was to be worked out by a complex formula based on the agency's earnings. Benton sold his name to the agency in perpetuity and agreed never again to enter the advertising business.

He put some of his money into the stock market and rapidly lost great chunks of it in the 1937 crash. This traumatic experience made him change course slightly. He didn't particularly want to make more money, but he didn't want to lose what he had, either. "It was obvious to him," says a friend, "that he wasn't cut out to be a stock-market player. He figured that anytime he bought a stock, some other guy was selling, and that guy might be an insider who knew more about the company than he did. What Benton wanted was a situation where he could invest his money and derive income from it but still retain some control over the situation without making a full-time job out of it."

Benton now launched himself on a crazy career of making money by mistake.

To help a friend, he put $5000 of new capital into a small shoe company that was suffering from depression problems. In ten years the value of Benton's equity soared to $125,000.

He put some money into a new company called Muzak, which was in the business of piping music over closed circuits to restaurants, office buildings and other customers. Benton started with the intention of being a one-third stockholder, with control over his investment but without day-to-day executive responsibilities. Because of a quarrel among the other owners, he ended as sole stockholder, with a total investment of about $130,000. Muzak leaped to success, and Benton, the reluctant moneymaker, eventually came out of the deal richer by some four million dollars.

And so it went. The biggest accidental bonanza of all came along in the early 1940s. This was the fabulous piece of property—fabulous today, not then—called Encyclopaedia Britannica.

This dusty old company had begun its life in Scotland, had bumbled around in England for nearly two centuries and had then been acquired by the giant American merchandising outfit, Sears, Roebuck and Company. Sears had made some money by peddling the encyclopedia in the U.S. but had not made much and was beginning to regret the whole deal. The encyclopedia was badly out of date and growing more so. Worse, it was perhaps the most monumentally boring set of books ever perpetrated. As one customer gloomily remarked, "It's a hundred-pound sleeping pill." A new and completely revised edition was called for, but Sears had no stomach for the trouble and expense that would be involved and was in no mood to gamble on the *Britannica*'s future profit potential. To Sears the encyclopedia had become nothing but a damned nuisance.

Sears's headquarters were in Chicago, and a general awareness of the *Britannica*'s problems had seeped across the campus of the University of Chicago. Some professors and others thought it might be fun to work on *Britannica* revisions. Such a project would be a proper and scholarly undertaking for a university and might also (though nobody knew exactly how) bring the university some money. But this was just faculty-party talk. The practical problems involved were huge. Around the university the *Britannica* glimmered in people's imagination like some great treasure known to have sunk somewhere beneath a mile or two of water. It was fun to dream about this treasure and speculate about its worth, but nobody was willing to go down and get it, and the consensus was that it couldn't be had.

Then Bill Benton came around. After quitting Madison Avenue, he had been offered many part-time consultant jobs by businessmen and others who had watched his rise in the ad business. One temporary post that attracted him was offered by Robert Maynard Hutchins, a Yale classmate who had become president of the University of Chicago. Hutchins wanted Benton to help jazz up the university's public image so as to attract more students and more cash. Benton, magnetized by the idea of a new career in education, took on the job.

The *Britannica* situation grabbed him as soon as he learned about it. Like everybody else, he thought it would be a good idea for the university to get involved in a major encyclopedia project. Unlike everybody else, he came up with some practical suggestions on how the deal could be swung.

He began by making a suggestion to Sears. Since the company considered *Britannica* a damned headache, why not give this headache to the university and thereby reap a juicy harvest of both tax and public-relations benefits? Sears thought this was a dandy idea. Benton then went back to the university and presented the idea to the trustees. They were delighted at first. Then their smiles evaporated. Sure, they said, it would be great to own the world's best-known encyclopedia. But the needed A-to-Z revisions and start-up costs would take working capital—lots of it, more money than the university had.

After months of debate Benton finally came up with a proposal that was consummated in 1943. He pulled $100,000 of working capital out of his own pocket. The encyclopedia company, donated lock, stock and pastepot by Sears, was reorganized as an independent corporation, with Benton holding two-thirds of its common stock. The remaining third was held by the university (but was sold to Benton in 1959). A complicated formula was worked out under which the university would perpetually receive income and royalties from the company, would give its prestige and imprimatur to the encyclopedia and would provide a pool of scholars to revise the volumes and keep them up-to-date.

Many businessmen find it hard to believe Benton went into this deal as a favor to the university, not as a money-making investment. Many reporters have questioned him about it over the years, and I questioned him all over again in 1971. Was it really true, I asked, that he saw *Britannica* as a gift to the university and that the huge wealth that subsequently piled up in his name was an accident? He said, "Wholly true."

And so Bill Benton became one of the great rich without really trying.

Britannica didn't take off and fly right away. It went through some painful and nearly fatal financial illnesses in the 1940s. Benton, having started it up, had been attracted by a variety of public-service jobs and had left the encyclopedia operation in other men's hands. He worked in Washington for two years as assistant secretary of state for public affairs. In 1949 he was appointed a U.S. senator for Connecticut, taking over the unexpired term of a man who was resigning. He stayed in the Senate three years, absorbed with his duties and projects—chief among which was a long, bitter fight with the notorious right-wing extremist of the early 1950s, Senator Joseph McCarthy. Only when Benton was defeated for reelection in 1952 did he turn his full attention back to the *Britannica*.

It was probably lucky for him that there were only two stockholders in the company at the time: himself and the university. If the stock had been publicly traded, its market price would have sunk to so low a level in the late 1940s that Benton might have been tempted to sell out in disgust. The costs of revising and shining up the old encyclopedia had been huge. The company had gone steeply into debt. Most of the encyclopedia sets were sold in installments, and the machinery for collecting customers' payments had fallen apart. Other, more aggressive encyclopedia companies were moving into the market with armies of door-to-door salesmen and a heavy artillery of buying inducements: free atlases, free research services, free sets of dinnerware.

Benton shook up his company's management in the late 1940s and saw Britannica nursed back to fair health while he was in the Senate. Then, early in the 1950s, he set out to make the company grow. He introduced new book sets such as the 54-volume *Great Books of the Western World*. He had the *Britannica* translated into foreign languages. He bought other companies such as G. and C. Merriam, publisher of the original *Webster's Dictionary*.

Britannica grew spectacularly. In the years since Benton took it over in 1943, its sales have increased more than fiftyfold and it has paid the University of Chicago some $35 million in dividends and royalties.

William Benton, the man to whom one million dollars seemed like enough, is now conservatively estimated to be worth about 150 times that much.

4

The Salesmanship Route

Salesmanship is the most purely personal of all routes to wealth. A salesman's only tools are in his own psyche. He needs a capacity to drive himself and an ability to manipulate other people. He needs virtually nothing else—no seed capital, no college degree, no profound technical knowledge. The seed of his success, if it exists, is implanted somewhere deep inside his mind.

It is probably because of this that some of the most astounding gutter-to-mountaintop stories are to be found in the careers of salesmen. A boy born poor and a boy born rich have equal chances to make it as salesmen. A man can go all the way through college and spend years on graduate studies and spend still more years polishing himself like a diamond. No matter. The likelihood of his getting rich as a salesman is still no better, on the basis of these qualifications alone, than that of a kid who quit school after ninth grade.

"Nobody knows exactly what makes a good salesman," says O. William Battalia, a New York executive recruiter who has tracked down many high-level sales executives for his client companies. "I mean, the qualifications can't be put down on paper in a precise way. Salesmanship is a thing you sense—an approach, an attitude, a *feeling* about a man. Some men have it, some don't. I know when a man has it and I know when he hasn't. But if you ask me *what* he has or doesn't have, I'm stumped."

As we'll see later, there are some students of sales psychology who believe they do know what this mysterious quality is. In fact, there are some who believe it can be taught—can be implanted in a man who previously lacked it and doubted he could ever acquire it. Others say that's balderdash. Selling ability, they maintain, is either an innate quality or is produced by one's character-forming emotional experiences in childhood. If you don't have it by the time you reach adulthood, you won't ever have it.

For the moment let's sidestep this debate. The interesting thing about sales ability is that, if you believe you have it or can acquire it, you need nothing else to make you rich.

The product or service you sell need not be new and startling. It can be old, familiar even to the point of boredom. Hundreds of other men may be out selling it and indeed may have been selling it for centuries. None of this counts. What counts is that, somehow, you sell it better than your competitors are selling it. That's how you make your millions.

The story that follows is the story of a master salesman who sold something that was neither new nor startling—insurance—and ended with something like $400 million.

W. Clement Stone: Four Hundred Million Dollars

He is, among other things, chairman of the board and chief stockholder of the Combined Insurance Company of America, a board member and major stockholder of Alberto-Culver Company and board chairman of Hawthorn Books. It is entirely conceivable that the market value of his stocks will rise enough within a year or two to put him in the half-billion-dollar class.

W. Clement Stone. He is one of the richest men in America and one of the hardest to put down on paper.

It isn't that he is deliberately elusive, in the manner of Howard Hughes and some other rich men. Stone doesn't dodge the press. He is highly publicity-conscious, in fact, and remarkably frank about his wealth and its sources. The difficulty is that he is a peculiar and maddening bundle of contradictions. A major magazine tried to put together a profile of him some years ago but gave up in despair. There were so many contradictory facets to his character that most of them seemed to cancel each other out. No clear picture of a man emerged. What emerged, instead, seemed to be a basket of ill-assorted fragments—not one man but several.

Stone seems insufferably pious to some; he reminds them of a small-town revivalist minister. Yet he reminds others of a big-city huckster or circus pitchman.

He is obviously a hardheaded pragmatist, a man who knows a lot about business and money and law. Yet on occasion he drifts into strange ethereal worlds: He supports studies of extrasensory perception, for instance.

He is among the biggest of big businessmen, financially well worthy of appearing on *Business Week*'s cover. Yet he has never appeared there, and it is extremely hard to imagine him there. He simply doesn't look like a big businessman. He looks more like a bit player from a cops-and-robbers movie of the 1930s. He is a short man with a round face. He wears his hair slicked straight back over his scalp. He wears an archaic pencil-line moustache in the style of Ronald Colman, colorful bow ties, dazzling cuff links, great flashy rings on his fingers. He incessantly smokes four-dollar Havana cigars, which he hoarded in a warehouse before political events cut off the supply.

He sometimes talks and writes as though the acquisition of money is life's only purpose. Yet he gives with unimpeachable generosity to boys' clubs and treatment centers for drug addicts, and he does other good works. He gives not only money but time. His philanthropies must be counted as genuine, not simply tax gimmicks.

He says the secret of his success is something called Positive Mental Attitude (PMA), and he publishes books and a magazine to spread the word. Some say his publishing ventures are cynically designed for profits. Others say he sincerely believes in PMA and genuinely wants other men to succeed as he did.

He is an enigma, this Clement Stone. But let's see what his life can teach us.

If his story were fiction, it would be too corny to take seriously. W. Clement Stone, born on May 4, 1902, helped support his impoverished family on Chicago's south side by selling newspapers.

Selling newspapers. Does it actually happen in real life?

Evidently it does. Clem Stone, true to the classic tradition, was a spunky kid who fought hard to win and keep his selling territories. He was thrown out of one restaurant several times but kept sneaking back with more papers to peddle. The customers were so amused by his gall that they finally prevailed on the owner to stop heaving the youngster out on the sidewalk. With a bruised bottom but a full pocket, Stone went away to ponder the meaning of this episode.

He was that kind of kid—and, later, that kind of man. He was fond of mulling over his experiences to see what could be milked out of them for future profit. "What did I do right?" he would ask himself. "What did I do wrong? How will I approach that kind of situation next time?" He badgered himself with such questions throughout his life. He tried, in fact, to reduce all of life to a formula. He wanted to write a kind of code by which to guide himself, a set of short, pithy instructions that would lead him safely and profitably through any thicket of personal or business problems.

He believes he has succeeded in that aim. He has arrived at just such a set of instructions. As we'll note later (chapter 5), the instructions aren't totally clear to everybody else. But they are obviously quite clear to Stone—and in his case, at least, they have worked magnificently.

Stone, an only child, was raised by his mother. His father died when the boy was very young. The books and articles Clem Stone wrote in later life indicate that his mother had a profound influence on his character. She managed somehow to combine a deeply felt piety with a tigerishly aggressive business instinct—a combination that shows up today in Stone himself. She and he alike seemed to see God as a kind of business partner or moral stockholder. They prayed for courage, guidance and luck in their business ventures. Rewarded, they felt obligated to pay their divine stockholder dividends in the form of personal virtue, good works and more prayer. In the success formulas that Stone wrote as an older man, he classified the Bible as a kind of self-help book.

Stone was also influenced, he says, by the works of Horatio Alger. He read some 50 Alger books as a boy and was impressed by Alger's suggestion that God rewards the virtuous with cash.

Stone's mother worked for several years as a seamstress. She managed to save a little money. When young Clem was in his teens, she invested her savings in a small insurance agency in Detroit.

It was a risky move. The investment actually bought nothing more than a business connection and a spoonful of goodwill. The agency was in business to sell health-and-accident policies of a single company, U.S. Casualty Company of Detroit. For each policy sold, the agency kept a commission —and that was its only income. The agency bore all expenses except those of printing the policies and paying the claims. Its only assets were a small, dusty rented office, a few items of office equipment and the abilities of its sales force.

The sales force—in fact, the entire staff—consisted of one woman, Stone's mother. She sold nothing on her first day of business. That night, according to Stone's own account, she prayed. She prayed some more the next morning. And then she went to Detroit's biggest bank, sold a policy to one of its officers, got permission to roam about the building and ended the day with 44 sales. Horatio Alger would have loved her.

The agency prospered. And in the summer before his junior year of high school, young Clem went out to try his hand as a salesman.

His mother instructed him to go to a certain office building and cold-canvass it from top to bottom. He was frightened. But his days as a newsboy came back to him, and as he stood trembling on the sidewalk outside the office building, he reviewed some of the pithy self-goads with which he had prodded himself back then. One went something like "When there's nothing to lose and much to gain by trying, try." Another went, "Do it now!"

So he did it. He marched into the building. Had he been thrown out, he was prepared to go back in just as he had gone back into the restaurant years before to peddle papers. He wasn't thrown out. He went from office to office. The phrase "Do it now!" kept thundering in his head. Each time he stepped out of one office without a sale to show for his efforts, he found himself scared to hit the next office and face the next rejection. But he forced himself to go to the next office without hesitating. In fact, before the day ended, he had developed the technique of *rushing* to the next office so as to allow no time for his panic to arise and defeat him.

He sold two policies that day. It wasn't a successful day in those terms, but it was highly successful in terms of what he was beginning to learn about himself and salesmanship.

A good salesman, as we've noted, has the mysterious ability to drive himself. In situations where most people would slow down and stop—indeed, situations many people wouldn't care to enter at all—the salesman somehow keeps himself going at high speed. From some deep well of optimism or confidence or hope or just plain self-powering mental oomph, the salesman dredges up whatever it is that helps him overcome his fear of the hostility and rejection he may meet at the next office.

Young Clem Stone sat down at the end of that day, with a few dollars of commissions in his agency account, and decided it hadn't been such a bad day after all. He knew he had the guts to overcome fear, and he had worked out a technique to help him do it. With luck, he thought, he might one day become a good salesman.

He sold four policies the next day and six the day after. His career was launched.

He continued to sell health-and-accident insurance for his mother during that vacation and during subsequent time off from school. He boosted his sales average to ten policies a day, then fifteen, then twenty. And all the time he was analyzing himself. Why was he succeeding? He finally decided it was because he had something called Positive Mental Attitude. He spent the rest of his life trying to explain this PMA to other people. Sometimes he got it across and sometimes he didn't.

There came a day in school when he was sent to the principal's office to discuss some minor infraction of the rules. The principal grumbled that young Stone was wasting a lot of the taxpayers' money by using up his, the principal's, high-salaried time.

It suddenly occurred to Stone that he, a high-school junior, was making more money per day worked than the principal. And so Stone quit school on the spot. (Later in life he completed high school and began, but didn't finish, a college law course.)

He roamed all over Michigan selling for his mother's agency. His sales average edged past 30 policies a day and in some towns topped 40. His PMA, whatever it was, appeared to be working beautifully.

At the age of 20 he moved to Chicago and set up his own one-man insurance agency. He called it Combined Registry Company. He was determined to make it live up to its grandiose name. He prayed, recited self-needling phrases to himself, stoked up his PMA until it must nearly have blown the top of his head off. And on his first day of business he prospected up and down North Clark Street and sold 54 policies.

There could hardly have been much doubt in anyone's mind after that first day that this new agency was going to grow. There was no doubt at all in Stone's mind. He sold policies around Chicago and then in other Illinois cities, and he grew better at it all the time. In Joliet he averaged more than 70 sales a day, and there was one magnificent day in which he reached the almost unbelievable total of 122 sales. On the basis of an eight-hour working day, that figures out to one sale every four minutes.

Stone was obviously doing something right. He had started by selling two policies on his first day as a salesman. After about four years of self-training and self-needling he had reached totals beyond which it hardly seemed humanly possible to go. Meanwhile, repeat business was flowing in at an ever-faster rate: People were renewing their policies, and the one-man agency was collecting commissions through no sales effort on Stone's part.

The time had come, he felt, to hire an assistant salesman or two. In later years he enunciated a principle about this early growth of a business. The principle, stripped of its PMA trappings, is a simple and apparently sound one: Don't try to make a business grow too rapidly at first. Get it solidly established in the beginning, doing all or most of the work yourself. Stone feels today that if he had tried to multiply his agency by hiring a lot of salesmen before the enterprise was ready to absorb them, he might have gone down to defeat. The agency couldn't have lived on its cut of their commissions. As it was, the agency had reached a state of radiant health by living on Stone's personal commissions alone. It was now in a position to absorb other salesmen and support them, perhaps unprofitably at first, while they learned the business.

Stone placed a help-wanted ad in a Chicago newspaper: "Exceptional opportunity to earn. . . ." He received a bundle of replies from towns all over Illinois. He hired several men. Replies also came in from Indiana, Wisconsin and other states in which Stone's agency was not then authorized to do business. He promptly wrote to the insurance company whose policies he was peddling and asked permission to sell in those other states. The company was happy with the volume of business he had been bringing in. Sure, said the company, go ahead.

Stone went ahead. He hired some men in Wisconsin and Indiana. Then he began advertising for help in still other states' newspapers. He expanded his sales force eastward, southward and westward. Soon he was advertising for salesmen in national magazines, and by the late 1920s he had more than 1000 men operating from coast to coast. He appointed state sales chiefs to help him manage the salesmen, then regional chiefs to help him manage the state chiefs, then assistant national chiefs to help him administer the entire army from his Chicago headquarters.

He was not yet 30 years old.

The Stone agency seemed to be embarked on a course of eternal multiplication. But then the Great Depression settled its huge weight on the country. Many small and medium-size businesses were crushed flat. For a while it looked as though Stone's business might be among them. The 1000-man army found sales resistance stiffening. People didn't have the money to buy health-and-accident insurance, and those who did have money were inclined to save it for the still rainier days that seemed to lie ahead. The agency's once-huge sales volume dwindled like ice melting on a summer day. The morale of the sales force sank in black despair.

Sitting in his Chicago office, W. Clement Stone puzzled over these problems and ended by adding a few new principles to his success code. One was a generalized statement about hard times. Its drift was that if you approach adversity in a determined and optimistic way, you can always find an advantage in it. Another principle had to do with salesmanship specifically: "Sales are contingent on the attitude of the salesman, not the prospect."

And to prove to his dispirited sales chiefs that these weren't just empty platitudes, Stone got up from his desk, put on his hat and went on a selling trip in New York State. In the depths of the depression, he sold as many policies per day as he had ever sold in the halcyon 1920s.

"You see?" he said.

They saw, but they weren't quite sure what to do about it.

Stone knew, however. It was now obvious to him that he would have to inoculate his salesmen with the all-purpose success medicine, PMA. Having built his business in the booming 1920s, when almost anybody could sell almost anything, he hadn't paid much attention to the individual salesmen and their selling methods and attitudes. He had simply hired them—by mail in many cases—had given them some standard insurance sales literature to read and had then turned them loose. Most had done tolerably well in those golden years of surplus money. But now, up against a real test, they were collapsing.

So Clement Stone launched his first sales-training campaign. He began sending out bulletins to his sales offices enunciating general PMA principles and giving specific pointers on salesmanship. Simultaneously he embarked on an 18-month tour of the country. He talked to his troubled salesmen and went out on selling trips with them. He showed them how he, the master, approached his art. *The attitude of the salesman, not the prospect. . . .*

Many of the salesmen were too weary and discouraged to absorb the medicine. Many quit. The 1000-man force shrank to fewer than 200. But those 200 were now well trained and thoroughly turned on with PMA. By the mid-1930s they were producing a bigger sales volume for Stone's agency than the 1000 had produced before. By the end of that decade Clem Stone was a millionaire.

He now decided it might be pleasant and profitable to set up his own insurance company instead of just selling other companies' policies. Looking around for a feasible way of accomplishing this end, he found what seemed to be a perfect setup. The Pennsylvania Casualty Company, once a thriving organization, had run into sundry depression-bred problems and had suspended operations. Its owner, the Commercial Credit Company of Baltimore, wanted to sell it for $1,600,-000, exactly the worth of the defunct company's liquid assets.

Stone wasn't much interested in the liquid assets. What caught his eye was a nonliquid asset, potentially much more valuable: Pennsylvania Casualty, though out of business, still owned valid licenses to sell insurance in 35 states.

"Do it now!" said Stone to himself. The morning after he learned about this setup, he was in Baltimore with his lawyer to see the people at Commercial Credit. In condensed form the conversation went something like this:

STONE: "I want to buy your insurance outfit."

COMMERCIAL CREDIT: "Fine. Cost you a million-six. You got that much?"

STONE: "No, but I can borrow it."

CC: "Who from?"

STONE: "You."

It was an audacious gambit. But, as Stone quite reasonably pointed out, Commercial Credit was in the business of lending money. It was true that the proposed deal had a peculiar round-robin quality: Commercial Credit was to sell a piece of property to a buyer who, in payment, would simply give Commercial Credit its own money back. Yet it wasn't an impossible deal to conceive, and after some initial grumbling, Commercial Credit went along with it.

This was the foundation of Clem Stone's present empire. The original small insurance company evolved step by step into today's giant Combined Insurance Company of America, which sells in all states and abroad (1970 sales volume: $213 million) and has some 5000 salesmen, all inoculated with PMA in regular doses. (At sales meetings they all stand up and shout, "I feel ter-*riffic!*") Most of them are comfortably well off. At last count 20 or so were millionaires.

While building Combined Insurance, Stone was getting involved in other lucrative ventures. In the mid-1950s a brilliant young man named Leonard Lavin came to him with a request for a loan. Lavin wanted to start a small cosmetics company. Stone listened to the request and found it praiseworthy, for his purchase of Pennsylvania Casualty had taught him that one way to get rich is to use what he reverently calls OPM— Other People's Money. He gave young Lavin a brief, fatherly lecture about the business benefits of wise borrowing. He then cooked up a deal in which he and Lavin both used OPM. Instead of directly putting up his own money, Stone guaranteed a bank loan of $450,000 to Lavin. In return Stone got a one-fourth interest in Lavin's new company.

The company Lavin formed was Alberto-Culver, one of the more impressive growth companies of the 1960s. Stone's share of the stock, which he had acquired without actually spending a dime of his own, reached a value of roughly $30 million by the end of that decade.

Meanwhile, Stone was off on another venture. He was going into the publishing business.

In 1960, acting more out of missionary zeal than any need to make money, he collaborated on a book called *Success Through a Positive Mental Attitude*. His coauthor was the late Napoleon Hill, who had previously struck pay dirt with an inspirational best seller called *Think and Grow Rich*. The Stone-Hill book sold over a quarter million copies. Delighted to see the PMA faith being spread so well, Stone in 1962 wrote another book covering substantially the same subject matter: *The Success System That Never Fails*. This book, too, sold to thousands of would-be tycoons.

To keep the faith spreading, Stone next founded a magazine named *Success Unlimited*. It was set up as a subsidiary of his insurance operations. It contains articles by and about successful men, an occasional inspirational treatise by Stone himself, great dollops of PMA and a wide selection of start-your-own-business ads placed by franchising companies and others. The magazine is heavily soaked in Stone's own Bible Belt morality and right-wing political philosophy (a recent article grumbled about the current liberalizing of pornography laws, for instance), but somehow it avoids the dreary, sermonizing sound that might be expected of such a publication. Many readers have been startled to find it sprightly, informative and even directly useful in the task of getting rich.

Stone's final step in the publishing world was to buy his own book company in the mid-1960s. The original publisher of his success books, Prentice-Hall, owned an imprint called Hawthorn Books. Hawthorn wasn't making any money, and Prentice was glad to get rid of it. Stone merged it with some other publishing properties that he bought—among them the old Appleton-Century-Crofts textbook business—and rapidly quadrupled Hawthorn's sales volume. Today, though Hawthorn is a mere bag of peanuts next to the giant Combined Insurance and Alberto-Culver enterprises, it makes money. And it gives Stone a pulpit from which to preach PMA.

Some of Stone's other activities are less easy to explain in terms of the main roads of his life. For a while he helped finance the ESP studies of Dr. Joseph Banks Rhine at Duke University. He is also involved with an odd organization called the Foundation for the Study of Cycles, which thinks many cyclical phenomena such as economic booms and busts, sunspots, weather and suicide rates may be interrelated.

But PMA will always remain Stone's most absorbing interest. He likes to talk of the famous men to whom he has given copies of his books. One of them is Richard Nixon (to whose election campaigns Stone has been a heavy cash contributor).

Has the president read the books? The White House says yes. Does he use PMA, and does it help? The White House declines further comment.

5

Can Fortune Building Be Taught?

Clement Stone, the remarkable man whose financial odyssey we've just surveyed, is interesting not only for his personality and his monumental wealth. He is also interesting for his philosophy. He believes people can be taught to become wealthy.

Stone has spent much of his life trying to codify and articulate the principles that he believes lead to success in the capitalist system. He has written books on the subject. He runs a magazine devoted to it. He teaches it to his huge captive student body—his employees. He believes the lessons can be learned by ordinary men like you and me.

Is it really possible to learn such lessons—to sit, read, listen, absorb and finally go out armed with some surefire formula and become magnificently rich? Or is the whole idea of make-a-fortune schooling a waste of time? A well-meant but fruitless attempt to map the unmappable? A glittering con game?

One thing, at least, seems reasonably certain: Whether or not the accumulation of capital can be taught, standard schools and colleges don't teach it. I went through 16 years of school and college and learned nothing that I can remember as having been directly relevant to the problem of getting rich. Today my son, a college freshman and a reasonably clever lad, knows much about many things but knows little, for example, about the stock market. Or about the ways in which businesses grow by borrowing. Or about the various routes a man might take to capitalize on an invention or a commercial idea. These are subjects we are expected to learn simply by keeping our eyes and ears open *after* we finish our formal schooling.

Indeed, it is remarkable how few of the very rich went to

46

college or even bothered to finish high school. Clement Stone quit high school specifically because he found it irrelevant to his self-imposed goal of making money. Howard Hughes had money and leisure to attend college but dismissed the idea as a waste of four good years. William Lear didn't even reach high school. If any general truths can be extracted from the lives of such men, one truth seems to be that a standard education in American schools teaches little or nothing about building a fortune.

Possibly this is why success schools and how-to-get-rich textbooks find so ready a market of students. A lack is felt. People come out of school or college, bumble along for a few years, discover they aren't getting as rich as they'd envisioned in their youthful dreams and so feel compelled to seek the missing chunk of education.

One of Clement Stone's inspirational books bears the intoxicating title *The Success System That Never Fails*. The promise implied in that title may not be literally fulfillable. *Never* is a big, big word. Yet the promise alone, fulfilled or not, can engender dreams so gorgeous, a high so euphoric and long-lasting, that the book's cost must certainly be counted as modest in relation to the value received. A quart of gin or a few high-quality reefers cost more, after all. And whether or not the "success system" actually works in the terms under which it is presented, the euphoria alone—the hope, the optimism—may become the switch that finally turns the student on to success. Unless you're optimistic about a proposed business venture, obviously, you will never launch it. Once launched, it may fail. But if it is never launched at all, its chances of success are plain, flat zero. Optimism is undeniably a necessary ingredient in any kind of fortune-building formula and may be the main ingredient.

Optimism is, in fact, the most clearly valuable commodity with which fortune teachers deal. They don't all stand there flat-footed and claim to sell systems that "never fail." Most are somewhat more timid. They sell systems that "almost never . . ." or "never, if used as directed . . ." or "never, as long as you're patient. . . ." They offer no money-back guarantees. You can never come up with a proof of final failure on which to base a breach-of-contract suit. (You're lying on your deathbed, age 92, flat broke. "Your goddamn system failed!" you croak, grabbing your fortune teacher's lapels with quivering hands. "Gee, that's too bad," he says. "If only you could have given it another year. . . .") Ah, but what you have really bought is optimism. This is the main thing that fortune teachers—some of them rather cleverly—teach.

Let's wander down the groves of this peculiar academe and look in at a few classes.

Horatio Alger

Strictly speaking, Horatio Alger was not a fortune teacher in the modern sense of the phrase. He offered no mail-order course. His books bore no titles such as *The Success System That . . .* or *How to. . . .* Yet he thought of himself as a teacher, and many men in subsequent years have so categorized him. Clement Stone, for example, claims to have been inspired and to have begun the first vague formulations of his own success system when he read a bundle of Alger books as a boy.

Horatio Alger was, in fact, the granddaddy of all capitalist success teachers. His very name is a cliché used to describe a man's rise from humble beginnings to large wealth. "His is a Horatio Alger story," it might be said (and indeed has been, several million times) of Clement Stone and most other men you will meet in this book. The cliché, like an old horse, is tired and deserves to be led out to the fields where it can die peacefully. But before we bestow our last affectionate pat on its rump and send it on its way, let's see where the old horse came from and what races it has run.

Horatio Alger, Jr., was born at Revere, Massachusetts, in 1834. His father was a Unitarian minister and evidently a dourly sanctimonious one. He preached at the boy endlessly, made him memorize virtually the entire Bible, filled him so full of religious mumblings that the kids in school called the boy Holy Horatio. But while one half of young Horatio was striving to obey and emulate his pious parent, the other half was seething with typical youthful rebellion. The result, as he grew to manhood, was a double personality of the bizarre type later fictionalized by Robert Louis Stevenson in *The Strange Case of Dr. Jekyll and Mr. Hyde.*

Psychoanalysts have since speculated that Alger was a schizophrenic. Who knows? The fact is, he spent much of his adult life—until he grew old and the flame burned down—

shuttling back and forth between piety and high jinks. One year he would be the very model of his clergyman father, a sour, stern, cold-eyed man who seemed to feel any form of fun was against God's will. The next year he would abruptly turn into the 19th Century version of a swinger—or, as the phrase went in those days, a dissolute and degenerate rake.

First he went to divinity school, dutifully preparing himself for the ministry as his father wished. He supported himself by tutoring and by selling scholarly and inspirational articles to newspapers and magazines. After graduation, instead of getting himself ordained and going to work as a minister, he suddenly disappeared. He turned up in Paris. (Where did he get the money? Nobody knows for sure.) He did what young Americans in Paris have always done: drank, gambled, kept company with young ladies of low inhibition, slept till noon and generally defied the good old Protestant ethic.

Just as abruptly, he returned to Massachusetts at age 30, was ordained as a minister and preached fervently against everything he had just finished doing in Paris.

Two years later he quit the ministry, went to New York and did everything he had just finished preaching against in Massachusetts.

Then came a period of relative calm. There was a generous, warmhearted side to Alger's sundered psyche, and while prowling New York's streets at night, he became aware of the great numbers of drifting, apparently homeless kids—street urchins, as they were then called. Wondering about their fate, he began asking questions about various charitable institutions that had been set up to house, feed and educate the urchins. One such outfit, the Newsboys' Lodging House, was near the seedy tenement where he lived, and he got into the habit of dropping in there whenever he felt like talking to somebody. He became friendly with the superintendent, started doing odd jobs around the place, read biblical and other stories to the boys at night, tutored some of them, preached at them, ended by becoming a kind of general busybody and unpaid assistant superintendent.

Meanwhile, he had been earning his meager living as a journalist. Since his Paris days he had harbored the dream of writing a great novel about Love, Death, Truth, Humanity and grand things like that. One night, chatting with the lodging-house superintendent, he speculated on what might become of all these homeless boys as adults. Would they all go down the drain? Or would some of them, perhaps, through prayer, thrift, industry, honesty, pluck, perseverance and other admired attributes of the Protestant ethic, rise to material wealth? Was it inconceivable that one of them might someday become president? Or a great merchant? Or . . . ?

And so Horatio Alger's famous books were born. The first was a serial story called *Ragged Dick*. Alger sold it to a boys' magazine. Boys and parents alike gobbled it up. A Boston publisher immediately commissioned Alger to write more books about the same character, following Dick's zigzag fortunes all the way from his boyhood in a city orphanage to his young manhood as a budding entrepreneur. This series was followed by dozens more, including *Luck and Pluck* and *Tattered Tom*. Alger went on to write well over 100 books, and some 20 million copies were sold during his lifetime.

The astounding success of Alger's books is difficult to explain today. All followed essentially the same formula: A street urchin triumphs over adversity by applying rules from the good book. Sheer coincidence helps him on his climb (a rich benefactor can always be counted on to turn up at the darkest hour), but the implication is that such lucky breaks come the young hero's way because he deserves them: works hard, prays a lot, thinks clean thoughts. The books offer little in the way of narrative momentum or suspense, and as for characterization, it isn't there at all. Every Ragged Dick and Tattered Tom is the perfect model of upright, clench-jawed, stiff-spined, red-blooded American boyhood, while the villains are the meanest, wiliest, sneakiest aggregation of blackguards ever to skulk the streets. Their hobby is foreclosing orphanage mortgages.

Every Alger book is this way. When you've read one you've read all. Yet millions of people bought book after book after book.

Sociologists and economists and others have speculated ever since about the reasons behind this popularity. One likely surmise is that the Alger type of rags-to-riches story was just then (mid-19th Century) beginning to seem possible in America. Only a few times before in the whole history of the world had a nation, a society and an economic setup existed in which the masses of poor and middle-income people could seriously dream about the possibility of getting rich. The

Dutch had enjoyed such a setup in the early 17th Century, but it had all gone down the drain a century later. Ever since, and through most of history before that, a man born poor could do little but resign himself to his fate. You're born poor, you die poor; such was God's will. To struggle was futile. Some lucky individuals did get rich, but the percentage was so small and the odds against the average man so large that to dream any such dream was universally considered to be ridiculous.

But now, quite suddenly, a crazy new place called America had arisen before the world's startled gaze. This America had existed for a long time without attracting much attention. It was widely considered to be, and, in fact, for a century was, a vast, empty place dotted with rural villages, most of whose inhabitants were poor and had virtually no chance of ever becoming otherwise. But at the beginning of the Industrial Revolution, while the world wasn't looking, this huge country in the middle of nowhere had become an economic colossus. And not only that—it had become the kind of place in which poor men could get rich.

They were calling it the "land of opportunity." Among the poverty-trapped millions of Europe, there were many in the late 1800s who came to believe literally that New York's or Boston's streets were paved with gold. Obviously, America wasn't quite that wealthy. Indeed, many of the ragged immigrants who poured into the country so hopefully not only failed to grow rich—they grew poorer. But the dream of making a fortune was fulfilled enough times to keep the dream alive. Andrew Carnegie emigrated from Scotland, landed in New York with less than a dollar in his pocket, went on to become the multimillionaire founder of U.S. Steel. John D. Rockefeller, the oil tycoon, began his career as an underpaid, half-starved clerk in a Cleveland shipping office. Joseph P. Kennedy's father fled a potato famine in Ireland, landed in Boston with an empty belly and no worldly assets whatever, lifted himself by his own bootstraps into a comfortable middle-income bracket, saw his son go on to become a multimillionaire.

Real-life stories such as these made Horatio Alger's yarns seem believable. People read Alger's books to reinforce their hopes and dreams. Alger was saying, "See, this is what can happen to people in America."

He was also saying something else that may have been still more interesting to some. For centuries the major Western religions had been trying to convince people that virtue is its own reward—that, in fact, poverty is preferable to wealth, since too much money inevitably leads to dissolution and damnation. Money was conceived to be the root of evil. A wise man didn't work for money but for the sake of the work itself. Work was purifying. Sweat was holy in the eyes of the Lord. Millions of poverty-trapped people had been forced to swallow this philosophy, for it was the only consolation they had. A man could think, "I may be starving, but, by God, I'm holy!"

And now Alger came on the scene with a different view. He suggested that money is fine in the Lord's eyes. He went even further. He preached that the Lord will reward virtue with money. To get rich, he said, all you need do is combine virtue with a certain degree of ordinary business acumen. The payoff will be in cash.

It was a grand new way to look at things. Alger wasn't its originator, of course, only one of its key spokesmen. The originators were the very businessmen who were then building what was to become the world's greatest economic power. Men such as Rockefeller, Carnegie and J. P. Morgan sincerely believed the accumulation of capital was a thoroughly righteous activity, something like prayer. In fact, some of them actually felt themselves to be divinely appointed custodians of the nation's cash. Because of their upright characters, God had singled them out to be great gatherers of money. It was their job to watch over this money for the welfare of less prudent and less virtuous men.

Horatio Alger, preaching this new financial religion, touched a nerve in millions of people. He gave them a heady dose of optimism. He assured them they could get rich simply by developing the attributes ordained in the good book, plus a few others such as thrift, pluck (the willingness to take a business risk) and perseverance.

Alger himself, as it turned out, failed to apply his own formula with what could be called smashing success. His book royalties brought him a very big income, but he never seemed to master the virtue of thrift. Some of the money went out in the form of generous gifts to the Newsboys' Lodging House and to individual orphans and foundlings whom Alger unofficially adopted as sons in all but name. (He never married and is not known ever to have fathered a child of his own.) The rest of the money simply vanished in plain, old-fashioned profligacy. Alger savored wine and women in New York, Paris, San Francisco and other scarlet places where a man's money could be drained away rapidly. Finally, old and tired, he crept back to the green tranquility of rural Massachusetts and moved in with his sister. He died there in 1899, flat broke.

The Magical PMA

Clement Stone's philosophy of Positive Mental Attitude is partly derived from, and would without doubt be whole-heartedly approved by, the old master Horatio Alger. Stone's books counsel the aspiring tycoon to observe all the usual Alger-type and biblical virtues. Stone doesn't explain clearly just what these virtues have to do with PMA, but he leaves no doubt that he considers them absolutely necessary for business success.

In *The Success System That Never Fails* he lists what he calls the "four basic causes of failure." These are "illicit sex, alcohol, deception and stealing." Certain highly successful entrepreneurs whom you'll meet later in this book—men with a well-developed appreciation of good booze and bad girls— would be interested to learn they have been nurturing the seeds of failure all their adult lives. But Stone states his beliefs as though stating plain, demonstrable facts. He *knows* illicit sex will bring your business tumbling down upon your sinful head. Clem Stone is nothing if not positive.

"If you want results," he says in another part of the book, "try a prayer." Again he fails to explain the relevance of piety to PMA, but he manifestly *knows* he's right.

This is the nature of Stone's books and articles and speeches and sales-meeting pep talks. They are a peculiar and often confusing mixture of folksy platitudes, sanctimonious warnings and chamber-of-commerce exhortations. God and money are somehow equated. The tone is always one of total assurance. Theories and suppositions are stated as facts. Surmises that could be argued with are presented in such a way that argument is clearly discouraged. No questions are invited.

And yet, in the midst of all this, like a diamond in a bowl of cold oatmeal, lies the gem of PMA. You have to eat the damned oatmeal before you find the gem, and even then it requires considerable cleaning off before you can see precisely what it is. But it may be a real gem after all. Many of Stone's star salesmen, while admitting they sometimes gag on the platitudes with which they are daily force-fed, insist PMA is a genuine, workable formula for success.

What is it? Basically it is a type of autosuggestion. It is somewhat similar to psychotherapist Émile Coué's formula for getting rid of psychosomatic illness: You endlessly repeat the statement "Every day, in every way, I am getting better and better." After repeating it for weeks, months or years, with luck you come to believe it. Your body then (so the theory goes) responds to your mind, and the end result is that you actually do get better.

Thus PMA. You start your success course by repeating slogans to yourself—"self-motivators," as Stone calls them. You recite them every morning and night and at odd hours through the day. They float about on the surface of your mind for a while. Then, after sufficient repetition, they begin to sink like waterlogged seeds. They sink to the depths, settle into the muck at the bottom, take root and become integral components of your psyche. From then on you barely need to think about them. In the midst of any business situation, the correct self-motivator will assert itself and will automatically guide you in the direction of success.

Among the slogans:

"Do it now!"

"Success is achieved and maintained by those who keep trying."

"Go where you fear to go."

"When there is much to gain and nothing to lose by trying. . . ."

And so on. Corny? Of course. Thunderingly obvious? Indeed. Yet it must be admitted that successful men do in fact obey these little rules, whether or not the rules are articulated thus, in the form of slogans. Illicit sex may not necessarily lead to entrepreneurial failure, but an unwillingness to try a business venture certainly does. So does procrastination—withdrawing from action, failing to "do it now." So does fear of the unknown, of rejection, of necessary risk.

Stone's point is that many or most people fail to develop all the useful self-motivators naturally as they grow to adulthood. They fail to develop the "do it now" habit, for example. Confronted with a scary opportunity, they tend to back off. They diddle around. The opportunity evaporates before their eyes. They then blame a malicious fate for their bad luck. This kind of experience, repeated over and over again throughout their lives, confirms them in the belief that they are born losers. They may cry over the situation or laugh at it good-humoredly, but the fact remains that they believe themselves destined not to succeed.

A man with this crippling attitude rooted in his psyche, Stone points out, obviously will not succeed except by sheer blind luck. Since he has failed to develop the right self-motivators naturally while growing to manhood, it's necessary to implant them in him artificially by the slogan-repeating technique. The slogans may be corny, but they represent useful habits that the man needs to swap for destructive ones. If the technique works, he will eventually reach a point where his immediate reaction to a situation will be, "Do it now," instead of "Well, maybe next week. . . ."

This is the basis of PMA. Is it valid? It will cost you only a few bucks to buy one of Stone's books and find out.

You may feel skeptical even after studying what the man says. It is easy to poke fun at Clem Stone, at his folksy clichés, his Bible Belt moralisms, his flashy cuff links and archaic Ronald Colman moustache. On the other hand, it is rather hard to argue with a man who came from nowhere and made $400 million.

The Tenth-Multiple Man

Paul J. Meyer is a multimillionaire from Waco, Texas, who runs a fortune school called the Success Motivation Institute. Meyer and his outfit are worth a brief look if for no other reason than that SMI is probably the most successful of all success academies. It is certainly the most successful of all those that are publicly owned (you can buy its stock on the over-the-counter market if you like) and that publish sales and earnings data. The value of the books, records and other course materials sold by SMI tops $20 million a year.

Paul Meyer is a tall, lean, athletic, urbane man in his middle 40s with a faint resemblance to Gregory Peck. He doesn't look or act anything like W. Clement Stone, but at certain key points the two men's careers have been remarkably alike.

Like Stone, Meyer cut his formal education short because he found it irrelevant to his personal goals and purposes. He started college but dropped out after three months, disappointed with what he called the "cookie-cutter" approach to education. He felt the system allowed too little room for students who heard a different drummer.

Like Stone, Meyer began his adult career as an insurance salesman. (Meyer was 20 at the time; Stone had started in his teens.) Also like Stone, he began with an empty wallet and no perceptible advantages over anybody else. In fact, the 20-year-old Meyer began with what seemed like a distinct disadvantage: He was afflicted with a stammer. The speech defect wasn't severe, but it was noticeable enough to make prospective employers nervous. Meyer was repeatedly advised that selling insurance was probably not his dish.

Some native streak of stubbornness pushed him into the business anyway. Unlike Stone, Meyer didn't try at that stage of the game to reduce life to a formula. He composed no codes of rules for himself, recited no slogans into his shaving mirror. It would be more accurate to say that, at first, Meyer simply felt his way along as most of us do—groped about in the dark, grabbed some ideas and rejected others without adherence to any formal plan or pattern. And suddenly he found himself succeeding wildly. He sold more insurance than seemed possible—sold it almost as fast as his company could print the policies. By 27, Paul Meyer was a millionaire.

Why? How had he done it?

These were the questions he asked himself. And when he thought he had the answers, he founded SMI, in 1959, to teach the secrets to other people.

The basic SMI principle, if it can be put in a nutshell, is that everybody is locked into the world of his own imagination. Your imagination, in other words, describes the limits of what you can do or become. Except by blind luck—unexpectedly winning a million-dollar lottery prize, for instance —you can never get out beyond the horizons that are severely and starkly outlined in your mind. If you see yourself as a middle-income salary earner, says Meyer, and if you find it ludicrous to think of yourself as anything else, the odds stack up to near certitude that you will not in fact become anything else.

The main thrust of SMI's fortune courses is to expand the narrow inner horizons that thus, in the Meyer theory, cramp men's lives. *Expand* may be too tame a word. SMI attempts not merely to stretch its students' horizons but to explode them.

Meyer believes success came to him when his own horizons detonated. At some point he stopped thinking of himself as an impecunious young fellow with a speech defect. He thought, "I *could* become a millionaire." The more often he pondered this astounding notion (as with Stone's slogans), the less ridiculous it sounded. Eventually he was able to take himself perfectly seriously in the role of potential millionaire. He was then in a position to plan, with cool deliberation, just how he was going to get there. Because he took his self-image seriously, he was able to take the plan seriously. And, by golly. . . .

Well, before we get too excited, it would be advisable to consider a couple of truths. First, what works for one man may not work for another. And second, just because a man can do a thing, it doesn't necessarily follow that he can teach it.

The SMI approach may indeed work for some people. Just as Clement Stone can point proudly to the salesmen who became millionaires under his tutelage, so Meyer produces an alumni honor roll similarly sprinkled with millionaires. Impressive. Yet a question will always hang in the air: Might not these honor students have become millionaires in any case, without ever meeting PMA or SMI?

The question cannot be answered. In the end each man must decide for himself whether he can benefit from fortune schooling.

You may not become a multimillionaire, but at least you aren't likely to be bored. The SMI courses (you get them by mail: tape recordings, printed material, self-needling forms to fill out) have something of the effect of mind-expanding drugs. The major object is to rev you up until your internal cogs and flywheels are screaming white-hot on their shafts. SMI's copyrighted slogan states that it is in the business of "Motivating People to Their Full Potential." Like an old car, you are oiled, greased and filled with high-octane gas; then your accelerator is bolted to the floor.

As one illustration of Meyer's horizon-exploding technique, consider his concept of what he calls the Tenth Multiple. "People don't realize," he says, "that the distance from thinking very small to thinking very big is actually a minor distance —just a few steps." He asks his listeners to think of $1000. It isn't an enormous sum. Most middle-income Americans accumulate that much, in property if not cash, fairly early in life. To most of us it is a *conceivable* sum.

But to most of us the sum of a million dollars—a thousand thousand—isn't conceivable. This is what Meyer means by cramped horizons. For he points out that you need only double $1000 ten times in order to have more than a million ($1,024,000, to be exact).

As a matter of fact, he adds, you can start by thinking even smaller, if it makes you more comfortable. Start with a dime. If you began on the first day of a 31-day month and doubled the amount every day, you'd end the month with more than $100 million. (You want precision? Very well: $107,374,182.40.)

These are heady thoughts. SMI is that kind of place. As its sales figures indicate, its approach has attracted large numbers of eager students. There are obviously many who believe fortune making can be taught and SMI can teach it.

Students aren't the only ones to hold this belief. It is apparently shared by large numbers of outside observers. When SMI went public, in 1969, its common shares jumped in three months from an offering price of $15 to $48 bid, $50 asked.

Even those who might be considered Meyer's competitors seem convinced the SMI approach is workable. One of SMI's stockholders, and once a member of its board of directors, is a man who has spent years preaching a different success gospel. He is a man, however, whose main doctrine is that fortune making *can* be taught—and he is obviously a man who believes in putting his money where his mouth is. He is W. Clement Stone.

6

The Stock Market:
Playing It

Of all the money dreams in the world, the one about making a killing on the stock market is without doubt the most common. This grand and intoxicating old dream is dreamed in every capitalist nation with a private equity trading system, and it is even dreamed in Communist nations that have no stock markets of their own. Visiting Russians seem fascinated by Wall Street, and, as a matter of fact, some wealthier Soviet citizens secretly play the market through intermediaries in Swiss and U.S. banks. Week-old *Wall Street Journal*s appear to circulate in Moscow along with other underground publications. The stock market's magnetism is so universal and so strong that a Russian will risk everything to get in on the action—will risk not only bankruptcy, as you and I might, but also arrest and a jail term.

What is the source of this magnetism? Obviously, part of it lies in the nearly irresistible lure of something for nothing—the market's promise that you will be given a 50-50 chance to sell something for more than you've paid. But there is more to it than that. The stock market offers the further promise—or seems to offer the promise—that to pile up money by this route is ridiculously easy.

That is the real grabber. *It looks easy.*

There are thousands of other types of enterprise that offer us poor old downtrodden, tax-bitten, inflation-riddled middle-income folks a chance to make it big. Take the retailing business. Any store owner does essentially what a stock speculator hopes to do: buy cheap, sell dear. Some retailers, like some equity speculators, get rich. But the retailing business looks a lot more difficult and complicated than the stock market. To set yourself up as a retailer, you need a store location, you need merchandise, you need a cash register, and you need umpteen other things. Horse racing, by contrast, at first glance looks easier. But everybody knows horse racing is—whisper the dreadful word—*gambling!* And everybody knows the odds are stacked high against making money by gambling. Therefore, horse racing isn't an easy route to riches any more than retailing.

But the stock market—ah, the stock market is something else. As all the brokers and exchange executives constantly assure us, stock trading is *investing,* not gambling. That's what they tell us, and that's what nearly everybody seems to believe. What's more, it is a plain and honest fact that putting your money into the market—getting into the action— *is* ridiculously easy, much easier than starting a retail store or even placing a track bet. Getting back out, or at least getting out whole, is another matter. But the process of starting, setting yourself up in the business of equity speculation, offers no difficulties at all. A quick phone call to a broker and you're in. There are no barriers based on race, religion, national origin, age, sex, physical appearance, education, social status or intelligence. Anybody may play, provided he has the required cash stake.

The game itself, once you're established in it, also looks easy. All you have to do is buy stocks when they're cheap and sell them when they're dear. Nothing to it. No lengthy education required, just an ability to do simple arithmetic. No textbooks to read. No examinations to take. Nothing to learn beyond that one simple rule: Buy low, sell high.

How easy, O Lord, how easy it looks.

The sad and baffling fact is that few people ever make much money on the stock market. The game isn't one-tenth so easy as it looks. But this fact never seems to get out in public—or, if it does drift out occasionally, is soon dismissed as mere hollow pessimism. The market's outward appearance never changes. It continues to look like the sweetest something-for-nothing deal on earth, the easiest money game of all. And the dream lives on.

We will now look at some men who made the dream real. It must be emphasized that these are men of a rare, rare breed. To make a hundred million bucks on the stock market, you must be somebody quite unusual, and the men we're about to meet are that, indeed. Yet perhaps we can afford a pinch of optimism after all. Rare though these men may be, they are still men. Not gods, not warlocks, not super-computers—simply men. And what one man can do, so can another. So can you or I . . . perhaps.

There are basically three ways to get rich in and around the stock market. You can play it—that is, buy and sell stocks. This is the route most people take and is the basis of the common market-killing dream. Or you can sell it. Instead of trading in stocks themselves, you make your money as a broker or advisor or other intermediary, selling stocks and stock schemes and the something-for-nothing idea to the millions of easy marks who are always milling around. Or, third, you can use it. You do this by creating companies or phantoms that look like companies, getting people to buy stock in those companies and manipulating the resulting flow of money so that some of it ends in your own pocket.

The third method will be discussed more fully in another part of the book, where we'll be studying the delightful trick of getting rich on other people's money. The exhibit we'll contemplate at that time (chapter 15) will be James Ling. As you'll see, he is acknowledged to be among the grand masters of this third approach to the stock market.

Meanwhile, the first and second approaches will occupy our startled gaze in this chapter and the next: the approaches of the market player and the market seller.

One of the most successful market players living today, and perhaps the most downright likable, is a man named Joseph Hirshhorn. He came out of the slums and made $100 million or so mainly by gambling in mining stocks. It is part of his charm that he himself admits it was gambling. There are many high-toned labels that he could apply to himself if he wanted to inflate his own importance and polish his image, as businessmen often like to do. He could call himself an investment banker or a natural-resource developer or any of several other grandiose-sounding things. But, no, Joe Hirshhorn could never be that stuffy. He stands there and looks you candidly in the eye, this preposterously rich man, and says he's a speculator.

Fortune reporter Emmet John Hughes visited the engaging Hirshhorn and wrote this fascinating and witty account of the great speculator's beginnings and early triumphs.

Joseph Hirshhorn:
One Hundred Million Dollars*
by Emmet John Hughes

Joseph Herman Hirshhorn . . . five feet, four inches high, stands at the glittering top of a world he made by and for himself. He looks a bit like Al Smith, walks a bit like Groucho Marx and thinks a bit (he hopes) like Bernard Baruch. He is bilingual: adequate English and fluent Brooklynese. He is an immigrant Jewish boy, a child of some of Brooklyn's toughest slums who has grown into a scarred and supple veteran of New York's Wall Street and Toronto's Bay Street. Coincidentally with making himself rich, he has helped make the Western Hemisphere considerably more secure in that most vital of strategic minerals, uranium. "Uranium, ah, uranium!" Joe was once heard to enthuse. "It's got sex appeal!"

The twisting, turning career that Joseph Hirshhorn found to be the shortest distance between poverty and fortune zigzagged to a climax . . . [in 1955]. The scene was Joe's unpretentious 19th-floor suite in Toronto's Bank of Nova Scotia Building, on the walls of which hang landscapes, still lifes, abstracts (a part of his million-dollar collection of contemporary American art), a portrait of Lincoln and a framed aphorism: "IMAGINATION IS THE FIRST LAW OF CREATION." For the occasion there perched on Joe's desk a cake whose pink-and-green frosting proclaimed, "RIO TINTO-HIRSHHORN E PLURIBUS UNUM."

Towering at Joe's side stood the natty British figure of Roy William Wright, boss of the Rio Tinto Mining Company of Canada, a new offspring of Great Britain's venerable 83-year-old Rio Tinto Company, in which the Rothschilds have large interests. As the cake was cut, Joe sighed and sang, "I'll be loving you always and always." He had just traded Rio Tinto his equity in a vast sweep of Canadian mining properties—uranium, gold, iron, copper, acquired over a period of two decades at a cost of some $4,800,000 —for about $31 million in Canadian Rio Tinto stocks and debentures and the chairmanship of the Canadian company's board.

Behind the happy moment lay three years of work re-

*Reprinted from the November 1956 issue of *Fortune* magazine by special permission. Copyright © 1956 by Time Inc.

volving about a stretch of land whose name seems destined to match the Klondike in fable: Blind River. The name properly belongs to a depressed little lumber town on the Canadian Pacific Railway along the northern shore of Lake Huron. But the name is now used to cover the whole southern part of the Algoma Basin, an expanse of little lakes and jack-pine bush, which, until Hirshhorn came along, had been a cemetery for the hopes of many hollow-eyed prospectors.

Early in 1952 Joe had listened patiently to Franc. R. Joubin, a lean and scholarly man who had recently become managing director of Joe's Technical Mine Consultants. Joubin's theory was that the many assay tests made on sample surface ore from the Algoma area (all of which had been discouraging) had been misleading and that deep diamond drilling would uncover vast uranium beds.

Finally, in 1953, Joe put up $30,000 for Joubin to start diamond drilling. Two months later Joubin and Joe had the greatest uranium find outside Africa, a discovery that took Joe on to the sweeping deal with Rio Tinto.

The full story behind these events goes back a good deal more than three years. It goes back half a century and to quite another world—to a village in Latvia, in fact, where Joseph Herman Hirshhorn was born in 1899, the 12th of 13 children. His father died in Joe's infancy. Joe was six years old when by train and steerage, via Liverpool and Ellis Island, he landed to join his mother and the rest of her brood in a Brooklyn tenement. "I came out of a hell-hole," Joe recalls. "And I was lucky—some of my playmates in that neighborhood found their way to the electric chair."

It took Joe less than 24 hours after landing in America to get his first lesson in finance. Some neighborhood boys taught him to shoot craps. Joe, though he could speak no English, got the idea well enough to win, and his tutors had to beat him up to recover their losses. His mother, Amelia, bore with a more systematic kind of punishment in a sweatshop pocketbook factory, where she worked 12 hours a day, six days a week, for $12 weekly. With such resources, she moved her brood to a slightly more spacious slum on Humboldt Street.

Across the bleak scene flares one flaming memory: a three-alarm fire that in May 1908 gutted the Humboldt

Street tenement. Some upper-floor tenants died in flames—or impaled on the fence below. The Hirshhorns survived, but Amelia was taken to the hospital while her children scattered around the neighborhood to get along as best they could. "I stayed alive on garbage," Joe murmurs. "Poverty has a bitter taste. I swore I would never know it again."

In the spring of 1911, P.S. 145's fifth grade went on an excursion to Staten Island. Joe started out with his classmates, but he didn't get to Staten Island. As the group meandered down Lower Manhattan's Broad Street, heading for the ferry, Joe saw a sight—the fantastic, yammering New York Curb Market. He spent the day watching, bug-eyed. "It fascinated the hell outta me," he remembers. "The wigwagging like deaf-and-dumb signals between sidewalks and windows, the brokers with their colored hats. I made up my mind to come back. Three years later I did—still not knowing what the hell it was all about."

Joe was 14 years old when he returned to the Curb. His timing seemed a little faulty. His mother certainly thought so, for it was one of the rare times when she slapped him —for brashly quitting a $20-a-week job in a jewelry store to head for Broad and Wall streets. It looked as if mother was right. Joe recalls, "It was 1914. Both exchanges were closed [at the beginning of World War One], everybody was broke, and when I wandered onto the Curb, there were all these guys sitting around playing cards, and when I told them what I wanted, they just laughed at me. 'Hell, sonny, we're lookin' for jobs ourselves.' "

It was not to be the only time that Joe moved in on a situation at its lowest. Joe patiently plodded through the offices of lower Broadway until, working floor by floor through the Equitable Building at number 120, he found a job with the Emerson Phonograph Company as office boy and noon-hour switchboard operator (for which he breezily trained himself in 24 hours at the telephone company up the street).

Such a start was less than spectacular, but it sufficed. The gilded names on the doors of the Equitable Building—grand-sounding names like Guggenheim and American Smelting and Refining—signaled at least a proximity to the world he was looking for. He soon found out that Emerson's general manager, one Richard D. Wyckoff, was also editor and publisher of the *Magazine of Wall Street* and had an office with a ticker in it. "So after six months," Joe recalls, "I took my heart and my noodle in my hands and marched into Wyckoff one day and said I was no office boy, I wanted to be a broker." His brashness paid off: A fortnight later Joe was charting stocks for Wyckoff at $12 a week.

The next three years meant education in everything from the important names in New York society to the tricky wriggles of his stock charts. All the while, the Hirshhorn economy (ten cents a day for carfare, nine cents for lunch, six cents for splurging, the rest to his mother) was supplemented by an extra $12 weekly earned as a Western Union messenger, running daily from 6:00 P.M. to 2:00 A.M. Joe got his feet so badly blistered that, upon quitting, he never went back for his last fortnight's pay. (Recently he reminded the president of Western Union that he was still owed $24.) To make up for his loss of income, Joe devoted spare time to drawing more stock charts for the old Wall Street firm of Cyrus J. Lawrence and Company.

At 17 Joe struck out on his own, headed fast for his first killing and his first rude lesson. He had, to start with, a sum of $255. Within a year, as a broker on the Curb, he had made his first fortune: $168,000. In the process he was able to buy himself his first fine clothes and his mother a house on Long Island. But the armistice came, and Joe got too clever. He stubbornly bought Lackawanna Steel on the scale-down that followed the peace. "They took me to the cleaners, everything but four thousand dollars." But, as Joe is fond of saying, "Sure, I've made mistakes, plenty— only a liar would say he never did—but I've never made one I didn't learn something from." He learned on this occasion, "Never, but never, buy on a scale-down unless you're an insider and know what's really going on."

The Twenties saw Joe grow rich. In 1922 he married Jennie Berman of Brooklyn, who was to bear him four children. In 1924 he quit the Curb to trade in unlisted securities, first in a short-lived partnership and a year later in his own J. H. Hirshhorn and Company. By 1928 Joe Hirshhorn, strictly a broker's broker, was ringing up profits at a $200,000-a-month clip.

More memorable than the scaling of such heights, however, was Joe's tiptoeing back from the precipice that lay just ahead. In the glittering spring of 1929, when he was thinking of paying over $500,000 for a seat on the New York Stock Exchange, what impulse pulled him back from the brink? Joe remembers it this way: "When it got to where doctors and dentists were quitting their jobs to speculate, you knew it was all crazy. I could see IT coming. Nothing made sense. The big gamblers took the utility stocks and ran them way up. I got scared. I sold everything I had in August." He got out with a round four million dollars. To this general triumph he added a couple of final footnotes: After the crash, in December 1929, he started buying again, then in the following March and April sold his holdings, capping this with a swift succession of short sales. Joe recalls, "I was still a kid without much experience—otherwise I would have kept this up and made a mint."

He discovered a different route to the mint: He discovered Canada. He had been up there to look things over once or twice, and he had been much impressed by what he had heard about Canadian gold. And early in 1933 J. H. Hirshhorn and Company opened its doors, to be one of the few broker's brokers in Toronto. It was, in fact, exactly the day the banks closed in the U.S. But on Bay Street, Joe's fun and fortune were just beginning.

"MY NAME IS OPPORTUNITY AND I AM PAGING CANADA." So shouted the black headline across a full-page advertisement in Toronto's *Northern Miner*, November 16, 1933. The lusty summons read:

> "Canada, your day has come. The world is at your feet, begging you to release your riches cramped in Mother Earth. . . . Carry on until the pick strikes the hard, firm, yellow metal, until the cry of 'Gold' resounds through the virgin forest. . . . And as for us, we believe in the future of this great Country to the extent that we have made investments in gold mining and other industries in the Dominion and shall continue to do so."

It was not conventional broker's jargon; it was not poetry. It was pure Hirshhorn—a kind of rousing mating call from a man who had found the financial market of his dreams. "I'm not an investor," Joe explains. "I'm a speculator. I'm not interested in the blue chips and their dividends—they're OK for grandma and the kiddies. I've always wanted the proposition that costs a dime and pays ten dollars."

For quite a while, however, Canada was anything but hospitable to Joe. Neither Toronto society nor its stiffly conservative banking fraternity could understand, much less like, the man who worked like an American robot, chattered like a Brooklyn peddler and let his good spirits explode in such phrases as "I feel felonious!" Joe also managed to prove, while trading on his own account, that he had not lost all knack for the occasional big mistake. A flier in Tashota Gold cost him $400,000. It was a bad licking but, like the Lackawanna Steel fiasco, it had its educational value. The lesson this time read, "The engineering staff wasn't right. If it isn't right, you're in big trouble."

Joe plunged ahead, this time into Gunnar Gold. The upshot was an exciting profit and considerable notoriety. Joe went into Gunnar Gold with the LaBine brothers, Charles and Gilbert, two of Canada's best-known mine developers. To begin with, Joe owned 598,000 vendor's shares, which had cost him less than 20 cents apiece. In July 1934, three months after Gunnar Gold was put on the Toronto exchange, its stock had rocketed to $2.50. At about that time Joe began gradually unloading. Near the end of October, as the Toronto securities commissioner reported after a subsequent investigation, Joe "decided to withdraw all support from the market." The climax came on the morning of October 31, when Gunnar dived in the space of two hours from an opening price of $1.43 to 94 cents.

The commissioner's report theorized, "The process of manipulation is by buying and selling to create in the public mind the impression of great activity in the stock. . . . This Mr. Hirshhorn succeeded in doing with very great skill. . . . The manipulator can sit in the center of his operations surrounded by telephones and, by using a three- or four-way jitney, as it is called, can buy and sell stocks without brokers who are doing the buying and selling knowing that the manipulation is in process." But since it was conspiracy in stock manipulations that the Ontario laws forbade and Joe characteristically had operated alone, the commissioner conceded that Hirshhorn "has not committed any criminal act." As for Joe's side of the story, he denies that he ever manipulated Gunnar Gold. "I was in Europe," he explains. "When I came back, I found the price was down, and I didn't like what I saw; so I started selling."

It was in 1936 that there came along what Joe calls "a really big ticket." It was named Preston East Dome Mines. It established Joe's fame as a backer of long shots, it proved him more than a match for the sharpest shooters on Bay Street, and it marked his growth and transition from a pure speculator to creative promoter.

Preston East Dome was a gold-mining company formed early in the century in the hopeful shadow of a great gold strike in the Porcupine area of northern Ontario. A fire had swept the area, destroying the company's installations; Preston East Dome was out of funds, and its stock certificates, selling for less than five cents on the Toronto exchange, were used by their cheerless owners to make change in poker games. Everyone had given up hope of making something of Preston except a geologist named Douglas Wright. Knowing Joe Hirshhorn's reputation for being fast on his feet, Wright made his way to Joe's office to tell his story again. Joe liked it and put up $25,000 for a drilling program. Within a few months gold was struck—just 25 feet away from an old shaft.

As Preston stock started climbing upward, the hard-bitten skeptics jeered at reports of the strike, and Bay Street's "bandits" thought they had spotted an easy target. The stock (they assured themselves) must surely slide again, making it a setup for the short-sale snipers. They sold. Joe kept buying. He kept on buying until he had taken over a large part of Preston's whole capitalization. Preston's price kept rising —on past the two-dollar mark. The short sellers were trapped. Their intended victim had given them an expensive and humiliating licking.

The mine, presided over by Joe's old friend, sharp-witted Toronto lawyer William H. Bouck . . . [was] grossing an annual $2,500,000 [by the mid-1950s]. Joe managed judiciously to sell enough of his Preston shares at rising prices to leave himself at one point holding 500,000 shares, which, in effect, had cost him nothing. He sold a number of those at a fat profit, and . . . when he threw his remaining Preston holdings into the deal with Rio Tinto, they were valued at $7.55 a share. It was, as Joe says, quite a big ticket.

Thanks to such tickets, Joe, through the Thirties, found himself living in a world ever further removed from the bitter memory of Brooklyn. He now traveled a circuit of two apartments and three homes—the apartments in Toronto and New York, homes in Great Neck, Long Island, Miami and the Poconos. To soften the hours spent poring over corporate balance sheets, he installed a Capehart in every house and bought himself seven pianos. In the Poconos he built a splendid French-provincial house on the 470-acre Huckleberry Hill Farm, with handball courts, swimming pool, Guernsey herds and dormitories big enough to accommodate any 24 school chums his children might like to bring home. "It was built from the heart, that place," Joe remembers. "But—I was the only Jew around for twenty-five miles. People called us 'the castle on the hill.' We were left alone." Finally, in 1947, Joe sold Huckleberry Hill Farm to the Kress family for $100,000—less than a third of what it had cost him.

Meanwhile, other troubles shook the hand with the golden touch. In 1945 Joe was fined $8500 by the Canadian government for neglecting to get permits to take money (specifically $15,000) out of the country. "It was a stupid mistake," Joe admits. It was in 1945, too, that Joe's marriage ended in divorce. He is clinically honest about this misfortune. "To do what I did, you gotta work, you gotta work like crazy. I've always been married to my work. To do what I did, you've gotta make sacrifices. I sacrificed my family, my relations with my wife and my kids." In the emotional turmoil that followed the divorce he found two recourses: sustained psychoanalysis and a second marriage (1945), to the modern painter Lily Harmon. Joe believes that the analysis greatly increased his understanding of other people and himself. He stayed married to Lily nine years. Early . . . [in 1956] they were divorced, and several months later he was married again, to Brenda Hawley Heide of New York.

Through all those troubled years Joe kept at his steady zigzag run. Some people thought they saw something reprehensible in the zigzags. Mining has notoriously held an irresistible attraction for penny-stock tricksters, the "hit-and-run" boys, the vast and venal array that prompted Mark Twain to describe a gold mine as simply a big hole with a liar at the other end. The fast-talking boy from Brooklyn was in a business in which success itself was often a proof of skulduggery, especially in the sour judgment of those who had failed. Inevitably, many of the chances Joe took with his own and other people's money—a list of mining gambles with names like Anglo Rouyn, Armistice, Aquarius, Calder Bousquet—fell below high hopes. Yet Joe never has quit on a company. When, for instance, Anglo Rouyn's gold petered out, Joe switched the company into Saskatchewan copper (Anglo Rouyn was one of the biggest Hirshhorn properties in the Rio Tinto deal).

The verdict on Hirshhorn heard today in the Ontario Securities Commission's offices is that his financing has been sound, his geological advice the best and his legal counsel responsible and respected. Aside from the penalty for exporting Canadian dollars during the war, Joe has had only one encounter with the law. In 1950 New York State attorney general Nathaniel Goldstein, whom Joe had known back in the Brooklyn days, took to the press to warn the public away from a stock offering by a company called American-Canadian Uranium Company, in which Hirshhorn was involved. . . . Goldstein submitted the facts to the SEC, but the SEC found no grounds for a hearing.

During the Forties Joe's happiest venture had involved a U.S. company, Mesabi Iron, owner of substantial taconite properties. "When I bought Mesabi stock," he says, "no one knew what taconite was—they thought it was a disease or a new product to clear your skin. I knew what it was, and I knew it was going to be big." Starting his buying at 1⅜ and moving in and out of the stock over a period of years, he netted in the end $1,550,000. Joe, as this demonstrates, does not have to be on the inside of a company to turn a profit.

Meanwhile, however, he managed to lose over $300,000 in a Philippine gold-mining venture. He found himself tangled in a web of nationalist laws and currency restrictions and learned another lesson: "Be sure you know all the facts before you dip into one of those foreign ventures."

It was in the late Forties that Joe first acquired his interest in uranium, which was to prove more fascinating than anything he had touched in his life. He had been reading about Canada's Precambrian shield and the meaning of the chatter of the Geiger counter. In 1949–50, in the Lake Athabaska region of northwestern Saskatchewan, Joe had bought the claims on 470 square miles of uranium-bearing land. It was a tribute to Joe's financing skill that Rix Athabasca, as this company was called, became Canada's first producing uranium mine operating on private risk capital. Not long afterward he hired Franc. Joubin to direct his Technical Mine Consultants—his key mine-exploring organization, which was overseeing more than a score of companies that Joe had acquired.

The scholarly Joubin was wrestling with a riddle: What was there beneath Ontario's bush-shrouded Algoma Basin that gave so mysterious a kick to Geiger counters? It was a heavily explored area. A parade of prospectors and geologists had tramped its game-filled acres. Everyone had seen his Geiger kick excitedly from time to time. All had taken samples for assays from the surface, which was where uranium was supposed to lie, and every assay had shown only negligible amounts of uranium. Everyone had settled for one explanation: The Geiger readings must have come mostly from thorium, for which there was no market.

This theory largely satisfied Joubin, but he began reading about the leaching of uranium-bearing land where sulfur is present, and this gave him an idea. One day he decided to test an old Algoma ore sample for thorium itself—and found there was hardly any. He was sure then that he knew the answer: Rain and snow and sulfur in the earth had leached away the radioactivity in surface outcroppings in the basin, and the Geigers had chattered the truth of big uranium-ore bodies *beneath* the surface. He tried to persuade a dozen different mining companies and promoters to make a definitive diamond-drill test. All refused the gamble as senseless waste. So Joubin went to Joe.

When, early in 1952, Hirshhorn listened to Joubin expound his theory, Joe was a man with some knowledge of geology. But, as he says: "I bought on my faith in the man talking to me. That's what counts with me. I don't ask my grandmother or a fortune-teller."

Diamond drilling began on April 6, 1953. Joe put up $30,000. Joubin enjoyed an arrangement that was standard in his dealings with Joe (an option to buy a ten-percent share of the deal). In this instance Joubin's ten percent was to make him a multimillionaire. The core samples were sent to Vancouver for assaying. One Saturday morning in May a bulky legal-size envelope came back to Joubin's desk. The report was that out of 56 samples, 50 contained uranium. Grinning, Joubin exclaimed to a friend, "That lucky Joe!"

Beyond this point, however, luck would not suffice. A fast-moving organization was needed to stake more claims, and Joe turned for money and manpower to his success of the Thirties, Preston East Dome, in which his ten percent of stock still made him biggest shareholder. Joe sat down with Preston's president, William Bouck, over a map of the Algoma area. Bouck flashed a pencil line across the map and proposed that everything below that line belong to a newly formed Hirshhorn company, Peach Uranium; the costs and profits of everything above that line would be split 50-50 between Hirshhorn personally and Preston East Dome. Most of the trained men to stake the northern area would be supplied by Preston.

The speculator now began to operate like a general directing a massive secret maneuver. The area to be staked was filled with hunters and vacationers and lay close to both a major highway and a Canadian Pacific rail line, and the risk of the operation's becoming known was enormous. Geigers, tents, sleeping bags and tons of food had to be quietly assembled. To escape attention, Hirshhorn and his colleagues purchased mining licenses in scattered spots all over Ontario. Bases were set up at scattered points, one even at South Porcupine, 200 miles above Blind River. Lawyers were lined up to draft claim papers as fast as the staking parties made their way through the bush.

When the expedition's pontoon planes took off from South Porcupine, they headed north, then swung southwest to Algoma and there deposited in the bush some of the four score stakers, who still did not know exactly where they were. For six weeks the crews snaked along a 90-mile Z, following their chattering Geigers. A halt was called July 9. And on July 11, in mining recorders' offices all over Ontario, lawyers and engineers raced in to enter a total of 1400 claims covering 56,000 acres. Bay Street was stunned. Joe and his friends had secretly staked out one of the most fabulous claims in Canadian history.

Like many a wondrous wish come true, the triumph of Blind River posed, for Joe, an old problem: Now that you've got it, what are you going to do with it? Two decades of speculating had involved him in operations spanning Canada—oil and real estate, gold, copper, iron ore ("In mining I have no favorites; I'll mine granite if it will pay"). Blind River, on top of all this, was, in a way, just too much. The moment obviously called for stock taking in the fullest sense —combing all the corporations out of the pockets of Joe's old clothes, adding them up and putting them together in some sane order. Joe had reached the point where one day he dropped a roll of several hundred dollars on the floor of his office without missing it. This sort of thing could get serious. Joe was getting exhausted trying to keep an eye on all his wealth.

As is his custom, Joe sought out some expert help—in New York, attorney Sam Harris, who became his most intimate counselor; and in Washington, the dignified former secretary of state, Dean Acheson. Acheson discovered that New Jersey Zinc and Phelps Dodge might be interested in taking over the Algom properties and problems. After poring over test drillings and cost-projection charts, the two firms offered to buy a two-thirds interest in Algom, but at a price so low that the offer was rejected—as Acheson wryly recalls, "It was too early for Christmas." By November 1954, however, Christmas, in a businesslike way, came to Joe—in the shape of Rio Tinto Company of London. Rio Tinto had just finished selling the bulk of its great Spanish holdings in copper, sulfur and iron pyrites, and it was especially interested in a uranium investment. This news came by the international grapevine to Sam Harris, who lost no time in urging upon his client the chance to gather the pieces of his scattered empire into one neat pile.

. . . [It soon] became clear that longer-range interests of both Joe and Rio Tinto were neatly intersecting: Rio Tinto wanted permanent control over his whole Canadian mining empire, and Joe still needed a corporate package for all his holdings. The negotiations were complicated and delayed by Joe's need to get a favorable tax ruling from the U.S. Treasury governing the transfer of his assets to a foreign concern. This ruling Dean Acheson succeeded in getting. The result . . . was Rio Tinto Mining Company of Canada. Into this elegant new receptacle Joe dropped all of his holdings in 46 different Canadian mining companies (one of which was itself a package of 17 earlier companies). Although Joe did not get voting control, he owned the biggest single slice of equity (55 percent).

There were some memorable moments during the long months of negotiating that threw Hirshhorn of Brooklyn into a room full of London's financial aristocrats. As a personality, Joe made a sweeping conquest of his British confreres by remaining utterly, stubbornly himself. In conference with Rio Tinto's Roy Wright, he would carelessly throw his feet on the furniture, chew his unlit cigar unremittingly and jar leisurely British discourse to an end with a phrase like "Let's cut the baloney and make a decision, eh?" When Rio Tinto's stately 75-year-old chairman, the earl of Bessborough (recently deceased), solicitously warned Joe to slow down and conserve his energy, Joe turned to him and said, "Look here, Earl, I got plenty of health." When the whole improbable encounter of these men was concluded, there prevailed a mutual and affectionate respect. In Joe's estimate, "Those British fellows—they're *wonderful.*" Said one of Rio Tinto's executives, "Mr. Hirshhorn is called just a promoter, and *promoter* is sometimes supposed to be a dirty word. But where would Canada be without promoters? There are people who will try to belittle him, but in a way he's a great man."

Hirshhorn is most impressive when—with unlit cigar jammed between tight lips, hand towel clutched tightly, ready for a sweating brow—he reaches for a telephone. To any broker the telephone is an indispensable tool of the trade. To Joe it is like a vital physical organ, certainly to be valued, for example, above one kidney or some miscellaneous glands or even countless pints of blood. This is not entirely figurative. His son Gordon recalls one night in 1947 when he and his sister were summoned to Joe's bedside in a New York hospital, where Joe lay gravely ill with peritonitis. Joe was coming out of the anesthesia, both arms pinned beneath devices for transfusion and intravenous feeding. As the children tiptoed into the room, the semidarkness was rent with the scream: "Get this goddamn thing outta my arm—I gotta make a phone call." The children softly retired, reassured.

The phone is where Joe works. He plays upon its switch buttons like a pianist, and the rhythm of his nasal "Yeah. . . . Yeah. . . . Yeah" is the pulse of his whole office. Into the telephone rattles the sense and humor of the man. To a nuisance: "Not interested, pal, not interested—I don't wanna make any more money, get it? Take it to somebody else, *please*." To a charitable solicitation: "OK, OK, OK, I got the idea—how much you want?—just tell me that . . . one hundred? . . . I'll make it a hundred fifty." On being asked his opinion of an able executive: "He's terrific, first-class —he took the company over when it was strictly ham and eggs, and he's made it into a steak." On a different kind of executive: "He knows as much about the market as I do about Latin. He's crazy. He is also a dope." To an exciting proposition: "I'm with you—put me on your team, kid—I wanna fix up the world, too—just gimme a hammer and nails and tell me what's to be done. . . . Yeah. . . . Yeah. . . . Yeah. . . . Got it. . . . You're wonderful, you're *wonderful*. You, my friend, are *wonderful*."

"I have never," his son Gordon relates, "seen him dead serious for a solid stretch of twenty minutes." But much of this is planned therapy, Joe's substitute for the medicine that other executives find on the fairways by day or at the poker table by night. At times his prankishness can get rather frenzied, as when he opens a board meeting by crooning a few bars of *I'm in the Mood for Love*—and doing a buck-and-wing as he leaves. But at any time the wrong wisecrack could cost him a couple hundred thousand dollars. He is not a man who stops thinking when he grins.

The chemistry of success is always hard to analyze. In the case of Joseph Hirshhorn only a few elements can be clearly isolated. Joe, irrepressibly articulate, tenders his own terse formula: "Time, guts and money—that's what it takes." Applied to himself, this sheds no dazzling light. He has had no more time than most others his age, and, to begin with, he had much less money than many. The element of "guts" has counted. He has always been a stranger to panic.

At the right time he was on exactly the right stage—that is, Canada, which for the last decade has spilled such wealth from its rocky earth, and Toronto, which, with less than one-tenth as many members as the New York Stock Exchange, last year traded almost 135 percent more shares.

He learned to hire good men, and as one aide notes, "He never tries to outsmart his experts—when he talks to his lawyers, he asks them, he doesn't tell them." More important still, he has known how to deal, wisely and warmly, with the mining prospectors. They like him. They trust him. And so, when they plod back from the bush to the big city, to report a staking and to seek financing, they are quite likely to head first for the Bank of Nova Scotia Building.

He has always been the lone wolf, disdainful of the well-worn track of the pack. His administrative methods are unorthodox, owe nothing to Wharton or Harvard. One of his office aides says plaintively, "He may at any moment send me out to get his pants pressed—and to pick up a box factory on the way back." Dean Acheson, appraising Joe's business methods, offers a historical note: "Joe reminds me often of Harry Truman in his early days in the White House. Mr. Truman thought it Napoleonic to make fast decisions, and he drove us nearly crazy until we were able to convince him that there might be some merit in the considered opinion."

There has never been any master design to Joe's course of action. There has simply been that spur to action, the passion of the born speculator. "Just to test my judgment —that's what gives me the great kick," Joe explains. "The money doesn't matter—not after the first million. How could it? You can't wear more than two shirts a day or eat more than three meals." As a speculator he preaches only a couple of axioms that he has practiced. One: "Don't tell me how much I may win, but how much can I lose."

But beyond that, according to one of Joe's friends, there is in him a "passion for discovery," a fervor for making something out of nothing. "I'm not interested in the industrial or manufacturing picture," Joe explains. "That's strictly competitive, not truly creative. . . . No, I don't have a very high regard for Wall Street—it's parasitical—what does it *create?* But *resources*—that's something else. There you're in the world of the Harrimans and the Huntingtons and the men who really *built.* So look at Blind River. It took a lousy thirty thousand dollars to get it started—and now there's four, maybe eight billion dollars in wealth there. But that isn't all. There will be twenty thousand people making their living there by the end of next year. There are railroads. There are mills. There are homes. There are schools. The whole works. It's new. It's just born. And I'm glad I helped build it."

He is no easy bargainer. He gives equally hard scrutiny to a new mining proposition, to his architect's estimates for a new house or to a dinner check. Meanwhile, he is a ready donator to Columbia University or Manhattan College or the Truman Library or the hospital at Blind River. His generosity sometimes is well hidden. When he has subsidized young American artists, he has carefully avoided publicity. When he has ventured upon a promising new enterprise, he has seen that everyone in his office—and the elevator boy —has had a chance to share in it. When his second marriage proved childless, he added two adopted children to the four children of his first marriage. And if he proved considerably less than generous of his time with that family, he could find an hour to pore over the pitiful problems of some mortgage-burdened miner or farmer who once met Joe somewhere and thought maybe Joe would see some way out of the awful muddle.

He has a scorn for the more conspicuous paraphernalia of the wealthy. Private yachts and planes strike him as preposterous. (His chauffeur-driven Cadillac is a matter of sheer self-preservation. As a friend observes, "At the pace he strikes in everything, if he drove, he'd be dead at the wheel in a matter of hours.") He likes simplicity, and when he thinks of the rich or great whom he admires, he thinks of them in some homely phrase: "What a wonderful mother those Ford boys must have—they're great people. Really nice. Simple."

. . . Even Joe's closest friends have no clear glimpse of his likely future moves. When Joe recently left for several months' rest in Europe, Gordon Dean could only remark, "His ship, I know, stops at Gibraltar. I would not be surprised if he came back with the Rock."

● ● ●

The story you've just read captured Joe Hirshhorn at the climax of his career. He has continued to develop mining ventures and prospect around the stock market since then, but the pace has slowed.

Among his major moves in the late 1950s and the 1960s were an Arctic oil-and-gas speculation and a tin-mining venture in England. "But I've spent less and less time on business in recent years," says Hirshhorn, today in his early

70s. "I've spent most of my time on what I guess you'd call my hobby—art."

The Hirshhorn Museum in Washington, D.C., has about 3000 sculptures (mostly European) and 6000 paintings (mostly American). This is the main fascination in Joe Hirshhorn's life at the moment. In this he is unlike most of the other rich men you'll meet here. Most are compulsive capital gatherers. They go on furiously making money throughout their lives, long after they've accumulated more than they can possibly spend. Some have hobbies and other nonbusiness interests, but these interests remain distinctly secondary to the main work of piling fortune upon fortune. Hirshhorn has gone the other way: His hobby has become more important than his business.

And yet he hasn't been able to retire completely. The very, very rich never do. On almost any weekday you'll find Joe Hirshhorn at his New York or Toronto office. He can't stay away. "I don't keep a market tape around anymore," he says, "but I keep in touch with the stock market. I've got to. I like the action. I'd miss it too much if I went away."

He is addicted to the stock market. He has been able to cut down the dosage somewhat, but he will never be quite free. The addiction is known to be incurable.

7

The Stock Market: Selling It

Joe Hirshhorn's speculative approach to the stock market is extremely, even frighteningly, risky. The fact that he came out a winner doesn't alter the fact that he often operated from positions of high jeopardy. One false step, one thunderbolt of ill fortune, and he could have been smashed flat in an instant. There are thousands of men who have tried to parlay Canadian gold and uranium stocks into a fortune as Hirshhorn did and who haven't made it. Many are broke. Many curse the miserable day they threw their first starcrossed dollars into the action.

Now let's look at another poor kid from Brooklyn, who took a somewhat safer route to a market killing—the seller's route. Bernard Cornfeld blundered into his life's great work by sheer accident. Previously he had had little or no interest in the stock market. As a friend remarked, it was probable that Cornfeld had never before seen a stock certificate or known anything about the market or given a damn. But when he finally tripped, half-asleep, and fell into the action, he looked around and saw something that jolted him wide awake. What he saw, and what he developed for himself after a while, was an absolutely 100-percent-foolproof system for making money out of the stock market. The system didn't depend on equity speculation. It depended on selling the speculative idea to other people.

It didn't last. After a few years the amazing system began to go awry. There may be some obscure kind of poetic justice in this fact, for somehow it seems that nothing so golden should be allowed to last forever. The world's puritan morality would never stand for it. The perfect get-rich-quick scheme belongs in dreams, not real life. But while Cornfeld's system did last, its flash and glitter dazzled the eyes of businessmen all over the world.

The system could have come to fruition only in the warm, cozy, euphoric environment of a long-lived bull market. People in general had to be optimistic about stocks over the long term; the system needed that environment as a seed needs moisture to germinate. The early and middle 1960s were perfect from this point of view, and Cornfeld had the unbeatable three-way combination that makes men rich: He was in the right place at the right time with the right idea. The life-giving environment disintegrated in the late 1960s and has not been hospitable since. But if another long bull market develops and maintains itself later in this decade, Cornfeld's system or a similar one can be nurtured again. If Cornfeld himself doesn't do it (he is still only in his middle 40s), somebody else inevitably will.

The story you are about to read is not only the story of a complex and interesting man. It is also, in a sense, a recipe for somebody's future success.

Bernard Cornfeld: One Hundred Fifty Million Dollars

Consider the butterfly. He spends most of his life as a caterpillar, grubbing about amid the leaves, ugly, unwanted, unnoticed. The struggle seems to be too much for him, for after a while he abandons it. He wraps himself in a cocoon and retires from life in gloomy solitude. And then suddenly he emerges as a butterfly. For a few glorious summer days he flies from flower to flower under the sun, a piece of sheer living color, startling the eye with his brilliance. His whole life has led up to this brief climax of joy. Has it been worth the effort? The butterfly may wonder, for he quickly fades and is seen no more.

Thus it was with Bernard Cornfeld. He started as nobody in particular—an ordinary man like you and me, grubbing for money to pay bills and taxes, holding hard to a slippery lower rung of the lower middle class. And then, in the 1960s, his short, bright summer arrived. He became the international king of the mutual-fund business and an acknowledged prince of the global jet set.

Nobody ever went quite so far as to call him one of the

Beautiful People. *Beautiful* wasn't a word that could be accurately applied to Bernie Cornfeld. He was a man of middle height, somewhat plump, with a roundness of face accentuated by early baldness. But in all other respects he was a standout member of that leisured, highly visible, supremely affluent class. He had châteaus in Switzerland and great, expensively decorated apartments in Paris and London and New York. He wore custom-made French suits and Italian shoes in the latest of moneyed Mod styles. He affected a small, tufty beard at one time, though it failed to square or lengthen the moon-round face. He traveled everywhere with a covey of lesser, female butterflies, also brilliantly hued: long-legged, miniskirted young ladies of sundry nationalities, most of them ten or twenty years younger than he.

And then the summer ended as abruptly as it had begun. The empire collapsed, and Bernie Cornfeld was seen no more.

He went out with money in his pocket, of course. How much? The question is hard to answer. Cornfeld himself has never offered any enlightenment on the subject. There have been a number of guesses, but that is all they really are—guesses. To settle on a median guess, let's say Cornfeld's net worth today is probably somewhere near $50 million. At the height of his fortune he was worth easily $150 million.

The specific figures may be in error, but the generality is correct. Bernie Cornfeld is very, very rich at the age of 44. He was very, very rich before he was 40, in fact. He has proven once again what other men in our gilded gallery have proven: that even in this era of high taxes and high costs and other apparent barriers, it is still possible to go financially from nowhere to somewhere rather rapidly.

Let's see how on earth he did it.

Bernard Cornfeld was born in Turkey on August 17, 1927. His parents were Jews from central Europe, well educated, moderately well off. When Bernie was a grade-schooler they moved to America, impelled partly by a rising tide of anti-Semitism that was soon to engulf most of Europe. They settled in New York City's unprepossessing but friendly borough, Brooklyn. The father, a theatrical promoter and actor, died shortly afterward. The family's sole support from then on was the mother, who scrounged a meager living as a nurse while recalling past glories in Europe. Young Cornfeld thus grew up in an atmosphere of shabby intellectual-style gentility.

Unlike many of the other moneyed folk we've met and are to meet in this gallery, Bernard Cornfeld seems to have been a perfectly satisfactory student in school. He graduated from high school with a B-plus average, served in the U.S. Merchant Marine during and after World War Two, went to Brooklyn College and came out with a bachelor's degree in psychology.

"Nobody back then was predicting old Bernie would become a multimillionaire," says Tom Pinker, a New York advertising man who was casually acquainted with Cornfeld in his college days. "In fact, he often talked as though he hated money. He was one of those campus reform-the-world nuts. You know, always going to weird political meetings and yakking about socialism and negative taxation and nutty stuff like that. Hell, I don't think he even knew what a stock certificate looked like."

After college Bernie Cornfeld drifted through a number of minor jobs, obviously and admittedly uncertain of the course his life should take. "Sometimes I think money is the answer," he said once to a girlfriend, "and sometimes I think money is a damned illusion." For a time it seemed as though he was going to turn his back on money and follow the world-reforming urge he had displayed in college. He went to work for a Jewish social-cultural organization in Philadelphia as a kind of youth counselor.

"That was the kind of job we all thought Bernie would end up in," reminisces Tom Pinker. "Most of us were actually more interested in money and security than he was. We were the silent generation, you may remember—the generation that was all shot up and beat down by the war. All we wanted from life was a steady job with guaranteed raises and free hospital insurance and a retirement plan. It wasn't usual in those days for a college kid to go into social work the way kids do today. Social work didn't pay the kind of money or offer the kind of security we were looking for. But Bernie wasn't one of us in that sense. He didn't seem to want money. He was heading in the opposite direction from the rest of us. It's strange, when you think of it, that he was the one who finally ended by hitting the jack-pot."

Bernard Cornfeld, social worker. The cocoon stage.

What actually happened to him emotionally and intellec-tually in that cocoon, what transformations took place in his developing mind, is hard to say. Cornfeld himself has tried to analyze the transformations in logical fashion, but he hasn't succeeded well, and neither has anybody else. It may be that this part of Cornfeld's story cannot be told in rational terms. For it is a curious fact that some of the most momentous changes in a man's life can spring from the most trivial circumstances—indeed, from external circum-stances having nothing at all to do with the man's strengths and weaknesses, his hopes and fears, his internal aches and itches. A man can drift into his life's most colossal happen-ing without meaning to and without even knowing where he is going. (For a fuller discussion of this baffling fact, see chapter 10, on luck.) Something like this appears to have happened to Bernard Cornfeld in 1954.

For no particularly compelling reason he left Philadel-phia, drifted to New York and got a job as a mutual-fund salesman. It was an easy job to land, and that is certainly one reason why he took it. A psychology major with a back-ground in social work could not choose from a great wealth of job opportunities in those pragmatic days. Few com-panies had any use for such a man. But mutual funds, then lustily growing in the postwar bull market, were desperately raking the undergrowth for salesmen. Almost anybody who could speak English and smile was welcomed in off the street, shot through a quick training course and shot back out to sell fund shares to an apparently limitless public of easy marks. Thus the young social worker was pulled into the fund business.

And thus, with no noticeable long-range planning and no fanfare and no awareness that anything very terrific had happened, Bernard Cornfeld launched himself on his life's great work.

A mutual fund is ostensibly an outfit that, for the mutual enrichment of its shareholders, gathers money from them, puts the money into a pool and invests it—most commonly in stocks. If the investments are sound, the pool gets bigger and so does each investor's share. In hustling fund shares to the public, salesmen usually stress two points: (1) that a small investor can command a greater diversity of stocks through fund ownership than he could by buying individual stocks himself, and (2) that he gets the advantage of what is portentously called "professional money management."

What the small investor doesn't always realize is how much this is going to cost him.

The salesman's commission, management fee, performance fee and other charges can add up to well over ten percent of what the investor kicks in. Thus, if he puts up $1000, $100 or more will disappear rapidly, and he is left with shares worth $900 or less. This $900 is what he will get if he decides he has made a mistake and elects to cash out. The per-share value of the fund will have to rise by more than 11 percent before the poor sucker can so much as break even, let alone score a capital gain.

Indeed, he may be even worse off than that. The lucky salesman may sell him a so-called contractual plan, under which the investor mails in a stated amount per month for a stated number of years. ("See how it can build up!" enthuses the salesman, flashing gorgeous colored charts with Everest-steep lines climbing toward infinity.) What the salesman fails to explain is that the contractual plan is "front-end loaded," meaning that all or most of the salesman's commission for the entire five-year or ten-year deal will be scooped out of the first year's payments. If the shareholder decides to cash out early ("That's your privilege," the salesman assures him, making a virtue out of it), he may find his actual shareholdings are worth only 50 percent or 75 percent of the money he has forked over.

In fairness it must be said that many investors have been served well by mutual funds—especially investors who were smart or lucky enough to get in at the beginnings of bull markets and who then were smart or lucky enough to stick with it for an appreciable time and thus outearn the commissions and fees. Mutual-fund managers obviously would rather have their shareholders make money than lose; it's better advertising and makes the salesmen's job easier. But Bernard Cornfeld was introduced to the business by salesmen-teachers who viewed it from a special angle. It didn't make any difference to them whether a given customer won or lost. They, the salesmen, won every time a new investor was brought into the fold.

What the salesmen had, in the booming 1950s, was a 100-percent-foolproof system for making money out of the stock market. There aren't many such systems. No system that depends on *investing* in the market is foolproof. Most, in fact, offer little better than 50-50 odds. The salesmen, however, were in the lovely position of claiming a win every time somebody else's money was invested.

Things aren't so easy for fund salesmen today. With the 1969–70 market collapse not far behind us, we are now keenly aware that stock prices can go down far and fast—and, once down, can sit and sit and sit. But in the middle 1950s many people believed the Final Permanent Bull Market had at last been established. Fund salesmen didn't have to talk very hard to convince people that one's money could grow faster in the stock market than in a savings account—and not only faster but with equal safety. Everybody knew there weren't going to be any more wars, depressions or bear markets of any great consequence or duration. Putting your money into a mutual fund, the salesmen could argue (quite reasonably, so it seemed at the time), was the same as putting it in a bank with an almost guaranteed annual interest rate of 20 percent or so.

No, it wasn't hard for a salesman to find customers in those days. And young Bernard Cornfeld must have thought, *How long has this been going on? Why didn't I get here sooner?* He plunged into his newfound profession with astonishment and delight.

His employer in those early New York days was a mutual fund called IPC—Investors Planning Corporation. (Later, one of Cornfeld's companies was to buy IPC.) His colleagues there remember him as a competent but not brilliant salesman. He earned a good living for a young man of the period—enough, at any rate, to afford a car and an attractive Manhattan pad and an endless supply of girls. But he seemed not to be throwing his whole heart and soul into the salesman's job. Having learned this much about the fund business, he wanted to know more. The more he learned, the more fascinated he became.

Up above the lowly salesmen's level he saw worlds beyond worlds. There were supervisory salesmen, who took cuts from the commissions of salesmen under them; and there were district and national executives, who took cuts from the supervisory salesmen's cuts; and up at the top were the fund organizers, who took cuts from everybody. Cornfeld, in those early New York days, spent nearly as much time learning about the fund's financial engineering as he did selling.

He had now found himself in terms of profession but not in terms of environment. New York left him dissatisfied for a number of reasons. Competition among fund salesmen there was savage, for one thing. Cornfeld thought there might be other areas of the world less crowded with competitors. Moreover, he was still a young bachelor in a drifting mood. He had seen a little of the world with the Merchant Marine and had felt drawn by the romance of foreign lands. And so, late in 1955, he went to Paris (with IPC's blessing but at his own expense) to see what could be done about selling mutual-fund shares there.

It turned out that a lot could be done. Most European governments forbade him to sell to their citizens, because they didn't want scarce capital drained off to America. So Cornfeld looked around and discovered the American-expatriate market. Europe in those days was full of American troops, diplomats and businessmen, most of them stationed overseas for protracted periods with their families. Their U.S. paychecks went a long way in the European economy, which was growing more affluent but which still lagged far behind booming postwar America. They had a lot of spare dollars. Many of them had read about the grand times that were being had on Wall Street, but being far from the action, they had no convenient way to move their money in and out of U.S. stocks. Cornfeld offered them a convenient way.

He sold enough IPC shares to demonstrate that a large, rich market for U.S. mutual funds existed overseas. He then severed relations with IPC and turned his attention to a mutual fund that he considered much more exciting and more salable: the Dreyfus Fund. This was an early version— perhaps the ancestor and archetype—of the go-go funds that were to leap to high prominence in the 1960s. Instead of being satisfied with slow, steady capital appreciation, the Dreyfus Fund went after killings—and sold its shares on that basis. One of its more famous killings was Polaroid. Dreyfus bought this stock when it was selling at slightly over $30 a share in the late 1940s. As far as anybody then knew, the stock was a dog. But Jack Dreyfus's hunch about it proved brilliantly right. His original shares, after numerous splits, eventually soared in value to more than $6000 apiece.

Cornfeld wrote to the Dreyfus Fund, offered some juicy statistics about the market he had uncovered in Europe and asked to be appointed Dreyfus's European dealer on a commission basis. Dreyfus, having no full-time European operative and having nothing to lose, said OK.

Cornfeld gave his new firm the grandiose name of Investors Overseas Service (IOS). He started by selling Dreyfus Fund shares himself—a one-man dealership. Then he began recruiting other salesmen one by one to work under him. The setup was the standard one of fund hierarchies: Cornfeld kept about a fifth of each salesman's commission on each sale.

At first the IOS sales force was small enough so that the whole crew—including Cornfeld—could pile into Cornfeld's car. They would drive to some likely city, put up at its medium-priced hotel if it had one, sell Dreyfus at the local U.S. Air Force base by day and sample the local booze and girls by night. Gradually the force grew too big for this omnibus wandering technique, and in any case Cornfeld was earning enough from the dealership commission cuts so that he no longer needed to sell in person. He established a combination pad-office in Paris and concentrated on recruiting new salesmen, opening up new territories and building the dealership. When the French government grumped that he was illegally selling to French citizens and began making trouble for him, he moved the operation to Switzerland.

By the late 1950s IOS had nearly 100 salesmen wandering about the earth on its behalf. They were not only in Europe but were beginning to spread into other parts of the world where there were concentrations of Americans with money: Africa, India, South America. The sales force was growing too big for Bernie Cornfeld to manage alone; so he established new, intermediate levels in the hierarchy. Some of the original salesmen moved up to become supervisors, with authority to recruit and train their own stables of salesmen in various countries and regions—plus, of course, authority to extract cuts from those salesmen's commissions. In time each of these supervisors built a stable big enough so that he had to set up subsupervisory levels below himself, and some of the supervisors eventually appointed sub-subsupervisors.

Each level took its bite from the money that the share buyers believed themselves to be investing in the stock market. The final bite, of course, went into the capacious pocket of Bernard Cornfeld. By 1960, at the age of 33, without having invested any important amounts of his own money, he had made himself a millionaire.

And now he was ready to take the final breathtaking step in his climb upward through the mutual-fund business. He was ready to organize his own fund.

"It was very easy to set up a mutual fund back then," says a Zurich banker, now in New York, who began dealing with IOS at about this time. "You couldn't do it easily in America, Switzerland or any country with strict laws for protection of investors. But if you chose some other country whose laws were more easygoing, all you really needed was a mailing address, the names of a few important-sounding banks and directors to put on your prospectus and a good printer who could turn out expensive-looking share certificates. You then went out, sold shares, collected money and invested it in practically any stock that caught your eye."

Cornfeld's first mutual fund was named International Investment Trust (IIT). It was incorporated in Luxembourg, a tiny country that stresses the *free* in free enterprise. The fund's mailing address and actual operating headquarters, however, remained in Switzerland with the rest of IOS. Cornfeld's seasoned and aggressive salesmen were able to give prospective investors the impression that this new IIT was a large, rock-solid, Swiss-based outfit. The shares sold like glamour stocks in a bull market. At the end of 12 months IIT had some three and a half million dollars of other people's money to invest, and the size of the fund kept growing until it finally reached nearly three-quarters of a billion dollars.

Cornfeld had long been irritated by the restriction of selling only to American citizens. Several foreign governments had complained in the late 1950s that IOS salesmen (perhaps without Cornfeld's blessing) were secretly evading this restriction—were in fact selling Dreyfus shares in volume to non-Americans through various banking and currency-changing subterfuges. Cornfeld now set about the task of getting the restriction lifted, country by country. He went to each country's monetary authorities and said, in effect, "You're worried about capital flowing out of the country, right? OK, I'll tell you what I'll do. My new fund, IIT, will invest some of its money in your country's stocks. In return, you must let me sell shares to your citizens."

As this deal was concluded in one nation after another, IIT's stock portfolio became highly diverse, to put it kindly. The stocks held ranged from solid Swiss and Dutch and American blue chips to obscure little companies and speculative ventures scattered all over the world—ventures that no regulated U.S. fund would have been allowed to touch. Not all these investments proved sound. IIT's shares, originally offered at five dollars, lost about 25 percent of their market value in the first two years of operation and didn't struggle back to five dollars until the fourth year. But Cornfeld's salesmen obviously didn't stress this fact when discussing IIT with new prospects, and the prospects continued to buy new shares, and the raw size of the fund continued to grow without letup.

Cornfeld thus phased himself from supersalesman to fund manager. His personal income no longer flowed mainly from sales commissions but from much richer sources. He now commanded management fees (calculated as percentages of the fund's total value), performance fees (calculated on the quarterly growth in per-share value, if any) and sundry brokerage and other bites that an alert fund operator could extract from the vast sums under his control.

If operating one fund was nice, Cornfeld and his top lieutenants figured, operating more than one would probably be still nicer. In 1962 they generated what may have been the most brilliant of all their ideas. This was the Fund of Funds.

The sonorous, faintly biblical name was without doubt a stroke of genius. The idea behind FOF was also highly salable, though it didn't make a great deal of sense when you analyzed it in sober quiet after the salesman had left. FOF was set up and promoted as a mutual fund that would invest mainly in other mutual funds.

"Look at it this way," the salesman would say. "You invest in a mutual fund to get diversity and professional management, check? So if you invest in the Fund of Funds, you get both *double*. You can't lose!"

You could, in fact, lose easily. In the first place, you paid two sets of fees—one directly to the Fund of Funds, the other indirectly to the funds invested in. In the second place, the sales pitch was based on two entirely unwarranted assumptions.

First assumption: that the professional management and diversity offered by a mutual fund will automatically protect investors against loss when the market turns sour. As was demonstrated with poignant clarity in the late 1960s, this simply is not true. Mutual funds went down the drain in 1969 and 1970 along with everything else.

Second assumption: that a master fund or fund-of-funds setup can be counted on to pick those funds that will fare best in a market downturn—or at least, through its diversity, to pick a cluster of funds in which the majority will stay afloat in foul weather. This had already been shown up as mere wishful thinking in 1929, when layers of investment companies, built one on top of the other in fund-of-funds style, all came tumbling down together in a single mighty crash. As a Securities and Exchange Commission official put it in 1971, "If a single mutual fund can't guarantee to pick the right stocks, why should anyone suppose a superfund can guarantee to pick the right funds?"

Yet the somewhat leaky logic behind the Fund of Funds made sense to thousands upon thousands of people, and IOS salesmen rapidly grew rich. And Bernard Cornfeld grew richer.

The Fund of Funds was incorporated in Canada as a subsidiary of the parent company, IOS. Why Canada? Because Canadian securities laws were friendly to this type of enterprise. United States law specifically bars any publicly owned investment company such as a mutual fund from owning more than a small percentage of any other public investment company's shares. The law was written to prevent a repetition of the disastrous 1929 chain-reaction effect in which the first layer of funds buckles under the second layer, which in turn buckles under the third layer. Canadian law in the 1960s, however, had no prohibitions against the fund-of-funds approach. One fund was allowed to own a sizable portion of another.

There was nothing to prevent FOF from buying shares of U.S. mutual funds on the open international markets. And so the Fund of Funds, in the first phase of its notable career, concentrated on investing in hot Wall Street funds that were known and admired by investors all over the world.

The second phase came when Cornfeld and his aides were struck by an intriguing idea: Suppose IOS were to set up some new funds of its own, and suppose the Fund of Funds were then to buy their shares. This way IOS could collect two sets of management and performance fees—one for the first layer of funds, the other for FOF.

This led to a still more intriguing notion. The U.S. law against multilayered funds applied only to publicly owned companies—that is, companies whose shares were sold to the public. But a privately owned company could behave in this respect as it wished. If IOS were to set up a fund with just one shareholder, namely FOF, that would fulfill the definition of *private company*. Such a privately owned fund could operate without legal interference in the United States— indeed, could set up shop right on Wall Street, the center of the big action. To IOS, long denied direct access to Wall Street and the rest of the U.S., the notion was hugely attractive.

And so, one by one, privately owned IOS funds came into existence. They invested in all kinds of stocks from blue chips to hair-raising speculations; they invested in real estate (an investment area in which heavy restrictions are imposed on public open-end funds in the U.S.) and in Arctic oil exploration and sundry other ventures, some more prudent than others. Gradually FOF ceased to be what it had set out to be—a superfund investing in other mutual funds. It became, instead, a kind of holding company operating a string of ventures that were all ultimately managed by one central group of wheeler-dealers.

Bernard Cornfeld was now, in the middle and late 1960s, enjoying the fullest flowering of his brief summer. "The IOS structure had become so huge and complicated," says one of Cornfeld's Zurich banker friends, "that almost nobody could sort it out. Every time I thought I had it figured out, a new piece would turn up and I'd have to take the puzzle apart again to fit the new piece in." But though few men knew exactly where all Cornfeld's wealth lay or exactly how it was pieced together, almost every newspaper reader in the Western world knew the round-faced social worker from

Brooklyn had become improbably rich.

Cornfeld would turn up at such jet-set watering spots as Acapulco, Mexico, and make headlines simply by arriving. Photographers would scramble to take leggy pictures of the famous miniskirt platoon with which he traveled. He threw enormous parties and seemed delighted when *Life* or the *New Yorker* sent reporters around to cover the festivities. "He sometimes acted like a college boy bragging about all the girlfriends he has collected," says the Zurich banker.

Warren Avis, the millionaire who founded the Avis Rent-A-Car System, owns a house in Acapulco and was occasionally invited to Cornfeld's parties. Avis is a serious-minded man with no great interest in such affairs, but he strolled over to Cornfeld's place one night out of curiosity. When he saw that the party was degenerating into an orgy and that reporters were present, he turned around and went back home. "I told Bernie," he recalls, "that he should cool it. He had set himself up as an international financier, handling millions of other people's dollars. It seemed to me he was projecting altogether the wrong image. People expect a financier to be quiet, sober, prudent. . . ."

Bernie Cornfeld's public image as an international swinger may indeed have contributed to his summer's abrupt end. The image certainly didn't help him.

Trouble began in the late 1960s when some of the less prudent fund speculations turned sour. It wasn't serious trouble at first, but it was aggravated by some internal management and cost problems—by sheer mismanagement, unhappy shareholders later charged. The result was a painful cash shortage.

Partly to raise cash, IOS decided to go public in 1969. The parent company's stock, until then privately held by Cornfeld and his aides and salesmen, was offered to the public at ten dollars per share. This not only raised cash for the company; it also enabled Cornfeld and his colleagues to cash out of the business in varying degrees. Previously they had been private stockholders in a company whose shares weren't traded on any public market. They could cash out only by finding private buyers—which might have been difficult. But now the shares were publicly traded, and Cornfeld and his men could sell as many shares as the market cared to absorb—and could come out with cash.

Those who sold their shares right away fared well. Those who hung on hoping the market price would rise far above ten dollars soon regretted it. For shortly after IOS stock was publicly floated, the world's stock markets faltered, slumped, recovered briefly and then crashed.

Ah, woe! The whole structure of IOS collapsed beneath the horrified shareholders' feet. The market value of the funds' dizzy speculations plummeted one by one. Some investments were wiped out completely, reduced to flat zero.

A decade back, buyers of the various IOS mutual funds had been assured by salesmen that their money was going to grow by something like 20 percent compounded yearly. It now turned out that these promises had been, to put it gently, exaggerated. People who in 1960 had bought the first IOS fund, IIT, discovered by the end of 1970 that their money had grown by somewhat less than three percent per year over the decade. They would have been far better off putting their money in savings banks. People who had bought FOF shares when the superfund was launched would have been far better off keeping their money under a mattress. The shares were issued at ten dollars apiece in 1962. Eight years later they were worth less than eight dollars.

Nobody in his right mind wanted to buy IOS fund shares anymore. In fact, hordes of fund shareholders wanted to cash out as fast as possible. The once-rich salesmen could no longer earn a dime. The glory days were over. IOS began to come apart.

A group of directors and major stockholders got together in 1970, frantically sought a scapegoat and picked Bernie Cornfeld. Charging him with gross mismanagement and other failings, they voted him out of the company he had founded. He made several attempts to regain control. When these failed, he vanished from the IOS scene.

He went out with less wealth than he had once had. But he was by no means a poor man. According to one authoritative Zurich guess, the value of his personal holdings as he departed was about $50 million. "He certainly has enough," one Zurich banker says, "to support him for the rest of his days in the rather lavish style he likes."

The directors who blamed him for the company's collapse were not altogether justified in their action. True, Cornfeld himself had performed much of the basic engineering on this huge and shaky structure. But dozens of other men helped, and it wasn't fair to blame Cornfeld alone. Booting him out certainly didn't solve the company's problems. IOS continued to go downhill after Cornfeld left. The company ended the year 1970 by reporting a staggering loss of some $60 million.

The IOS shares, issued at ten dollars apiece in 1969, plummeted to a low of 38 cents in 1971. In fact, they were virtually unsalable. As this book goes to press, bickering groups of stockholders are still gloomily seeking ways to bring the shattered company back to life.

And Bernie Cornfeld? The poor boy from Brooklyn who started it all seems to be out of it for good. He may be glad he is. He may laugh secretly at the efforts to revive IOS. On the other hand, he may wish he were in there helping. He may miss the action.

He isn't as visible as he used to be. He turns up once in a while at his favorite spots in Geneva, Acapulco and elsewhere. But he turns up quietly and often by himself. He prowls the world alone, a remote and brooding figure. His old friends sometimes feel sorry for him.

But perhaps there is no real reason to feel sorry for Bernie Cornfeld. He is certainly rich in terms of money. Not as rich as he might be, but quite rich enough to be reckoned an outstanding financial success. And he also has another form of wealth to enjoy. He has a 20-year hoard of memories richer than most men could pile up in 20 lifetimes.

8

The Scatterseeds
Approach

Most of the wealthy men we've visited so far have been, to some extent, specialists. Each has made his fortune predominantly in a single industry or a single characteristic type of venture. Though he might have wandered into other territories at various times in his life, each was continually drawn back to his primary field—the field about which he felt he knew the most, in which he felt the most confident, the most comfortable. This primary field is the one with which the world associates the man and by which it labels him. Thus Clement Stone, though he has toe-dipped and waded and sometimes plunged into many ventures during the course of a busy life, is still inescapably labeled as an insurance man. Conrad Hilton is unequivocally a hotel man, William Benton an advertising man, and so on.

Now we'll look at a different breed—a type of man for whom no such handy label offers itself. This type of man doesn't become wedded to a single industry or a single, identifiable manipulative mechanism. His approach is to scatter seeds in all directions. Some of the seeds shrivel and die. Others mature into enormous trees. The man becomes rich. And in the end, looking back on it all, neither he nor anybody else can find a convenient tag with which to describe the means by which his wealth was piled up. You can't say of him, "He was a such-and-such man," or, "He made his pile in this-or-that business." You can only mumble, "He's—well, rich."

Such a man is Howard Hughes.

Howard Hughes:
One Billion Dollars

In one sense it might be argued that Hughes doesn't belong in the group we've gathered here. All the men whose portraits we've hung thus far in our gilded gallery have been men who struggled up from humble, if not downright ragged, beginnings. They began as men like you and me—men with no particular economic advantages except the magnificent thoughts that were drifting about inside their skulls. That's what makes them interesting. In that sense Howard Hughes is not one of our men, for he began with a handsome inheritance.

But there are at least two sound reasons for including Hughes despite that disqualifying fact. For one thing, Hughes is so staggeringly, so monumentally rich that it is hard to ignore him no matter what qualifying rules one might set up. He is one of the two or three richest men in America—and, for all anybody knows, in the world. Ignoring him would be something like staring into a million-candlepower arc lamp and saying, "Never mind, it isn't there, look at all those other pretty little lights down below."

For another thing, it can be fairly said of Hughes that he made most of this colossal wealth himself, with his own brain and backbone. His life can therefore teach us something, perhaps. He didn't become one of the world's richest man simply by sitting on his father's fortune and watching the dividends pile up around him. His inheritance was not that big, after all—roughly half a million dollars in appraised value. Howard Hughes, when he began his remarkable career in the 1920s, was only one of thousands of Texas sons and daughters whose fathers had struck it rich in the state's oil boom. Most of those sons and daughters went nowhere in particular—went, in fact, to oblivion. Their names ring no bells today. Young Howard Hughes took a distinctly different route. He saw his father's capital not as a cushion upon which to sit and grow fat but as a bag of seeds that could be made to grow—provided someone stood up, went out into the world and sowed them.

Howard Hughes did that. The forest he planted contained many peculiar and fascinating trees.

It is an illuminating fact about Howard Hughes that,

throughout most of his life, he lacked anything resembling a headquarters office.

He conducted his business from public telephone booths, hotel rooms, wherever he happened to be. Most of the information he needed to run his bewilderingly diverse enterprises—information that the average systematic businessman would store in file cabinets—he stored in his head. His employees and even his close associates seldom knew where he was on any given day. He would dart about among his far-flung ventures with an apparent lack of plan and a total lack of formal scheduling that irritated and confounded the more orderly-minded of his executives.

If you wanted to get in touch with him, you called a phone number and were plugged into a switchboard that, at various stages of his career, might be in Hollywood, Las Vegas or Houston. You gave your message to a secretary. A few weeks might go by. Finally, if Hughes felt like talking to you, he would phone you back, perhaps from a neighboring city, perhaps from halfway around the world. The call might come at 1:00 A.M. your time. Hughes wouldn't consider this important. It might be 4:00 A.M. his time.

The formal structures of the business world meant nothing to Hughes: its chains of command, its documents, its timetables. He worked when he wanted to work, sometimes 36 or more hours at a stretch. The fit of work might seize him as readily on a weekend as on a standard business day, as readily after midnight as between 9:00 A.M. and 5:00 P.M. "He was the kind of man," says a Hollywood press agent who knew him in his moviemaking days, "who broke every rule taught by the Harvard Business School. Every rule except the one that says you should make money."

He has often seemed like an extremely disordered man, even a scatterbrained one. The impression is wrong. Howard Hughes may be a genius. He has a mind that feeds on problems as greedily as a dog feeds on meat. When one problem has been swallowed and digested, Hughes goes out and looks for more. His range of interests is huge. He is curious about everything. His mind is immensely retentive, capable of being interested in a dozen things at once. He could never be satisfied operating in just one business, for there was always another business on the horizon that attracted his attention and demanded, by its very presence, that he assault it with his brain. Thus, he never had a head-quarters office. His inquisitiveness, his hunger for facts and firsthand experience, was such that he couldn't let other men run parts of his empire while he sat and counted money in a centralized palace. As the actress Katharine Hepburn once put it, "He was never anywhere; he was always en route to somewhere else."

Today, in his late 60s, Hughes has apparently settled down somewhat. He never talks to the press and shrouds all his movements in elaborate secrecy; so it is hard to know at all times where he is. But he seems to spend part of his time in the Caribbean and part in Las Vegas, where he owns fabulously valuable real-estate holdings. He may be feeling old and tired. Perhaps some of his aircraft-crash injuries, of which he has had many in his lifetime, have been aggravated by age and are troubling him. On the other hand, perhaps this apparent hiatus in his life is nothing more than a period of reflection and reorientation. He may be planning bold new moves into still different lines of business.

Howard Hughes's life is a lesson in how to get rich through diversity. Diversity is, of course, a time-honored technique of certain prudent stock-market players. It is also a technique for operating a corporation. (Harvard B-School types, with their penchant for adding unnecessary syllables, generally refer to it as "diversification.") The idea is to have many things going for you and thus get the law of averages on your side. One thing may fail, but others, with luck, will succeed.

The technique isn't foolproof, and, indeed, there are some who say it's nonsense. Certainly, it can be carried too far. Your affairs can become so diverse that you have too little time to devote to any one of them, and some or all collapse. (Even Hughes seemed to have overdone it at one point.) Nor is diversity, even moderate diversity, everybody's cup of tea. There are some men, such as Hughes, whose minds are capable of switching back and forth between wildly dissimilar fields of thought without getting confused or feeling pressured—in fact, who are bored and restless when denied the opportunity for such switching. There are other men, such as Conrad Hilton, who are more comfort-able and effective when they can concentrate narrowly on one small, tight bundle of thoughts. Neither type of mind is necessarily superior to the other, but the two are distinctly different, and neither seems to operate well in the other's milieu. Each man must recognize how his own mind works best. If you want to try Howard Hughes's route to riches, first be sure you have Hughes's type of mind.

Howard Hughes was born in Houston on December 24, 1905. His father was an oil speculator and wildcatter—not a notably successful one up to then. But there was a valuable idea in the senior Hughes's head, and the idea came to fruition when young Howard was still a toddler. It was an idea for a new kind of oil-drilling bit—one which, if it worked, would cut through hard rock far beneath the earth's surface and thus open up huge reservoirs of oil that so far had been unattainable.

It worked. The senior Hughes patented it and founded a company to manufacture and lease it. The enterprise evolved into the small but prosperous Hughes Tool Company.

The senior Hughes died in 1924, when Howard was 18. The estate, of which Hughes Tool was the main component, was appraised at slightly over $600,000. Under his father's will, the teen-age Howard received title to three-quarters of the company's stock, with the remaining quarter going to a gaggle of relatives.

The law, under normal circumstances, is reluctant to let minors vote capital stock in cases where they inherit a controlling interest in a company. It was assumed that young Howard Hughes would follow the usual pattern in such cases: He'd allow his stock to be handled by some kind of voting trust until he reached 21.

"Most teen-age boys would have taken that route," says a New York banker who dealt with Hughes in later years. "After all, why not? What the hell, there were only three years to wait. What's more, those were boom times, and the company was doing nicely. It was running itself. The kid could assume dividends would keep piling up and the value of his stock would keep appreciating. Any normal kid would have been happy to sit on his ass for three years and spend the money without doing any work. But this particular kid, this Hughes—he wasn't a normal kid."

Indeed, he wasn't. Curiously, up to that time he hadn't shown many signs of being out of the ordinary. Dozens of biographers have interviewed his schoolteachers and boyhood friends in the hope of spotting peculiarities, but the search has produced only dry holes. The people who knew Hughes in his youth can only shrug helplessly and say, "He was just—you know, an average kid."

Like many of the very rich whom we've met and are yet to meet in the book, Hughes was decidedly a late bloomer. Except for a certain brilliance in mathematics and the physical sciences, he was a mediocre student in school. He liked to tinker with a ham radio set and other gadgetry in his spare time but, as far as anybody can recall, showed no particular inventiveness during his boyhood. Nor did he show any notably thrusting entrepreneurial spirit: He neither hawked newspapers nor did anything else that Horatio Alger would have considered worthy of mention. Socially he was just as drab. Girls seem to have been somewhat uninterested in him, and the nonpassion was reciprocated. (Photographs of Hughes in his late teens show a puppy-dog face that was just beginning to take on a masculine handsomeness, but he was too tall for his weight, gangly, awkward and shy.) Indeed, Hughes appears to have shambled dimly around the outer fringes of teen society. He was one of those quiet, ghostly youngsters who drift through a school without leaving any tracks. They come to class, they do their unspectacular work, they go home. Years later people say, "Who the hell was he? Did he really sit in *my* classroom?"

But suddenly, at the age of 18, for reasons that neither Hughes nor anyone else has ever explained satisfactorily, the quiet kid caught fire.

He decided he didn't want to spend three years merely sitting. To the amazement of everybody (especially the relatives who held the remaining 25 percent of Hughes Tool's stock), he went to court and argued that he was competent to vote his own shares. A seldom-invoked Texas law permitted the court to give him this voting power if he presented a reasonable case. He did.

"I would like to suggest, Mr. Hughes," said the judge in handing down his decision, "that you find older men to help you carry the burden of your new responsibility for a few years. Your education should not stop here. You should go on to college."

Hughes nodded politely, but he had no intention of going back into any classroom. He was impatient to try himself against the real world. Like many others in our gallery of the rich, he never earned a college degree. But he did follow another part of the judge's suggestion: He looked for able men to help him run Hughes Tool.

"Despite his tender years," says John Keats in his biography, *Howard Hughes,* "despite his awkward nervousness, his look of abstracted melancholy and his somewhat lonesome life, the youth was a rare judge of people. . . ." Sitting in his father's office at Hughes Tool a few weeks after the court decision, he interviewed men who were applying for an accountant's job. The man he hired was Noah Dietrich. This hard, bright man quickly became Hughes Tool's chief operating executive and, for the next three decades, ran it and the other Hughes enterprises when the boss was off doing something else—which was most of the time.

The teen-age Hughes was already beginning to formulate a business methodology. "He treated a business something like a clock," says a banker acquaintance. "He'd start by taking it apart to see what made it tick, and then he'd put it back together and tinker with it until it was in good working order, and finally he'd wind it up, walk away and forget it. He'd only come back to it after that if it broke down or needed rewinding."

Thus with Hughes Tool. The young owner studied the business carefully, tinkered with it, adjusted this part and that. He fired some men and hired some, such as Dietrich. He bought his relatives' shareholdings so as to gain 100-percent control. And finally, with Dietrich at the helm and everything running smoothly and money pouring in, Hughes went away.

A different kind of business had caught his eye and captured his restless curiosity: motion pictures.

An actor friend, learning of Hughes's wealth, approached him with a movie idea and asked him to back it. Hughes agreed to invest about $50,000. The movie was a miserable failure, but Hughes extracted something of high value from it: an education. His curiosity was such that he hadn't been able to sit in Houston, an anonymous angel, while the film was being made in Hollywood. He had watched and even participated in the entire process, from the first script discussions to the final film editing.

The experience exhilarated him. It seemed to him that, with luck and management, money could be made in Hollywood as easily as in Texas. Step by step he began investing in Hollywood companies of various kinds, including a production studio, a lab that was experimenting with color film and another that was dabbling with talkies. (In those days the public was watching only silent films.) The corporate setup behind all these speculations grew increasingly complex. In most cases Hughes Tool became the principal stockholder and/or creditor of each new movieland venture, but the tool company's presence was shadowy, and there were many in Hollywood who didn't know exactly who this brash young newcomer was or where he was getting his seemingly bottomless supply of capital.

Hughes's next three films, following his initial failure, were financial successes. The critics considered them empty, rankly commercial and shallow, but Hughes didn't seem to care—a fact that made the critics all the more irritable with him in later years. This once-lonesome young man, who in his teens had seemed to be learning very little about people, had somehow developed an almost unerring sense of public tastes in humor, sex, violence, gore and other salable items of film fare. His films were designed to grab the gut, not tickle the intellect. "This is a business," he is said once to have snapped at an arty intellectual young woman who was carping at him during a Hollywood party. "The purpose of a business is to make money. If it happens to make art, too, that would be secondary and accidental."

Hughes has also been credited with another bit of folk wisdom that journalists still whisper to each other today. According to legend, some damned busybody approached him during the filming of a historical epic and suggested that a certain detail might not be quite factual. The detail was important; an entire scene hung on it. The busybody thought somebody should go to the library and check the detail in a history book. "No!" shouted Hughes. "Never check an interesting fact!"

Hughes's fifth film was a staggering costly epic named *Hell's Angels,* dealing with air fighting in World War One. It was first made as a silent at a cost of over one million dollars. Just as it was about to be released, talkies abruptly caught the public's imagination. To the horror of his financial advisors, including Noah Dietrich, Hughes scrapped the entire film and started it all over again as a talkie. The original lead actress had been a European who could barely speak

English; so he hired an obscure blonde starlet named Jean Harlow. Some said Jean Harlow couldn't act, but she could speak English and her every gesture spoke the universal language of sex.

Hughes worked on the film personally, constantly changing hats as he flitted from scriptwriting to directing to set designing to editing. He often worked more than 24 hours at a stretch without even pausing for a nap. "I never saw a man who could concentrate that hard or for that long," said Jean Harlow, who seemed to be amorously interested in Hughes but who never received a tumble in return. (As a rich and moderately handsome young man, Hughes enjoyed an interesting and diverse sex life among the starlets. But he didn't often become involved with the star actresses of his own shows. Such was his capacity for concentration that he viewed those particular ladies as strictly business properties. Jean Harlow's bright-blonde hair and sultry eyes made him think of money, not sex.)

Hell's Angels was released in 1930. Critics grumped at it, as usual. But once again Hughes's mental barometer had measured the public emotional climate with uncanny accuracy. The film became a smash hit, and Jean Harlow became a star of world renown whose very name meant female libido. Hughes had put more than three million dollars into the film. It went on to gross some eight million.

Meanwhile, Hughes Tool had been spinning along smoothly. It now manufactured not only oil-field drill bits but also a growing variety of other industrial tools and equipment. The value of its stock couldn't be gauged accurately, since it had never been traded on a public market, but its worth had certainly risen sharply under the capable hands of Dietrich and the occasional attentions of the young semiabsent owner. The Hollywood properties were similarly rising in value as Hughes attempted ever-bigger ventures in the search for ever-bigger profits.

At the end of 1930 Hughes reached his 25th birthday. He had inherited half a million dollars at the age of 18. His net worth now was conservatively guessed at around $20 million.

And once more his attention was wandering to a new field of business.

He had wound up Hughes Tool like a clock and walked

away from it, and it had gone on ticking. He had then wound up a battery of Hollywood ventures, and they were now ticking steadily. Leaving them under the command of handpicked managers, he now began to back away from them exactly as he had left Hughes Tool.

What new business had caught his curious eye? Aircraft.

He had apparently become fascinated by airplanes during the filming of *Hell's Angels*. He had pestered pilots and mechanics with questions, had watched with childlike wonder as planes were taken apart for repair, had even taken flying lessons and earned a pilot's license. "His mind is like a damned attic!" said an actor who played a bit part as a pilot. "He keeps storing stuff in it. I never heard a guy ask so many questions!"

Shortly after *Hell's Angels* was finished, Hughes began to absent himself from Hollywood for long periods of time. He would be gone a month, would return for a few days to see that his clocks were still ticking, then would vanish again. Nobody knew where he went. When asked for explanations he would only say, "Oh, I've been traveling."

In fact, this astoundingly knowledge-hungry man was busy learning more about airplanes. Using a false name, he had secretly gone to Texas and found a job as copilot with a small airline.

Airline wages in those days were meager. The young millionaire, whose growing collection of businesses were then earning more in a day than he could earn in a whole year as a copilot, obviously had no need for the money. Though he never troubled to explain his motives to anybody, it seems evident that he had only one reason for taking this secret job: He wanted to learn.

When he felt he had learned enough, he quit. Over the next few years he bought himself a number of private planes. He established a small service-and-repair shop in California to keep the planes in flying condition. But basic service and repair weren't interesting enough for Hughes. He was a compulsive tinkerer: He had to modify his planes, build more oomph into their engines, experiment with their aerodynamics. The service shop rapidly evolved into a rebuilding plant. Flying his own rebuilt planes, Hughes began to win air races. A rebuilt Lockheed, with Hughes at the controls, flew around the world and made headlines in

1938. Eventually other plane owners were coming to Hughes and asking whether he would do some tinkering for them. Thus, the onetime service shop grew into a small but rich operation eventually named Hughes Aircraft Company.

While this was happening, in the late 1930s, Hughes was looking around the airline industry for a possible investment. The industry was young and not very healthy. The Great Depression had slowed—in fact, nearly halted—the growth that had begun amid the euphoria of the 1920s. Most airlines were desperately short of customers and cash. If anyone was foolish enough to want to buy an airline, he could choose from a large, ragged and droopy-winged assortment on the bargain counter.

Hughes was convinced that somebody, someday, would make a lot of money from intercontinental airline service. He figured it might as well be he. And so, for a sum of money reputed to be in the neighborhood of $10 to $15 million, he bought roughly three-quarters of the outstanding common stock of a seedy but (he thought) promising little outfit called Transcontinental and Western Airline.

The name may have attracted him. Later he changed it to Trans World, reflecting the little company's expanding horizons but keeping the initials that were eventually to become one of the world's best-known trademarks. (When he finally sold his TWA stock, in 1966, the bundle brought him considerably more than half a billion dollars. Subtracting the long-term capital-gains tax, his profit on the deal was presumably somewhere near $400 million.)

By the time of World War Two, Howard Hughes was shuttling back and forth between so many business ventures that some were likely to suffer. At this point he may have been overdiversified. There were many men in the federal government who complained that this was indeed the case. Hughes Aircraft Company got involved in several design-and-development contracts for warplanes of various kinds, spent millions of the government's dollars but ended by producing not one usable plane for the war effort. Frustrated military officers howled that the main reason was Hughes's ghostly habit of vanishing.

Whenever the aircraft company's executives and engineers needed Hughes's OK on some key decision or his signature on a document, nobody could find out where he was. Frantic phone calls would be made to his Hollywood headquarters or to Hughes Tool in Texas, and the pleasant young lady on the phone would promise to pass on the message, and days or weeks later Hughes would call in from New York or Toronto or some remote town nobody had ever heard of. Meanwhile, the aircraft work would have ground to a shuddering stop, and engineers and military procurement officers would be running around in circles weeping with impotent rage.

The Hollywood business fared better. Following the smash success of *Hell's Angels* in the early 1930s, Hughes produced an equally successful gangster film called *Scarface*. This film was made at a time when Hughes was getting involved with the airplane business. There was a lull in the Hollywood operation for the next few years. Then, abruptly, in the midst of World War Two, when everybody assumed Hughes was so busy with his aircraft problems and his tool company's defense contracts that he couldn't find an hour to call his own, he plunged into what was to be his most colossal Hollywood success.

The film was called *The Outlaw*. The plot was barely noticeable, as Hughes himself acknowledged: just another horse opera dealing with Billy the Kid. But the star was a young woman, hitherto unknown, who had been working as an obscure photographer's model until she was spotted by Hughes's unerring eye. Her name was Jane Russell.

As an actress Miss Russell was, to put it charitably, less than brilliant. She had a rather uninteresting face. When she strove for the look of sultry passion that Jean Harlow had achieved so well, it somehow came across as a look of either dyspepsia or boredom. Her voice had an irritatingly mechanical quality. But she had something that very adequately made up for all these drawbacks: a mammary development the likes of which had never before been exposed to the popeyed gaze of the moviegoing public.

As one of Hughes's own press agents put it in a later year, "She had only two things to recommend her. Either one would probably have been enough."

Some of Hughes's film advisors, watching Jane Russell's early screen tests, argued vehemently against hiring her. But Hughes had once again gauged the public mood with uncanny precision. Sexual taboos were being stretched and, in fact, were breaking in the turbulent wartime society. The public in general was starting to talk of sex as a type of entertainment, a means of escape from the harsh realities of war. The ponderously solemn attitude with which it had once been approached was now being laughed at. Moreover, millions of men who were heading for combat, and the women who were being left behind, were swinging to the view that one might as well enjoy one's sexual adventures while the chance was still at hand, for another chance might not come for a long time or, indeed, forever. For reasons that psychiatrists are still arguing about today, these changing attitudes found overt expression in a thunderous, nationwide obsession with the female breast.

The Outlaw was by no means a pornographic film—certainly not by today's standards and not even by those of the 1940s. The only element to which bluenoses of the time could object was the camera's tendency to linger for what seemed like unnecessarily long periods of time on Miss Russell's magnificent cleavage. Hughes carefully and cleverly capitalized on this minority objection. He instructed his publicity agents to pose as offended bluenoses. They phoned the police and other authorities in cities where the film was being shown, demanded that the theaters be closed in the name of public decency, raised so loud a hue and cry that the film became famous around the world.

It was really just a run-of-the-mill western. Hughes, through his expert handling of it, made it into perhaps the biggest box-office success in all the history of movies up to that time. His profit on it over the years is reputed to have added up to something like $15 million.

Most of Hughes's other ventures were similarly profitable during the 1940s and 1950s. Though his aircraft company failed ever to produce a warplane that the U.S. government wanted to buy, the company kept busy during and after the war by producing aircraft gun turrets, machine-gun parts and other armaments. Hughes Tool continued to grow during the war and in the peacetime boom that followed, and by 1950 its estimated net worth was at least 500 times what it had been when the teen-age Hughes inherited it.

TWA went through hard times after the war, as did almost all airlines throughout the world. Hughes wanted it to become a major intercontinental carrier. Another growing airline, Pan American, nurtured the same ambition. The two fought fiercely for routes. They pegged fares at ridiculously low levels, granted all kinds of financial concessions to various national and city governments. TWA lost so much money in 1946 that its stock price (adjusting for subsequent splits) fell from a wartime high of above $50 to less than four dollars.

Hughes, hospitalized in 1946 after the crash of an experimental airplane, was urged to sell his TWA stock before the bottom dropped out completely. (He had bought it at the equivalent of less than two dollars.) He refused. He could enjoy the comfort of diversity: Though this one venture was suffering, he didn't need to panic. He also understood the very interesting position in which TWA stock then found itself. Since he held 78 percent of the stock, there wasn't much left for trading on the public market. If TWA ever recovered from its financial ailments and began to show a profit (which Hughes was certain would happen eventually), the small amount of available stock would be sought by a large number of buyers. The price might then rise precipitously.

In fact, this was precisely what happened. Other investors who saw the picture as Hughes did were treated to a gorgeous ride uphill. By the time Hughes sold out in mid-1966, the stock was trading in the range of $100 a share.

(TWA stock warrants offered an even better ride during four short years in the 1960s. If you had put $1000 into TWA warrants at the right time in 1962 and sold out at the right time in 1966, you'd have ended with some $26,000. Nobody but Hughes's broker knows for sure whether Hughes or his companies invested in these warrants, but the likelihood is that they did.)

One would have thought Hughes had enough to do in the late 1940s. He was busy doctoring TWA, experimenting with new airplanes, negotiating new contracts for Hughes Tool, making more movies, planning sundry other investments such as a purchase of RKO movie studios and theaters. But apparently this wasn't enough for him. He abruptly plunged into a new field: electronics.

Both Hughes Tool and Hughes Aircraft had been moving into the fringes of the electronics business. Hughes, guessing the business would grow over the coming decades, now founded an electronics company as a subsidiary of Hughes Aircraft. And once again he demonstrated his amazing ability to pick people for jobs he wanted done. Among those he hired for the infant company's top management team were Charles B. ("Tex") Thornton, a clever administrator who later became chief architect of the mighty conglomerate named Litton Industries, and Drs. Simon Ramo and Dean Wooldridge, brilliant young scientists who later founded their own string of companies.

The young electronics company, with its bright young management, attracted attention right away. The army, the air force and (later) the National Aeronautics and Space Administration hired the little outfit to develop weapon-aiming devices, radar, missile-guidance systems, space gadgetry of all kinds. By the middle 1950s the company's sales were running at the astounding rate of a half-billion dollars a year.

The astonishing Howard Hughes, meanwhile, was off on yet another tangent. He had become fascinated by the city of Las Vegas. The reasons for this fascination aren't clear even in retrospect, and Hughes characteristically has never offered any enlightenment. Perhaps, some observers have suggested, Hughes was attracted by the transience of the gambling capital's people. The city has only a small population of permanent residents; all the rest are en route from and to somewhere else. Hughes, who never had a headquarters or even a permanent home, may have felt comfortable in this society of other drifters. At any rate, he began buying hotels, gambling casinos, vast tracts of real estate in and around the city.

This may have been the last straw—the step that finally turned diversity into chaos. For all at once Hughes's colossal and variegated empire began to come apart. His managers, his employees, his companies' important customers all started to complain that he was becoming even more ghost-like than before. Nobody ever knew where to find him. He made appointments with people and failed to keep them. He failed to return telephone calls. What had happened to Hughes Aircraft during the war now began to happen throughout the Hughes domain: One by one projects ground to a halt because the boss wasn't there to sign contracts or authorize purchases or make key decisions.

At TWA the storm of protests grew so extreme that Hughes was finally forced to divest himself of the stock. The same happened at RKO, whose employees and stockholders complained they were losing money because Hughes wouldn't authorize the company to make enough movies. The top managers of Hughes's new electronics company got disgusted and quit—first Thornton, then Ramo and Wooldridge. At Hughes Tool the situation grew unbearable even for faithful old Noah Dietrich, the man who had been Hughes's closest financial sidekick for over 30 years. Dietrich quit, and his departure seemed to signal the end of an era.

Hughes vanished into a limbolike retirement. He still had his vast stockholdings in Hughes Tool and Hughes Aircraft (now almost exclusively an electronics company), and he had a bundle of smaller shareholdings in other companies. But he no longer tried to use his shareholdings to control the companies. He was simply a faceless stockholder such as you or I might be—though, of course, on a monumental scale. He also had his Las Vegas land and his hotels, and he had a mountain of cash.

The total value of Hughes's known assets has been variously estimated at $900 million to $1½ billion. Let's settle on a billion. Our chances of being right seem as good as anybody else's.

That is sheer conjecture, of course. Nearly everything one might say about this wraithlike man is necessarily flawed by a component of guesswork, for Hughes has very seldom confirmed or denied any reports about himself. When he does step out of his limbo to confirm or deny something, the net effect has only been to increase the mystery that surrounds him.

This happened early in 1972, when two New York publishers proposed to bring out what they claimed was an autobiographical book about Hughes—a book said to have been dictated largely by the ghostly billionaire himself. Hughes, or a man claiming to be Hughes, arranged a telephone press conference in which he denied having authorized any such autobiography and denounced the book as a fraud.

Was the book authentic or wasn't it? Was the voice on the phone Hughes's voice or wasn't it? Nobody knew—except Hughes and perhaps some of his trusted aides.

Perhaps the two most descriptive words that can be said about Howard Hughes are, after all, Nobody knows.

9

Diggers and Drillers

There is a vast amount of treasure buried underground, as everybody knows: iron, copper, gold, uranium, oil, diamonds—a varied and fabulous array. But it's treasure only when it's brought up to the surface.

If all these romantic commodities were lying about on the surface where any fool could pick them up, they would be cheap. But they aren't. They lie hidden. Finding them and bringing them up takes work, money and a willingness to live with high risk. Men who undertake this kind of task have a right to be well paid, and the world has always seen to it that they are—when they succeed.

The world's richest treasure digger is oilman Jean Paul Getty. His story is a textbook study of how to get improbably wealthy by finding a valuable commodity underground and taking it to places where it can be put to use.

It might be argued that Getty, like Hughes, is out of place in this gallery. Getty had a rich father. But, as you'll see in the story that follows, this gave young Getty few, if any, unusual advantages. It is a popular misconception that the senior Getty set his son up in business by handing him umpteen and a half million dollars and that young J. Paul simply invested this juicy fistful and spent the rest of his life sitting Buddhalike on his rump while great green mountains of money piled up around him. Not so.

The facts are quite otherwise. When the senior Getty died, he left his son just half a million dollars. That amount had little effect on the young man's subsequent fortunes. J. Paul Getty had already made millions of dollars by himself.

Unlike Howard Hughes, Getty is a frank and talkative man. He enjoys telling his own story, for he believes the

112

story embodies lessons for young men just starting the long climb. He is PLAYBOY's contributing editor for business and finance, and 34 of his articles have appeared in the magazine, plus three books. He obviously derives some kind of kick from this subsidiary career of writing. There was a time in his youth when he thought he might want to earn his living as a writer, and this old dream seems to be still with him. He turns out a clear, strong, straightforward brand of prose. Let's listen now while he recalls his remarkable career in his own words.

J. Paul Getty:
One Billion Dollars*
by J. Paul Getty

After many fruitless months of prospecting for oil in Oklahoma, I finally spudded my first test well not far from Stone Bluff, a tiny Muskogee County hamlet, in early January 1916.

On February 2 the bailer—the device that cleared formation rock from the drill hole—brought up a quantity of oil sand. This indicated that we were nearing the final stages of drilling. The next 24 hours would prove whether the well was a producer or a dry hole.

I was still very young and quite green. My nervousness and excitement rose to an intolerable pitch. I became more hindrance than help to the men on my drilling crew. To get out of their way and ease my own tension, I beat a strategic retreat to Tulsa, the nearest city of any size. I decided to wait there until the drilling operation was completed and the results were known. In Tulsa J. Carl Smith, a close friend who was considerably older and far less excitable than I, volunteered to go to the drilling site and supervise the work there for me.

There were no telephones in the remote area where my well was being drilled. The single line between Stone Bluff and Tulsa seldom worked. Hence, J. Carl Smith promised to return to Tulsa on the last train from Stone Bluff the next day and inform me of the latest developments.

On the following day—a chill, blustery February 3,

*Originally appeared in PLAYBOY magazine under the title *How I Made My First Billion.* Copyright © 1961, 1965, 1966 by Playboy.

1916—I was at the Tulsa railroad depot, anxiously pacing the windswept passenger platform more than an hour before the train was due to arrive. At last it pulled into the station. Endless seconds later J. Carl Smith's familiar figure emerged from one of the coaches. His face beamed, and my hopes soared.

"Congratulations, Paul!" he boomed when he saw me on the platform. "We brought in your well this afternoon. It's producing thirty barrels!"

I automatically assumed he meant 30 barrels a day, and my elation vanished instantly. Thirty barrels a day—why, that was a mere trickle compared to the gushers other oilmen were bringing in at the time.

"Yes, sir"—J. Carl grinned—"We're getting thirty barrels an hour. . . ."

Thirty barrels *an hour!*

That made a difference, a world of difference. That meant the well was producing 720 barrels of crude oil daily. It also meant that I was in the oil business—to stay.

Being the son of a successful oilman, I had been exposed to the virus of oil fever since childhood. My parents, George F. and Sarah Getty, and I first visited what was then the Oklahoma Territory in 1903, when I was ten. While there, my father, a prosperous Minneapolis attorney-at-law, found it impossible to resist the lure of the Oklahoma oil rush, which was then in full swing. He formed the Minnehoma Oil Company and began prospecting for oil.

My father, a self-made man who had known extreme poverty in his youth, had a practically limitless capacity for hard work, and he also had an almost uncanny talent for finding oil. After organizing Minnehoma Oil, he personally supervised the drilling of 43 oil wells, of which 42 proved to be producers!

I served a tough and valuable apprenticeship working as a roustabout and tooldresser in the oil fields in 1910 and 1911, but I didn't go into the oil business for myself until September 1914. I had but recently returned to the United States after attending Oxford University in England for two years. My original intent was to enter the U.S. diplomatic service, but I deferred that plan in order to try my luck as an independent operator—a wildcatter—in Oklahoma.

The times were favorable. It was a bonanza era for the

burgeoning American petroleum industry. A lusty, brawling pioneer spirit still prevailed in the oil fields. The great oil rush continued with unabated vigor and was given added impetus by the war that had broken out in Europe that year. Primitive boomtowns dotted the Oklahoma countryside. Many bore bare-knuckled frontier-era names such as those of the four "Right" towns: Drumright, Dropright, Allright and Damnright.

Streets and roads were unpaved—rivers of mushy clay and mud in spring and winter and sun-baked, rutted tracks perpetually shrouded by billowing clouds of harsh red or yellow dust in summer. Duckboard sidewalks installed outside the more prosperous business establishments and gambling halls were viewed as the very ultimate in civic improvements.

The atmosphere was identical to that which historians describe as prevailing in the California gold fields during the 1849 gold rush. In Oklahoma, the fever was to find oil, not gold, and it was an epidemic. There were few, indeed, who were immune to the contagion.

Fortunes were being made—and lost—daily. It was not unusual for a penniless wildcatter, down to his last bit and without cash or credit with which to buy more, to drill another hundred feet and bring in a well that made him a rich man. A lease that sold for a few hundred dollars one afternoon sometimes increased in value a hundredfold or even a thousandfold by the next morning.

On the other hand, there were men who invested all they owned in leases and drilling operations only to find that they had nothing to show for their money and efforts but a few dismally dry holes. Leases purchased at peak prices one day proved to be utterly valueless the next. It was all a gargantuan, supremely thrilling gamble for staggering stakes, and I plunged into the whirl hopefully. I had no capital of my own; my personal budget was $100 per month. My first year was anything but profitable. Large oil strikes were being reported regularly, and other wildcatters were bringing in gushers and big producers, but fortune seemed to elude me.

Then, in the late fall of 1915, a half interest in an oil lease near Stone Bluff in Muskogee County was offered for sale at public auction. I inspected the property and thought it highly promising. I knew other independent operators were interested in obtaining the lease, and this worried me. I didn't have much money at my disposal—certainly not enough to match the prices older, established oilmen would be able to offer. For this reason I requested my bank to have one of its representatives bid for me at the sale without revealing my identity as the real bidder.

Surprisingly enough, this rather transparent stratagem accomplished the purpose I intended. The sale, held in the town of Muskogee—the county seat—was attended by several independent oil operators eager to obtain the lease. The unexpected appearance of the well-known bank executive who bid for me unnerved the wildcatters. They assumed that if a banker was present at the auction, it could only mean that some large oil company was also interested in the property and was prepared to top any and all offers. The independents glumly decided it would be futile to bid and, in the end, I secured the lease for $500—a bargain-basement price!

Soon thereafter a corporation was formed to finance the drilling of a test well on the property. I, as a wildcatter with no capital of my own, received a modest 15-percent interest in the corporation. I assembled a crack drilling crew, and my men and I labored to erect the necessary wooden derrick and to rush the actual drilling operations. We spudded the well in early January 1916. I remained on the site night and day until the drilling went into its final stages. Then, as I've related, I found it impossible to stand the nervous strain and fled to Tulsa, where my friend J. Carl Smith brought me the news that the well had come in for an initial daily production of 720 barrels.

The lease on the property was sold to a producing oil company two weeks after that, and I realized $12,000 as my share of the profits. The amount was not very impressive when compared to the huge sums others were making, but it was enough to convince me that I should—and would—remain in the oil business as a wildcatter.

My father and I had previously formed a partnership. Under its terms he was to provide financing for any exploration and drilling I conducted and supervised for the partnership. In return he would receive 70 percent of the profits, while I received the remaining 30 percent. After my first success we incorporated the partnership and in May 1916 formed the Getty Oil Company, in which I received a 30-percent stock interest.

Many fanciful—and entirely erroneous—accounts of the business relationship between us have appeared in print. Contrary to some published reports, my father did not set me up in business by giving me any outright cash gifts. George F. Getty rejected any ideas that a successful man's son should be pampered or spoiled or given money as a gift after he was old enough to earn his own living. My father *did* finance some of my early operations—but solely on the 70-30-percent basis. Insofar as lease purchases and drilling or other operations I conducted on my own account were concerned, I financed these myself. My father neither provided the money for my private business ventures nor did he share in the profits I received from them.

Incidentally, there is another popular misconception I'd like to correct once and for all. It has been said that my father bequeathed me a huge fortune when he passed away in 1930. Actually, he left me $500,000 in his will—a considerable sum, I'll admit, but nonetheless a very small part of his fortune. It was a token bequest. My father was well aware that I had already made several million dollars on my own, and he left the bulk of his estate to my mother.

After father and I incorporated our partnership in 1916, I went right on prospecting and drilling for oil. My enthusiasm was not dampened when my second well proved to be a dry hole. By then wildcatting was in my blood, and I continued to buy and sell leases and to drill wells. I usually acted as my own geologist, legal advisor, drilling superintendent, explosives expert and even, on occasion, as roughneck and roustabout. The months that followed were extremely fortunate ones. In most instances the leases I bought were sold at a profit, and when I drilled on a property, I struck oil more often than not.

There were no secrets, no mystical formulas behind these successes. I operated in much the same manner as did almost all wildcatters—with one important exception. In those days the science of petroleum geology had not yet gained very wide acceptance in the oil fields. Many oilmen sneered openly at the idea that some "damned bookworm" could help them find oil. At best, the vast majority of oilmen were skeptical about geology as a practical science and put little stock in geologists' reports. I was among the few who believed in geology. I studied the subject avidly at every opportunity and applied what I learned to my operations.

The independent operator had to possess a certain amount of basic knowledge and skill. He also needed reliable, loyal and experienced men on his exploration and drilling crews. But, beyond these things, I believe the most important factor that determined whether a wildcatter would succeed or fail—whether he would bring in a producing well or wind up with a dry hole—was just plain luck.

There were some who didn't consider it luck, among them T. N. Barnsdall, one of the great Oklahoma oil pioneers. Multimillionaire Barnsdall often expounded his favorite theory about what he thought made the difference.

"It's not luck," he maintained stoutly. "A man either has a nose for oil or he doesn't. If he does, he smells the stuff even when it's three thousand feet down!"

Perhaps. But I rather doubt it myself. Personally, I was never able to sniff out the presence of a subterranean oil pool. Nor do I recall that I ever tingled with an oil dowser's extrasensory response while tramping across a potential drilling site. I still think my early successes were due mainly to pure luck.

However, lest there be those who imagine wildcatters had little to do but wait for the wheel of fortune to spin and then reap their profits, let me say that the oil business was never an easy one. It has always entailed work—hard work—and it has always been fraught with innumerable financial pitfalls, especially in the early days. Wells sometimes blew up, and profits—and often capital—were devoured with appalling speed by costly efforts to extinguish the resulting fires. Dry holes, equipment failures and breakdowns at crucial periods, squabbles and litigation over leases and rights-of-way—these were a few of the myriad problems and setbacks that frequently drained the independent operator's financial resources down to a point well below the danger mark.

In addition, all of us who operated independently often found ourselves facing heavy competition and opposition from major oil firms. Some of these huge companies did not always abide by Marquis of Queensberry rules when they engaged in legal or financial infighting to smother an independent who appeared to be growing too big or too fast.

Wildcatters developed traits and techniques that enabled them to stay in business and to do more than merely hold their own against the petroleum industry's behemoths. We became flexible, adaptable, and versatile—adept at improvisation and innovation—if for no other reason than because we *had* to in order to survive. For example, the big companies employed vast numbers of specialists and consultants, administrative personnel and office workers, housing them in large and expensive offices. We, the independents, found our experts among the hard-bitten veteran oil-field workers who formed our prospecting and drilling crews, or we relied on our own judgment and experience to solve our problems as they arose. We did our own administrative and paper work—keeping both to a minimum. As for our offices, these—more often than not—traveled with us in the mud-splotched automobiles we drove from one drilling site to another.

In my own case, as I have said before, I was lucky—very lucky. I made many profitable deals and brought in several producing wells in the months after I first struck oil on the Nancy Taylor Allotment site. The Getty Oil Company prospered. I was named one of the company's directors and elected its secretary, but this did not mean I exchanged my work clothes for a business suit. Notwithstanding my heady new titles, my work was still in the oil fields—and on the drilling rigs. My role in the company's affairs remained the same as it had been: I bought and sold oil leases and prospected and drilled for oil.

As the Getty Oil Company's wealth increased, so did my own in proportion to my 30-percent share in the firm—and I was also embarking on profitable ventures on my own account. All these things kept me very busy—too busy to pay more than cursory attention to how much money I was actually making. Then one day I stopped and took detailed stock of my financial situation. I suddenly realized that I had gone a very long way toward accomplishing what I'd set out to do in September 1914. I had built the foundations of a business of my own in the American oil industry.

I was not quite 24, but I had become a successful independent oil operator. And I had made my first million dollars. I was a millionaire!

Until then my life had been devoted chiefly to growing up, obtaining an education and establishing a business. Now, at 24, I found I'd made enough money to meet any personal requirements I might conceivably have in the foreseeable future. I made a headstrong snap decision to forget all about work thereafter and to concentrate on playing, on enjoying myself.

My decision was influenced—at least in part—by the fact that there was a war raging in Europe. Although the United States had not yet entered World War One, I felt certain that American participation in the conflict was inevitable. I'd already filed official applications to serve in either the air service—my first choice—or the field artillery when and if the U.S. declared war. I was sure it would be only a matter of time before I received my orders, and I wanted to relax and have fun before they arrived.

My mother, father and I had made our permanent home in Los Angeles, California, since 1906. I'd attended school and college in California before going on to Oxford and then, later, starting my business career in the Oklahoma oil fields. I loved California and the easy, informal and extremely pleasant life that prevailed there in those days. Thus, it was only natural that I should choose Los Angeles as the place to enjoy the money I'd made in the oil fields.

"I've made my fortune—and I'm going to retire," I announced blandly to my startled parents.

Neither mother nor father was pleased with my decision. Both of them had worked very hard in their own youth. When first married, my mother had continued to work as a schoolteacher to help provide my father with the money he needed to put him through law school. Both of them firmly believed that an individual had to work to justify his existence and that a rich person had to keep his money working to justify its existence. My father tried to impress upon me that a businessman's money is capital to be invested and reinvested.

"You've got to use your money to create, operate and build businesses," he argued. "Your wealth represents potential jobs for countless others—and it can produce wealth and a better life for a great many people as well as yourself."

I'm afraid I didn't pay much attention to him—then. Later I was to realize the truth of what he said, but first I had to try things my own way. I owned a spanking new Cadillac roadster, good clothes and had all the money I could possibly need. I had made up my mind I wanted to play, and with these prerequisites I encountered no difficulty plunging full tilt into the southern California–Los Angeles– Hollywood whirl of fun and frolic. Although the United States entered the war, my call-up was first delayed, then postponed, by bureaucratic snarls, and finally I was informed that my "services would not be needed." I consequently spent the World War One years playing and enjoying myself.

It took me a while to wake up to the fact that I was only wasting time and that I was bored. By the end of 1918 I was thoroughly fed up. Early in 1919 I was back in the oil business—not a little abashed by the "I told you so" smile I got from my father when I informed him that, having retired at 24, I was coming out of retirement at 26!

In 1919 oilmen's attention was already shifting from Oklahoma to southern California, where new producing areas were being discovered and developed. A great new oil rush was in the making, and I was among those who wanted to be in on it from the beginning. My initial oil-prospecting venture in southern California was a fiasco. I drilled my first California well on the Didier Ranch near Puente, but the well proved to be a dry hole.

The luck that had stayed with me in Oklahoma had taken a brief holiday, but it hadn't deserted me. Subsequent tries were considerably more successful. I drilled several wells in the Santa Fe Springs, Torrance, Long Beach and other southern-California areas, and most of them proved to be producers, some of them sensational producers.

I spent most of my time in the field working on the drilling rigs with my men. This habit, formed in Oklahoma, paid many handsome and unexpected dividends. Not the least of these stemmed from the drilling crews' reaction to the presence of a working boss on the job. The men felt they were partners with the boss in a mutual effort rather than merely employees of some corporation run by executives they never saw and who had probably never set foot on a drilling platform in their lives. Morale—and production— soared as a result.

This was important, for with new wells being drilled by the hundreds throughout southern California, there was an acute shortage of experienced oil-field workers. The personnel managers of most large companies engaged in wild scrambles to find the necessary manpower for their operations. They bid frantically against each other in the labor market, offering special inducements and benefits to anyone who'd ever had any experience working on an oil rig.

Most old-timers resented the implication that they had to be bribed with frills to do an honest day's work. They preferred to sign on with wildcatting operators who offered no fancy extras but who spoke their language and worked side by side with them on the drilling sites.

I'll never forget the time I began drilling on a property not far from the site on which a major oil company was drilling a well. Carrying its employee-inducement program to ludicrous extremes, the firm had designed and built what its press agents glowingly described as the last word in drilling rigs.

The entire rig was steam-heated all the way up to the crown block. A neatly raked gravel drive led to the site. There were hot showers for the men and even a laundry that washed their work clothes while they waited! Early one afternoon not long after I'd spudded my well, a grizzled roughneck appeared on my site and announced that he wanted to see the boss. When I was pointed out to him, he came over and wasted no words asking me for a job.

"Are you working now?" I asked.

"Yeah," came the sour reply.

"Where?"

"Over there," the roughneck replied, nodding his head toward the deluxe drilling rig. There were no home comforts available for my crew, and I told the man so. And, I added, I couldn't understand why he would want to leave a job that offered such luxuries for one on my relatively primitive operation.

"I've been on that rig for five months," the roughneck growled unhappily, "and we've only gotten down four thousand feet!" I laughed. Four thousand feet in four months was a ridiculously slow rate for drilling through the type of soil formations to be found in that particular field.

"How long do you think it'll take me to get down that far?" I asked.

"From the looks of you—about ten days!" the old-timer

answered with a broad grin. "That's why I'd rather work for you than for that cream-puff outfit over there . . . !"

He got the job and stayed on my payroll for many years. As a footnote to the story, I might add that my well was drilled in record time and proved a good producer. The "last word" in drilling rigs brought in a dry hole and was finally abandoned.

Another good example of what close teamwork and mutual confidence between boss and crew could accomplish can be found in the story of how my men and I liked the "insoluble" problem of a certain oil lease.

The lease was on a tiny piece of property in the midst of a forest of oil wells in the rich Seal Beach, California, field. By some fluke the lease had been overlooked by the firms that were operating there. A company in which I held a substantial interest acquired the lease but was about to write it off as a dead loss. Everyone agreed that nothing could ever be done with the property. In the first place, it was a plot barely larger than the floor area of a small house. In the second, the only right-of-way providing access to a road was over a strip of ground several hundred feet long but less than four feet wide. It was impossible to get supplies and equipment to the property by truck over this constricted path. Even if it had been possible, the postage-stamp-size plot would not have accommodated a regular-size derrick and drilling rig. The companies holding leases on adjacent properties refused to grant any right-of-way over their sites, for if a producing well was brought in, it might diminish the production of their own wells, since it would be pumping oil from the same pool.

"Forget the lease," associates with whom I discussed the matter advised me. "You'll never get a well drilled there— not in a million years."

Stubbornly I insisted there must be a way. I put the problem before the men in whom I had the greatest confidence, the members of one of my drilling crews. They listened to me, and their reaction was the same as mine. They considered the problem an irresistible challenge.

"Let's go up and look at things, boss," a hard-bitten driller grunted. "We'll find some way—don't worry." Several men and I went to survey the situation firsthand, and we found that it did look fairly hopeless.

"I guess we could drill the well with an undersized rig," the driller mused after thinking things over. "If you could get somebody to design and build it, we could set it up—but I can't figure how we're going to bring everything we need in from the road. . . ."

The obstacle provided by the limited right-of-way seemed insuperable, until my mind began to turn over the driller's suggestion about a miniature drilling rig. If we could drill with a miniature rig, then why couldn't we solve our transportation problem with a miniature railway? It was a perfect solution: a narrow-gauge track and a car or two on which to bring the disassembled "baby" derrick and supplies and equipment from the road to the drilling site.

Mulish obstinacy? A desire to prove that we were able to accomplish what everyone else considered impossible? Possibly—even probably. But both the miniature rig and the miniature railway were procured. The former was moved in sections over the latter and assembled by hand on the microscopic plot of ground. The well was drilled—and we struck oil.

I recall other memorable strikes during the 1920s. Among them is the one I made in the so-called Athens Field in the southern suburbs of Los Angeles. I acquired the plot in question for something over $12,000. Because I was operating entirely on my own account and knew that I would be stretching my available cash resources thin before completing the first well, I elected to act as my own drilling superintendent. Among the men I hired for my crew were three of the finest drillers in the oil industry: Walter Phillips, Oscar Prowell and "Spot" McMurdo. We completed the first well on February 16, 1925, at a depth of 4350 feet for an initial daily yield of 1500 barrels. A short while later I brought in the second well on the site for an initial production of 2000 barrels per day. In the next nine years the two wells on the Athens property were to show over $400,000 excess recovery—clear profit over and above all costs and expenses.

Even more spectacular is the story of the Cleaver Lease in Alamitos Heights, which I bought with a personal check for $8000 in October 1926 from a man who had purchased it for $4000 only a few days before and who wanted to make a quick profit.

I spudded well number one on February 21, 1927, and

subsequently drilled three more wells on the property. All proved exceptional producers, bringing up a total of more than 17,000 barrels daily. Between 1927 and 1939 excess recovery on the Cleaver Lease wells was nearly $800,000—a 10,000-percent profit on my original investment. Yet, within a few weeks after the first well came in, I was not only close to losing a fortune but also close to losing the lease itself. Behind this apparent paradox lie two stories. One illustrates what the average wildcatter faced when he jousted with certain major oil companies. The other proves that while some large firms had no compunctions about strangling an independent operator, others were ready and willing to give him a break—and even a helping hand.

As soon as I'd brought in Cleaver well number one—which produced an impressive 5100 barrels a day—I cast about to find a buyer for my crude production. To my dismay, the firms I approached refused to deal with me. The motives behind this evident boycott became infuriatingly clear within a few days, when I received several calls from brokers offering to buy the Cleaver Lease at a very low price. The brokers refused to name the principals they represented.

By then I was an old hand in the petroleum industry. I recognized all the classic signs indicating a well-organized squeeze play. Certain interests wanted my lease. Either I sold out at a ridiculously low price or I would be left without any market for the oil produced by the wells on the property.

Unable to sell my oil, I had to find some way to store it. The only storage facilities available in the Los Angeles area were in a defunct refinery—two storage tanks with a total 155,000-barrel capacity, which I immediately leased. In the meantime, even while I was vainly seeking a buyer for the 5100 barrels of crude my number-one well was producing every 24 hours, well number two came in for a 5000-barrel daily production. This was followed in short order by number three, which produced 5100 barrels a day, then by number four, the runt of the litter, which brought up 2100 barrels daily.

This production rate was rapidly filling the two storage tanks—and I was still unable to find an outlet for the oil. I knew that when the tanks were topped off, I'd have no choice but to shut down my operation entirely.

Obviously, I was receiving no income from the four wells.

My fluid cash resources—already strained by drilling costs—
dwindled rapidly as I paid for leasing the tanks and for trucking my crude several miles from wells to storage. The
situation could have easily turned into financial disaster. I
decided to make a frontal attack on one of the biggest of all
the major oil companies—Shell Oil. By a fortunate coincidence, Sir George Legh-Jones, then the Shell company's
president, happened to be visiting in Los Angeles. In
desperation I aimed high, asked for an interview with him
personally and was informed that he would be happy to see
me.

A warm, friendly man, Sir George listened attentively to
what I had to say. The deepening scowl that etched across
his face as he heard me was all the proof I needed that his
firm was not a party to the boycott and that he heartily
disapproved of such tactics. When I finished talking, he
smiled his reassurance.

"Relax." He grinned. "We'll help you."

As a starter the company would buy the next 1,750,000
barrels of crude oil produced by my Cleaver Lease wells, Sir
George told me. In addition, a pipeline would be constructed
to link my wells with the Shell Oil Company's pipeline
network—and construction work was to commence the very
next day.

Sir George and the Shell company were as good as their
word. Shell's work crews arrived on my Cleaver site bright
and early the following morning and started to lay the
pipeline. The boycott was broken—and the Cleaver Lease
was safely and profitably mine!

As the 1920s drew to a close, the American petroleum
industry began to undergo a radical change. The industry
was rapidly growing more complex; the costs of finding and
producing oil were spiraling ever higher. Much greater capital
expenditures were needed to purchase leases, machinery and
equipment and to finance exploration and drilling. Most oil
pools that lay near the surface in known oil belts had been
located and were being exploited. It was necessary to prospect
ever farther afield and to drill ever deeper to find oil.

There were many mergers and consolidations of oil companies. Some independent operators were falling by the way-
side. Others were selling out to big oil companies. There was
also a strange, ominous undercurrent running through the

entire U.S. economy. The stock market listed shares at fantastic highs, but there were warnings and forebodings of economic trouble ahead.

It was a critical period for all wildcatters and a particularly difficult one for me. I had to look after my own mushrooming business interests—my own leases, producing wells and companies. Then, through the years, I'd bought sizable blocks of stock in my father's companies as well. Now his health began to fail, and I found it increasingly necessary to take an active part in managing the operations of those companies.

In 1929 the stock market crashed. The following year my father suffered a stroke. Although he was over 75, he fought death bravely and grimly for several weeks, but the battle was lost on May 31, 1930, when he passed away. My mother and I were allowed but little time to grieve. We had to keep his businesses going and his companies operating. The federal government pressed for rapid settlement of the inheritance taxes on the estate. These and many other matters demanded immediate attention, and all were complicated by the economic factor of the deepening depression. Many advised me to liquidate everything—to sell out not only my late father's holdings but my own firms and interests as well.

"The business situation can only get worse," they predicted. "The economy is going to disintegrate completely!"

I didn't see things that way at all. I was convinced the nation's economy was essentially sound—that though it might sag lower in the near future, it would eventually bounce back, healthier than ever. I thought it was the time to buy—not sell.

Many oil stocks were selling at all-time lows; they were spectacular bargains. I began to envision the organization of a completely integrated and self-contained oil business, one embracing not only exploration and production—the operations in which I'd been exclusively engaged until that time— but also transportation, refining and even retail marketing.

In business, as in politics, it is never easy to go against the beliefs and attitudes held by the majority. The businessman who moves counter to the tide of prevailing opinion must expect to be obstructed, derided and damned. So it was with me when, at the depths of the U.S. economic slump of the 1930s, I resolved to make large-scale stock purchases and build a self-contained oil business. My friends and acquaintances—to say nothing of my competitors—felt my buying spree would prove a fatal mistake. Then, when I announced my intention to buy into one of the seven major oil companies operating in California, even those who had been my supporters in the past were inclined to believe I had taken leave of my senses.

Major oil companies could, and often did, buy out independent operators' firms. But for an independent operator to buy a major oil company? That was heresy—an attempt to turn the established order upside down!

Nonetheless, I went ahead with my plans, for I was looking to the future. The oil companies I controlled or in which I held substantial interests were engaged exclusively in finding oil and getting it out of the ground. To insure markets for this oil and for that to be produced by new wells drilled in the future, I had to invest in a company that needed crude oil and that also had adequate refining and marketing facilities. There were only seven such companies in California —all majors.

The list was headed by the Standard Oil Company of California—obviously far too big a chunk for any independent to bite off and digest. The same held true for the Shell Oil Company. The next possibility was the Union Oil Company, but this firm had its own crude-oil sources. So did the General Petroleum Company, which, in any event, was virtually a closed corporation, and its stock was not available for purchase. That left three firms: Richfield Oil, then in receivership and consequently not a very tempting prospect; the Texas Oil Company, which was amply supplied with its own crude; and, lastly, the Tide Water Associated Oil Company.

Tide Water Associated seemed the logical choice. The company met only half its refineries' crude requirements from its own reserves, buying the rest from other producers. Tide Water also had a good marketing organization, and its products enjoyed a good reputation with the consuming public.

I saw great advantages in linking my companies up with Tide Water. My firms—George F. Getty Inc. and Pacific Western Oil Company among them—would have assured outlets for their crude production, and they would guarantee steady crude oil supplies for Tide Water's refineries. Further-more, with the firms working interdependently, large-scale economies could be effected. The savings could be passed on to the consumer in lower gasoline and oil prices and shared by Tide Water's 34,668 individual shareholders in the form of higher dividends.

I began my Tide Water campaign in March 1932 by pur-chasing 1200 common shares at $2.50 per share. Within the next six weeks I'd increased my holdings to 41,000 shares. Nearly 20 years were to pass before I gained clear-cut control of the firm. In that time my producing companies and I would buy millions of shares of Tide Water common. I didn't guess wrong when I started buying at depressed 1932 prices. In the next five years Tide Water's common shares rose to more than $16—and eventually each share came to be worth many times that amount.

It was not easy to gain control of the Tide Water Asso-ciated Oil Company. Many risks were taken, much opposition encountered, many no-holds-barred proxy and legal battles were fought. Countless critical situations developed. The out-come was often in doubt.

My first attempt to obtain a voice in Tide Water's man-agement was made in May 1932. I went to the annual stockholders' meeting armed with my own 41,000 shares, plus a proxy for 126,000 additional shares. At the last moment the proxy was revoked. My efforts ended in failure. I bought more stock and tried to sell my ideas to Tide Water's directors. They, however, did not see things my way and dug in for a long, hard fight. Why? Well, I suppose there were several reasons. First of all, I was an outsider. I'd had little or no experience in the heady atmosphere of board-rooms.

"Paul Getty should stay where he belongs—on a drilling rig," a Tide Water director supposedly snorted when told I was buying the company's stock right and left. I fear there were others on the board even less kindly disposed toward me and my ambitions.

I'd studied Tide Water's organization and operations care-fully and recommended that the company make certain changes and practice certain economies. These recommenda-tions, apparently too radical to suit the conservative directors, caused considerable resentment.

I'd also concluded that much of Tide Water's refining plant was obsolescent and would soon be obsolete. I believed the company should make provisions for modernization and replacement, but management was reluctant to make capital expenditures during the business slump. The directors called it "necessary caution." I viewed it as shortsighted and dangerous penny-pinching.

By 1933 Getty interests owned nearly 260,000 Tide Water shares—a block too large to be ignored. I was elected to the company's board, but it was a hollow victory. I was only one among many, and the other directors were still ranged solidly against me and my proposals. I continued to buy Tide Water stock. Proxy fights, lawsuits and countersuits ensued. Injunctions, restraining orders and writs flew in blizzards. By late 1937 Getty interests owned enough stock to obtain a voice in management. Three years later we held 1,734,577 shares —a shade over one-fourth the voting stock—and many changes I proposed were being implemented. By 1951 I held enough Tidewater stock to have numerical control. (By then the *Associated* had been dropped from the company name and *Tide Water* contracted into a single word.) Two years later, with all but one director elected by Getty interests, the campaign was finally over. Today Tidewater's assets exceed $800 million.

In 1938 I turned momentarily from the oil business and bought the Hotel Pierre in New York City, purchasing it for $2,350,000, less than one-fourth its original 1929–30 cost. Later I bought several hundred acres of land in Acapulco, Mexico, where I eventually built the Pierre Marques Hotel on Revolcadero Beach. These, contrary to reports that have me owning a string of hotels, are the only ones I own.

In 1937, as part of the Tide Water campaign, I obtained control of a firm known as the Mission Corporation. Among Mission's holdings was a 57-percent interest in the Skelly Oil Company, a major oil firm with headquarters in Tulsa, Oklahoma. Thus, almost as a windfall, I acquired the controlling interest in a company with a 1937 net income of $6,400,000—and which, today, has more than $330 million in assets.

But this is not the whole story. Among Skelly Oil's subsidiaries was the Spartan Aircraft Corporation, a Tulsa concern engaged since 1928 in manufacturing aircraft and training pilots and navigators. I paid my first visit to the Spartan plant on December 7, 1939. Its aircraft-manufacturing operations were rather limited; there were only some 60 workers employed in the factory. The pilot-training school was much more active. It was, in fact, the largest private flying school in the U.S.

I'd just returned from a trip to Europe, which was already at war. I was convinced that the United States would eventually have to throw its weight into the war against the Axis. Consequently, I felt Spartan Aircraft would have an increasingly important role in the nation's defense program—but I could not guess then how very important it was destined to be.

Two years to the day after my first visit to Spartan, the Japanese attacked Pearl Harbor and the United States was at war. It was in that same month that my beloved mother died. It was a heavy blow. Although I was by then almost 50, I felt the loss as keenly as though I had still been a youngster.

War news filled the newspapers. I had not been allowed to serve in World War One, and I now hoped for the chance to serve in the second world conflict. I had studied celestial navigation and had owned—at various times in my life—three yachts, the largest a 260-foot, 1500-tonner with a crew of 45. On the basis of this, I volunteered for service in the United States Navy. To my chagrin, I was politely but firmly informed that the navy didn't have much use for a middle-aged businessman unless he was willing to take a routine, shore-based administrative job. After exhausting all other avenues, I obtained an interview with Navy Secretary Frank Knox and pleaded my case. I told him I wanted a navy commission and sea duty.

"You qualify for a commission as an administrative or supply officer," Secretary Knox declared, "but sea duty is out of the question." He paused and studied me closely. "I understand you own the Spartan Aircraft Corporation," he said after a moment. I agreed that I did.

"The armed forces must have every aircraft factory in large-scale production as soon as possible," he told me. "The most important service you can render the war effort is to drop all your other business interests and take over direct personal management of Spartan."

I arrived in Tulsa as the working president of Spartan in February 1942. There was a tremendous amount to be done and very little time in which to do it. Manufacturing facilities—including factory space—had to be expanded, machinery and tools obtained, engineers and technicians recruited and workers hired and trained by the thousands. Despite bottlenecks, shortages and setbacks, peak production was attained in less than 18 months.

I remained in active and direct charge of Spartan's operations throughout the war. Before it ended, the Spartan flying school was training as many as 1700 fledgling aviators at a time. By V-J Day, the Spartan factory—employing more than 5500 workers at the peak—had turned out a vast array of airplane parts and components on subcontracts from major aircraft firms. Among these were 5800 sets of elevators, ailerons and rudders for B-24 bombers; 2500 engine-mount sets for P-47 fighters; Curtiss dive-bomber cowlings by the hundreds; Douglas dive-bomber control surfaces by the thousands; wings for Grumman Wildcat fighters; tail booms for Lockheed P-38 pursuits. Spartan also produced N-1 primary trainers on prime contract.

Spartan's production record brought high commendations from the armed forces—tributes to the efficiency and loyalty of the men and women who'd worked for the firm and who did their part in helping to win the war.

I stayed on at Spartan until 1948 to nurse the firm through the pangs of reconversion to peacetime production of house trailers. Then once more I went back to my first and greatest business love—oil.

My oil companies were prospering and were larger and more active than ever before, but it was time for additional expansion. Vast demands had been made on America's oil reserves by the war, and postwar petroleum consumption was rising sharply throughout the world. Oil prospectors were fanning out—to Canada, Central and South America, Africa and the Middle East—searching for new oil sources. Instinct, hunch, luck—call it what you will—told me the Middle East was the most promising locale, the best bet, for oil exploration. I had almost obtained an oil concession in the Middle East in the 1930s but had allowed my chance to go by. Now I decided to seek a concession to prospect and drill there and make up for the opportunity I had lost. In February 1949 my company obtained a 60-year concession on a half interest in the so-called Neutral Zone, and arid, virtually uninhabited and barely explored desert region lying between Saudi Arabia and Kuwait on the Persian Gulf.

The concession was granted by His Majesty, Ibn Saud, king of Saudi Arabia. In immediate consideration for the right to explore and drill for oil in the Neutral Zone, I paid the Saudi Arabian government $12,500,000. It was a gargantuan risk, and many people in the petroleum industry once again openly predicted I would bankrupt my firms and myself.

Four years and $40 million were needed before we brought in our first producing well in the Neutral Zone. But by 1954 I could relax and enjoy a private last laugh at the expense of those who had prophesied my ruin. The Neutral Zone had proved to be one of the world's most valuable oil properties. Well after well had come in, and petroleum geologists conservatively estimate proven reserves in places in the region covered by my concession to exceed 13 billion barrels!

With this tremendous reserve and with producing wells in the Middle East and elsewhere bringing up millions of barrels of crude oil annually, it has been necessary to expand even further in other directions. My companies have had to build and buy additional refineries to handle the enormous crude-oil production. Pipelines, storage facilities, housing projects for workers and innumerable other installations and facilities have been built or are abuilding.

A $200-million Tidewater Oil Company refinery was completed at Wilmington, Delaware, in 1957. Another Tidewater refinery near San Francisco has been modernized at a cost of $60 million. There is a new 40,000-barrel-a-day refinery in Gaeta, Italy, and another with a 20,000-barrel-a-day capacity in Denmark.

In 1954 and 1955 construction began on the first vessels in a fleet of supertankers. Several of these have been completed and are even now in operation. This tanker construction program is proceeding apace. Tonnage afloat and now under construction exceeds one million deadweight tons. Among the ships are truly giant supertankers displacing upwards of 70,000 tons.

My firms have recently built spanking new office buildings in Los Angeles, California; Tulsa, Oklahoma; and New York City—at a cost approaching $40 million. Regardless of what they produce, plants and businesses owned by Getty interests are oriented to steady expansion. Management is constantly seeking ways and means to increase output, and large-scale projects are under way to develop new products and to find new applications and uses for old ones. By no means the least of the activities in which my companies are engaged are oil and mineral explorations, which are being conducted energetically on four continents.

This, then, is the story of how I chose my road to success and how I traveled it from my wildcatting days in the Oklahoma oil fields, of how I've built my business and made my fortune. To it I would like to add a brief, highly personal— and mildly rueful—footnote.

For years I had managed—at least on the whole—to avoid personal publicity. Or, rather, since I did nothing either to seek or evade it, I suppose it would be more accurate to say that personal publicity avoided me. This state of peaceful near anonymity ended suddenly and forever in October 1957, when *Fortune* magazine published an article listing the wealthiest people in the United States. My name headed the list, and the article labeled me a billionaire and "The Richest Man in America." Subsequently other publications gave me the even more grandiloquent title of "The Richest Man in the World."

Since then I've been besieged by requests to reveal exactly how much money I have. I'm seldom believed when I reply in all honesty that I don't know, that there is no way I *can* know. Most of my wealth is invested in the businesses I own or control. I make no claims about the extent of my wealth, and I really don't care how rich I am.

Today my companies are thriving, and they're carrying out ambitious programs for further expansion. My primary concern and main interest lie in making certain that my companies continue to grow so that they can provide more employment and produce more goods and services for the benefit of all.

My associates and I are convinced that the overall economic trend is up and that despite the alarms and fears plaguing our era, the world is on the threshold of a prosperity greater than any in its history. We want to contribute our part to bringing this prosperity about—and to share in it, along with all peoples in all countries throughout the world.

10

Do You Need Luck to Make a Million?

The men in this gallery have used many and varied techniques to hoist themselves to the top of the financial heap. Salesmanship, borrowed money, technical innovation, plain old-fashioned audacity—we've watched and will watch these and other techniques and approaches being applied. We can analyze the techniques in a general way, for each is tangible enough so that you can grab it, turn it around and upside down, study it from this angle and that. Each seems capable of being taught, at least to a minor extent, by one man to another.

Now let's look at another component of success whose qualities are quite different: luck.

Luck can't be taught by or transferred from one man to another. It can't easily be analyzed. It isn't tangible; there are no convenient handles by which to grab it and examine it. Yet, bafflingly, it seems to be a necessary part of almost every man's climb to the top.

Luck, the totally unpredictable workings of a blind and uncaring fate. Its presence is more clearly felt in some men's lives, of course, than in others. J. Paul Getty credits luck for much of his success. Joe Hirshhorn, the stock-market player, had to have it in large measure. Many of his most successful plays, while founded partly on wisdom, still depended on the outcome of future events that could not be foreseen with any real clarity. He sold all his stockholdings just before the market crash in 1929, and he later admitted luck had a great deal to do with it. Hundreds of other men, less smart or less lucky, failed to sell out—and nobody knows their names today.

Luck isn't so clearly evident in the lives of other rich men, but if you look hard enough, you can always see it lurking somewhere in the background. Clement Stone, for example, appears to have battled his way from poverty to riches solely with his own brain and backbone. Yet there were many key points of his life when ill fortune could have squashed him flat as it has squashed other men. On his first day as a frightened young salesman he managed to peddle two insurance policies. Suppose, by chance, he had not met the two kindly gentlemen who bought those policies. Suppose his sales total that day had been—as it could easily have been, but for a quirk of fate—zero. It is conceivable that he might then have become discouraged and quit the insurance-selling business forever.

At any time of his life, too, he could have been stopped by sickness or automobile accident or any of a hundred other calamities. None of these things happened. And so Clem Stone kept going onward and upward.

It is instructive and somewhat scary to think that there might have been another teen-age salesman who began peddling insurance on the same day as young Clem Stone, in the same city, perhaps even the same office building. This other young fellow might have had latent sales talents equal to Stone's. Blundering in and out of offices just as Stone was doing, he had the bad luck not to meet two kindly gentlemen who happened to have a need for health-and-accident insurance. And so this other young man quit the business in disgust and went—who knows where? Downhill, perhaps. Stone, meanwhile, falling into two sales by sheer blind luck, gained enough encouragement to go on sharpening his then-unknown talents as a salesman and ended with $400 million in his bank account.

The other would-be salesman, age about 70 today, may be living in pinched and gloomy retirement from some penny-ante job. He may still be working for a few bucks a day to keep body and soul together. He may be on the Bowery. He may be dead.

But instead of just imagining this luckless man, is there any way in which we can track him down in the flesh, actually talk to him, find out exactly what his life has been like? *True* magazine once asked me to do exactly that. The assignment was to find two men who had been born and bred in the same year, in the same section of the same town, with the same advantages and disadvantages—one of whom had gone uphill and the other of whom had gone down. The story was to be a study of that elusive phenomenon, luck.

It was a fascinating assignment but a tough one. I had to approach it backward. I started by going down to New York's Bowery district, that depressing and grimy home of the homeless, the destitute, the washed-up. I went into the Majestic Bar, where you could buy wine for 15 cents a glass. I handed out a few bucks and briefly took down the life stories of all the ragged, bleary-eyed men who were lined up along the elbow-worn, drink-spotted bar. Then I went to a library and combed through *Who's Who* and other volumes until I found a successful man who had been born and brought up in the same town and circumstances as one of my Majestic bums. I then interviewed both men at length, and I interviewed other people who seemed to have something to say about luck, and here is the story.

The Theory and Practice of Luck*

Charles Alexander Wilson and Issur Danielovitch were both born in the grimy east end of Amsterdam, New York, during the First World War. They were equally endowed with a high native intelligence. The fathers were immigrant laborers, and their families' economic and social standings were exactly equal—which is to say, rock bottom. They were launched into life with about the same chances to succeed or fail.

They lived through the same sociological changes, the same historical events, the same world cataclysms. They grew up as boys in the Roaring Twenties. The Great Depression smacked them down as teen-agers. They were sucked into the vortex of the Second World War as young men in their 20s. They were spewed out again into the fantastic peacetime boom of the late 1940s and the 1950s. And today they are middle-aged men in the early autumn of life, looking back on spring and summer, on failure and on success.

Today Charles Alexander Wilson is known to his friends as Banana Nose. He is a Bowery bum. Issur Danielovitch is

*Originally published in *True* magazine under the title *Who Is the Dame Called Lady Luck?* Copyright © 1969 by Fawcett Publications, Inc., and Max Gunther. Reprinted with permission.

known as Kirk Douglas. He is a Hollywood star and a millionaire.

Fortune has treated them unequally. Why? Are their characters different? Of course. Has one tried harder than the other? Certainly. Heraclitus remarked some 25 centuries ago that character is destiny, and philosophers and novelists and moviemakers since then have made the point over and over again. To a large extent a man makes his own fate. But is that all there is to it? How about luck, pure, blind, random, uncontrollable chance? Did luck play any part in the diverse lives of Kirk Douglas and Banana Nose Wilson?

It did—a very big part. There were events in both men's lives that were seemingly beyond their control, events that took shape beyond their purview and then came crashing into their lives. These events helped one man reach a pinnacle of success—and knocked the other man flat.

Luck. It blunders in and out of our lives, unbidden, un-expected, sometimes welcome and sometimes not. It is the supreme insult to human reason: You can't ignore it; yet you can't plan for it. No matter how carefully you design your career, you cannot know how the design will be changed by the workings of random events. You can only know that the events will occur. You can only wait for them and hope that they're in your favor.

"Nobody has ever figured out a way to duck luck," says Sherlock Feldman of Las Vegas. Feldman lives in a world of raw luck, a world in which people deliberately expose themselves to the distilled essence of it. He is casino manager of the Dunes, one of Nevada's biggest gambling clubs. On duty from 2:00 A.M. to 10:00 A.M., he daily watches people who would rather play with raw luck than sleep. "The very fact that you exist at all is a matter of luck. If you want to scare yourself or amuse yourself—depending on your view-point—find out how your father chanced to meet your mother. Maybe they met at a party. Maybe your father was only at the party because he happened to run into a buddy on a street corner that day and the buddy invited him to drop in that night. That's how close you came to not existing."

Feldman, a beefy man with thick-rimmed glasses and a look of sad good humor, does a lot of thinking about luck. "It's a strange commodity," he says. "You can get super-stitious as hell about it if you let yourself. People come in here with rabbits' feet and astrology charts and all kinds of crazy ideas about how they're going to control their luck. I laugh. I say, 'There's no such thing as luck. It isn't a mystical something; it's just random events.' But then somebody comes in and does something that's statistically impossible and I have to say, 'Well, yes, he had luck.'"

Like the innocent tourist who dropped in one night recently —"a guy, I don't even know his name, a little guy from nowhere." The little guy had about $100 with him and was prepared to lose it all. He thought he would like to try shooting craps. He had never played the game before and had to be taught how. Normally a crapshooter thinks himself lucky if he holds the dice and continues winning for five or ten minutes, and a quarter hour is considered a superb run of luck. The little guy from nowhere held the dice for a fantastic two hours and forty minutes. When the incredible game ended, he had won about $30,000.

"How do you explain a thing like that?" asks Feldman, frankly puzzled. Many veteran gamblers around the table that night thought something was at work, though their definitions of this something differed. Some said the little guy was "hot"—meaning, essentially, that he was temporarily in a condition in which random events were influenced to fall his way. Influenced how, by what force or agency? Some of the onlookers said they didn't know, but others talked about something called "psychokinesis"—a presumed mental capacity by which the amateur gambler himself controlled the fall of dice. Others spoke of "precognition," the gambler's ability to look into the future and see how the dice would fall. Still others thought his luck resulted from mysterious forces operating around him but not within him, not under his control—forces exerted by the stars or other external agencies that, for reasons not known, were favorably disposed toward him on that particular night.

And a few thought the winning streak had no special significance at all. It was just a gathering together of random circumstances; it happened for no particular reason, without any intervention of unseen forces.

However you define luck, it patently exists. The phrase *streak of luck* is in the language because it articulates a common human experience. There are days when everything you touch turns to gold, and there are other days when everything turns to—well, let's be polite and call it dust and ashes. Some men seem consistently luckier than others—so much so, often, that friends of the fortune-blessed individual will talk as though luck is a built-in part of his career equipment, like education. "That lucky bastard," they'll say, "he can't do anything wrong!" His shoelace never breaks when he's hurrying to catch a plane. No waitress ever spilled coffee on his pants when he was on his way to an important appointment. When his car conks out, he's always half a block from a service station. It never rains when he goes to a ball game, but when he wants to ski, it snows.

Among the most famous of such lucky men was Jesse Livermore, a stock-market speculator who flourished early in this century and whose bets were consistently, outrageously right. The story of Livermore's luck would be too weird to believe if its main points were not documented in Wall Street's archives. Livermore was a farmer's son, born in Massachusetts, who drifted to Boston as a young man and got a clerical job in a brokerage house. He became fascinated by a type of gamble called short selling. In this hair-raisingly risky maneuver, you sell shares of a stock before you own them. You hope the price will drop before you're required to "cover" or deliver the shares. If the price does drop, you make money by buying the shares for less than the amount you've already sold them for. It is a way of manipulating big blocks of stock without needing big capital to start with. You stand to make huge profits without investing any of your own money—but conversely, of course, you face equally huge losses if the stock goes up in price.

Livermore quickly discovered that he had an uncanny ability—he could never fully explain it—to sense when a stock was about to drop in price. He began by making penny-ante bets with fellow clerks at the Boston brokerage house. He would bet that a certain stock would drop next week when everybody else, including seasoned traders who were customers of the house, thought it would rise. It would drop. When people asked him how he knew, he could only shrug and say, "Just luck, I guess."

He began selling short on the stock market itself. He became a multimillionaire. He was so consistently and uncannily successful that newspaper and magazine writers of the time, and even some hardened Wall Streeters, seriously believed he had the gift of precognition.

He denied it, but some of his parlays were hard to explain any other way. One morning in April 1906, he strolled into a broker's office and sold short several thousand shares of Union Pacific. It was a supremely foolhardy thing to do. The stock market was booming, and Union Pacific was one of the hottest growth issues on the board. The brokerage manager was sure Livermore had made a mistake. "You mean *buy*, don't you?" asked the manager. According to onlookers, Livermore picked up the order slip he had just filled out, stared at it with a faintly puzzled expression, then slowly shook his head. "No," he said, "I mean what I wrote." And with a distant smile, he left.

The next day he was back. The situation hadn't changed. All the news about Union Pacific was still overwhelmingly bullish. The vast majority of professional traders, far from selling it short, were greedily buying it on margin. But Livermore, still with that vaguely puzzled air yet oddly serene, sold more thousands of shares short.

On the next day, April 18, San Francisco was smashed by an earthquake. Millions of dollars in Union Pacific track and other property, and uncountable millions in potential earnings, vanished beneath the rubble. The company's stock fell like a stone. Livermore covered his short sales and came out of the deal more than $300,000 richer.

"Where did you get the hunch?" they asked him later. He could only shrug helplessly.

He was strongly aware of the enormous force exerted by luck in his life, however. He sometimes worried about what would happen if his luck deserted him. "When a man has lived by luck," he remarked once to a Swiss banker friend, "he lives with fear. If luck departs, where do you go for a new supply?" Livermore's luck began to evaporate during the giddy boom of the 1920s—a notably bad time for short selling. He recouped some of his losses in the 1930s, but his old flair seemed to be gone. In 1940, for reasons that never became clear, perhaps brooding about departed luck, he shot himself.

Kirk Douglas and Banana Nose Wilson, of Amsterdam, New York, are two more men who think long thoughts about luck. Oddly, Wilson seems more comfortably at home with his bad luck than Douglas does with his good luck.

Wilson says, "I stopped fighting it long ago. The hell with it. Life can take me where it wants. I'll go quietly."

Douglas says, "A man likes to feel he's in control of his life, but it's a damned illusion. The X factor is always there: luck, whatever you want to call it. You can have all the talent in the world, but without luck you go nowhere. It's frustrating because you can't control it; you can't do anything about it."

Issur Danielovitch was a tough kid from a tough neighborhood, with no apparent prospects for any great success. "I was going no place. I wasn't interested in anything except girls. I was the kind of kid who, as an adult, would end up as a clerk in an Amsterdam department store. But then this crazy X factor blew into my life for the first time. In high school, by chance, I was assigned to a class run by a teacher named Louise Livingston, and one day she asked me to take a small part in a school play. There was no reason for her to do it; it just happened—it was a fluke. If it hadn't happened, nobody outside Amsterdam would know my name today. But it did happen, and I got interested in acting, and Louise Livingston boosted me along, and that's how it started."

Young Danielovitch worked his way through college (partly as a clerk in an Amsterdam department store), went to New York City and tried to break into show business. "For a long while it looked as though luck had gone. I lived in a grubby little room in Greenwich Village, worked as a waiter in a Schrafft's restaurant. I got a couple of bit parts on Broadway. In one play I was an offstage echo— this was the kind of success I was having. When I went into the U.S. Navy in 1942, I seemed to be no further along in my acting career than when I'd started under Louise Livingston."

But luck was operating in its own secret way. One of the girls whom young Kirk Douglas kissed good-bye when he went to war was a struggling young actress named Lauren Bacall. While Douglas was out in the Pacific, Lauren Bacall enjoyed her own run of luck and abruptly became a Hollywood star. ("Your own luck depends on other people's luck. It's crazy, crazy.") She induced a Hollywood producer to watch Douglas act when he got back to civilian life, and his movie career began. "Oh, sure," he says, "I guess I had some kind of talent. But if I hadn't had this Lauren Bacall fluke, where would the talent have gone? Dozens of my friends back then had talent, too, but you don't see their names in movies today. They didn't have the luck."

After acting in obscure second-rate movies for a while, Douglas one day had a Jesse Livermore–style hunch. He was offered parts in two movies. One was a big, expensive production by a wealthy company that could offer him a lot of money. The other was a low-budget production by a small company that could offer only a bare minimum in earnings. "Why did I choose the little outfit? I didn't know then, and I still don't know today. It was a plain, wild hunch." The little company's movie was entitled *Champion,* and this was the movie that made Kirk Douglas a star.

One day in 1958, producer Mike Todd invited Kirk Douglas to fly with him from the West Coast to New York. "At the last moment I didn't go. There were circumstances— luck, I guess you'd call it. I had my bags packed, but I didn't get on the plane." The plane crashed, killing Mike Todd and everyone else aboard.

Luck. Issur Danielovitch plainly had it. Charles Alexander Wilson didn't. While Danielovitch was going up, Wilson was going down.

Wilson was born in the same tough section of Amsterdam. He did well in his early years of school; he recalls that his grades were mainly A's and B's. When he was about 12, his father chanced to hear of a semiskilled job in Providence, Rhode Island, and the family migrated. "It seemed like good luck for my old man, because his wages went up a bit, but it was bad luck for me. I'd been happy in school before, but somehow I never made it in the Providence schools. I ran into some bad teachers. There was one who kidded me about my big nose, and the kids took it up from her, and I never got to be anything but an outsider. I was Charlie the Beak, the kid everybody laughed at. Well, hell, that kind of thing bothers a kid. My grades fell. I guess from then on I was marked as a loser. I had the loser psychology. I'd only just started, but I was already finished."

Unlike young Danielovitch, whose chance contact with a good teacher showed him the value of education, unlucky Charlie Wilson understandably came to hate school. He dropped out before finishing high school. He worked as a laborer. "Every now and then I'd try for a better job, but

I had *loser* written all over me. I guess what I did was, I'd apply for a job believing I wasn't going to get it. I'd apologize to the guy for wasting his time. Naturally, he wouldn't give me the job."

In 1939 a break came Wilson's way. He got a job driving for a small trucking company. He and the owner of the business grew fond of each other. The owner, an older man, wanted to retire and began to talk about turning the business over to Wilson as manager and partner. Wilson saw a chance to succeed at last, grew excited over the deal, studied the company's books and the economics of the trucking business. "I was going to be a businessman! I thought, *I've finally made it!*"

But then the United States went to war. One of the first men drafted into the army from Providence was Charles Alexander Wilson. By the time he returned to civilian life in the mid-1940s, the little trucking business and the owner were both dead.

He drifted from job to job. He had learned to like whiskey in the army, but he was not yet drinking much. A new chance to succeed came his way when the Firestone Tire and Rubber Company hired him in 1948 as a warehouseman. Like many big companies in those days, Firestone had ambitious peacetime expansion plans but was hobbled by a postwar lack of technically trained young men. The company was continually dipping down into its pool of unskilled laborers, lifting them up, sending them to school and channeling them into what, for some, became golden new careers. Charlie Wilson, lacking education but impressively bright, was one man so lifted. Firestone began by training him as a tire retreader, and there was talk of sending him to night school to complete his high-school education and then perhaps on to a chemical technicians' school. "Once more I thought I had it made."

Once more he was wrong. One Saturday night he was driving an arthritic 1938 Buick in New Jersey, when the steering mechanism gave way. He found the wheel spinning freely in his hands. "I was on a kind of country road. There was only one house anywhere near me. The rest was open fields. The car could have gone in a thousand different directions and it would have been OK. But what happens? Christ, the car heads straight for the house. I smash into the side of the garage, and the whole goddamn garage roof collapses."

Charlie wasn't badly hurt, but his career was. He had been drinking that night—but, he steadfastly claimed, not heavily. "I think I'd had three glasses of beer, nothing else." He was charged with drunken driving. Nobody believed his story about the steering mechanism; the car was too badly smashed to yield supporting evidence. He was uninsured. The owner of the house sued him for several thousand dollars' worth of damage, and his wages at Firestone were garnisheed.

That ended his bright career at Firestone. He drifted some more. One day in 1950, jobless and hungry and without hope, he passed an army recruiting poster that promised to teach him skills and a trade if he would reenlist. "It seemed like an answer. Here was a new chance to learn something useful. I figured that since you didn't get shot at in the peacetime army, a man might as well earn his living there as anyplace else."

He enlisted on June 15, 1950. On June 25 North Korean troops unexpectedly invaded South Korea across the 38th parallel, and two days later U.S. forces were on their way to war, and a few months after that, Charlie Wilson was in Korea getting shot at.

"I figured, Nothing I do is ever going to turn out right. I figured, From now on, the hell with it. Korea is where I started drinking in earnest."

Out of the army again in the late 1950s, he drifted to New York City, blew all his back pay and his frontline bonus and started looking for a job. "I was forty. I thought I had to make it this time or I'd be through forever. I quit drinking, dried out completely, got myself a decent-looking set of clothes. I mean, I was really determined to give it one last try."

But he had no skills to offer any employer. And one day, sitting gloomily on a park bench scanning help-wanted ads in a newspaper, he had what he now considers the unluckiest break of his entire luckless life. "I'm sitting there, and a guy comes from nowhere and sits next to me. A bum, ragged, lushed up. He says, 'Out of a job?' I say yes, and he says, 'I'll tell you where to go.' I figure he's about to tell me about a job I can get. Instead, what he tells me is—well, it's my doom."

The bum told Charlie Wilson about New York's Municipal Lodge—"the Muni," its patrons call it—where destitute men can get free meal and bed tickets redeemable at restaurants and hotels in the Bowery. "When I got my free meal that night and went to bed in a free dormitory, I just gave up. The pressure was off. I didn't have to hunt a job anymore. From that day on, I was trapped."

Today he makes his daytime home at the Bowery's rather ill-named Majestic Bar, where wine is served at 15 cents a glass. Banana Nose, as they call him (and, curiously, he likes the name), still clings to his self-respect. He shaves daily, his hair is neatly combed, his fingernails are clipped short and perfectly clean, his clothes are old but neat. He also clings to a certain sad optimism. "Most of what has happened to me is probably my own goddamn fault," he told me recently, "but some of it has been plain bad luck, and I keep thinking maybe my luck will turn some day. Luck can turn, can't it?"

I nodded. Banana Nose Wilson's ugly but pleasant face suddenly brightened. "Maybe it just turned," he said, "just now when you came out of nowhere and buttonholed me. Out of a thousand bums, you happened to pick me. Now, is that luck or isn't it?"

I thought maybe it was. I had bought Banana Nose a meal and a carton of cigarettes. Now, as we parted, I gave Banana Nose ten bucks.

But what is luck? "You can read case histories like these in any of several ways," says Dr. Jean Rosenbaum, a New Mexico psychoanalyst who is fascinated by what he calls "the syndrome of the chronic loser." A man's own character may help shape his luck, says Dr. Rosenbaum, but luck may have shaped his character to begin with. "It's very hard to separate the two factors."

If you examine a chronic loser's life story, he says, you usually find that he invited much of his own bad luck. Dr. Rosenbaum once had a patient, for example, who was accident-prone to an almost ridiculous extent. He was a machinist. He had lost three fingers in three separate accidents. He had broken both arms and a leg at various times. He had been scalped in another accident and nearly blinded in another. "Around the plant where he worked, they called him Hard-Luck Harry. On the surface it did seem that he was a victim of outrageous and almost continual bad luck. But when he came to see me—he suspected his luck might be his own doing, you see—we discovered an interesting fact: Not more than a couple of hours before each of his accidents, he had had an argument with some supervisor or other. It seemed as though he then injured himself as a punishment for having bad thoughts about an authority figure."

Dr. Rosenbaum pauses. "So his luck was caused by his character. But what had shaped his character? Where did this hang-up about authority figures come from? It went back to his childhood and his relationship with his father—back to events that were not his doing at all. Luck, you see, had shaped his character."

This is one explanation of certain kinds of luck. But there are other kinds that cannot easily be explained that way. The kind Sherlock Feldman sees at the Dunes, for instance. "We have chronic losers around here, too," says Feldman. "The law of averages says everyone should win once in a while, in an honest game—but there are people who almost never win. Why? You tell me."

Feldman's most poignant story concerns a sad-looking man who wandered into the Dunes one night and stood around watching a roulette game. Noticing that somebody had dropped a five-dollar bill under the table, he shouted to the dealer, "There's a five on the floor!" The dealer misheard it amid the noise, thought the man had said, "Five on four!" Accordingly, the dealer put a five-dollar chip on the number four. The wheel spun, four came up, and the sad-looking man had won $175. The dealer shoved the chips across the table. Stunned, the man left them where they lay—by chance, on red. The wheel spun again, and red came up. The sad man had won again.

He was quivering with excitement. "My God," he said to a bystander, "this is the first time in my life I ever won anything! I'm the unluckiest guy alive. I've never even won a dime in a poker game!"

"Well," said the bystander, "if this is your lucky night at last, let it run."

He did. He played that wheel until he had won more than $5000. Then, unable to stand the tension any longer, he gathered his chips and went to cash them, laughing and singing.

A firm rule at Las Vegas states that if a player calls a bet without actually putting up cash, he must eventually show that he had the cash in his pocket to cover that first bet. Otherwise the house will refuse to cash his chips. In this case the sad man was required to show that he had five dollars on him—the price of his first chip.

He pulled out his wallet and looked inside. It was empty. His wife had emptied it that day to go shopping and had forgotten to tell him.

Luck of that kind cannot easily be explained by reference to character. Nor can the kind of luck that produces winning lottery tickets. "It comes at you from the blue, like being struck by lightning," says 62-year-old Sol Levin of Jersey City, New Jersey. Levin, a dental-supply man who had never before won anything in a lottery, pessimistically bought five tickets in the New York State Lottery one day. The chances that any one of his tickets would be picked in a prize drawing were roughly one in a thousand, and the chances that two would be picked were too microscopic to think about. But the nearly impossible happened: Two of Levin's tickets were picked, winning him a total of $400. "It wasn't much money," says Levin, "but it shows you that this thing called luck does exist. Every now and then it zeros in on somebody. I don't know why, but I do know—I mean, *now* I know—it happens."

Many people think they know why. Numerologists, for instance, believe Levin won twice because his tickets had lucky numbers. His two winning tickets bore the consecutive numbers 10,522,453 and 10,522,454. If you add all the individual digits in those numbers, numerologists point out, you get the total of 45—which is considered by some adherents of this mystical pseudoscience to be an overwhelmingly lucky number. (It is the "king number," the total of all the digits from 0 to 9.)

Many other people have many other explanations of luck. "With anything as unexplainable and uncontrollable as luck, it's only human to try to explain it and control it," says Penn Mutual Life Insurance executive Robert S. Johnson. As a fighter pilot over England and Germany in World War Two, Johnson had more luck than anybody could explain rationally. "It's silly, but you do it—you latch on to funny little superstitions."

Johnson shot down 28 German aircraft without ever

sustaining more than superficial damage to his plane and a minor wound in his leg. This was a fantastic record in the European theater of the war. Out in the Pacific, where the Japanese often fought with inferior aircraft and hastily trained pilots, it wasn't uncommon for American fliers to chalk up high scores. But German planes and pilots were superior. If an American scored as high as ten and lived to tell the tale, it was considered remarkable. How did Johnson survive?

Character must have had something to do with it. Johnson had obviously learned his deadly business conscientiously, and he obviously handled his plane with great skill and impeccable judgment. He didn't expose himself to unnecessary danger, never sacrificed safety in some wild quest for glory. "I didn't go out of my way looking for victories."

But at least some German pilots must have been equally excellent. How did Johnson elude their bullets? He grows almost apologetic as he talks about it. "Damned silly . . . I carried two lucky pieces all the time, a British farthing and a little steel knife. I knew it was silly, but I wouldn't have felt safe without them. And I called my plane 'Lucky.' I was trying to explain and control my luck, you see."

Today, a short, taut, graying man in his mid-40s, Johnson still worries about luck. "This tie I'm wearing today brings me luck. The thirteenth of the month is generally lucky for me. . . ." Silly, perhaps, as he says. Yet luck—whatever it is—once saved his life. It is understandable that he is mildly obsessed by thoughts about luck. In fact, it would be strange if he weren't.

Other students of luck have attempted more scientific examinations of the phenomenon. Probably the most famed is psychologist Joseph Banks Rhine, executive director of the Foundation for Research on the Nature of Man. First at Duke University and now at his foundation, Dr. Rhine has spent most of his professional life seeking the answer to one question: "Is there an element of direct mental action operating at times to influence results in games of skill and chance?" Rhine believes the answer is yes, but he has yet to convince a clear majority of fellow scientists.

In Rhine's view, luck may result partly from precognition, psychokinesis and other weird manifestations generally cataloged under the general heading of extrasensory perception, or ESP. Rhine, his wife and a few dozen other respected researchers scattered across the country have performed literally thousands of experiments to find out if ESP exists and, if so, what it is and how it operates. Generally these experiments have involved attempts to influence the roll of dice or guess what cards somebody else was holding. If such an ability actually exists, it would, of course, be useful not only at the gambling table but also on the stock market and in the game of life itself. It would help explain why Kirk Douglas failed to board Mike Todd's airplane (precognition) or why no enemy bullet ever found a vital spot in Robert Johnson's plane or body (psychokinesis) or why Sol Levin's two consecutive lottery tickets came up in a drawing.

If it exists. Some of Rhine's experiments seemed to show that it does. The most bizarre experiment took place in September 1933. Divinity student Hubert E. Pearce sat in a cubicle in the Duke University library and tried to guess what cards were being turned up in another building 100 yards away. The cards bore five different designs. Thus, in an average series of 300 tries, Hubert Pearce would have been expected to get 60 right answers by chance alone—one in five. But in one amazing series Pearce scored 119. The odds against this happening by chance were something like a quadrillion to one. Hence, said Rhine, it probably didn't happen by chance. Therefore, it must have happened because some other force was operating—ESP, controlled luck.

It was a tempting conclusion, but many other scientists didn't accept it. One of the more rigid rules of science is that an experimental result must be repeatable, and Hubert Pearce was never able to do the trick again (though he did have a number of other runs in which he scored significantly higher than the expectable pure-chance score). His life since then has been normally but not spectacularly lucky. He is now a Methodist minister in Kansas City, a quiet man who lays no claim to any future-foretelling or mind-reading abilities.

A somewhat more pragmatic approach to the causes of luck is that of economist A. H. Z. Carr. Carr, who was economic advisor to Presidents Roosevelt and Truman, became intrigued by questions about luck when he tried to sort out all the reasons why nations win or lose wars. He developed some theories about personal luck and expressed them in a 1952 book, *How to Attract Good Luck*. The book quickly sank into oblivion, but it made one sensible point.

You can't win a game without entering it, said Carr. This is obvious if you are talking about poker or the stock market, but less obvious if you are talking about life in general. To attract lucky chances, you must put yourself in a position to receive them—"expose yourself as fully as possible to the fluid circumstances of life." To boil this down to its essentials, this means simply to get into contact with as many people as possible.

Kirk Douglas hit Hollywood because he was in contact with Lauren Bacall. She was one of several hundred people whom the amiable young actor had taken the trouble to befriend. He had no way of knowing in advance which of these several hundred might bring him a stroke of luck or what that luck might be—but, by being in contact with that many people, he made the odds favorable. By contrast, one of Banana Nose Wilson's main problems was that he never made many friendly contacts. Knowing few people, he had relatively few chances of hearing about a good job or lucking into some pot-of-gold opportunity through a friend of a friend.

"Yes, that book is right," Wilson told me one day as we strolled down a crowded New York sidewalk. "Luck comes mostly from other people. If I could live my life over, I'd get to know a lot more people. That's the secret! That must be it!"

"Why not start today?" I asked. "You talk as though you're already dead, for God's sake."

"You're right!" Wilson's voice rose with enthusiasm. "I'll try it! People, that's what it's all about! There's no such thing as bad luck!"

But a little while later a pigeon emptied its bowels from a ledge high above the sidewalk. The dropping could have fallen on any of several hundred strollers. It landed on Banana Nose Wilson's sleeve.

"Oh, the hell with it," said Wilson.

11

The Technology Route: The Jack-of-All-Trades Approach

It is obvious that a lot of money can be made from advances in technology. The trick is to arrive on the scene with the right idea at the right time—to turn up just a split second before your competitors do with a new device or material or process that the world wants to buy.

There seem to be two basic ways of pulling off this trick. One way is to concentrate fairly narrowly on one specialized field of science, to dig in that one field, probe it to its depths, progressively uncovering one treasure below another below another. If you succeed, you become known as the master of that field and virtually its sole owner. You become its owner not only intellectually but also—if you have a good patent lawyer and a sound financial instinct—in terms of money as well. A man who performed this feat in a peculiarly brilliant way is Edwin Land, and we'll look at his star-dusted career in the next chapter.

The second approach to technology is that of the non-specialist. This kind of man isn't wedded to any particular science. Instead, he is in love with technology itself—all of it. He is typically a tinkerer. He loves to take devices apart and see what makes them go, then play around with them to see whether he can make them go better. He doesn't particularly care what kinds of devices they are, just as long as they offer him the opportunity to apply his own ingenuity. Unlike the specialist, who usually needs a fairly thorough education in his science, the nonspecialist doesn't seem to require much in the way of formal education. He may even have dropped out of school because books and abstract thought bored him: He was impatient to go out somewhere and get his hands on actual, working, nonabstract devices.

Such a man is William P. Lear, Sr. He is probably best known as the producer of the Lear Jet, the small, inexpensive airplane used mainly by companies wishing to reduce travel time for high-salaried executives. But he has had his hands on dozens of other technological advances, from early radio innovations to new kinds of pollution-free car engines. Consider his story, told here by the perceptive reporter C. P. Gilmore—who visited the restless, ebullient Lear for a few days and came back giddy and out of breath.

William Lear:
Two Hundred Million Dollars*
by C. P. Gilmore

It was a tough problem. The new hydraulic system wasn't developing enough pressure to start the plane's jet engine. A group of engineers around the table theorized about where the trouble might lie.

At one end of the polished walnut slab, a stocky, ruddy-faced, graying man, his chin crisscrossed by ancient, jagged scars, remnants of an air crash years earlier, was losing patience rapidly. "For crying out loud," he shouted, "let's cut out this mental masturbation and *try* something."

For most of his life William P. Lear, Sr., legendary aviation and electronics pioneer, inventor, tycoon, pilot, flamboyant extrovert, multimillionaire, has been trying things. Most of them have succeeded. Over the years Lear has revolutionized the flying business by inventing or vastly improving a wide range of flight instruments from autopilots to automatic direction finders. The old Majestic, first mass-produced radio for home use, was his idea. So was the first automobile radio. Lear holds more than 100 patents and is responsible for scores of basic innovations in electronics and aviation. He has been honored with virtually every significant award in the flying business.

With nothing but a grammar-school education, boundless energy and a fierce drive to succeed, Lear built a $100-million-a-year business, Lear, Inc., and accumulated vast wealth. Then [at the age of 60], an age when most men are

*Originally published in *True* magazine under the title *Hard-Nosed Gambler in the Plane Game.* Copyright © 1966 by Fawcett Publications, Inc., and C. P. Gilmore. Reprinted with permission.

beginning to look to shuffleboard for their greatest thrills, he sold his company and threw his entire fortune, reputation and prestige into a risky new business the experts said couldn't succeed: building jet airplanes.

The experts were wrong. Bill Lear has done it again. Today Lear's jet, produced at his Wichita plant, is the hottest thing in private aviation and [he has built] a new corporate empire.

Lear has made his several fortunes by being an all-around man. Despite his lack of formal education, he's an expert in every phase of business from finance to engineering and frequently comes up with solutions to problems that have stumped experts. When the trouble with the hydraulic system came up recently, for example, Lear listened to the engineers around the table and figured they were off the track. While they were still theorizing, he decided that a smaller nozzle at one point in the system would cure the trouble. It did.

Lear's entire approach to every aspect of the jet-airplane business is similarly offbeat. Most of the builders of plushy executive planes (actually small airliners) used by America's business leaders are convinced that businessmen, with millions in company funds to spend, want luxury. Most planes on the market, consequently, are opulent enough for a maharaja. "This is the royal-scow approach," says Lear, who grabs you by the elbow and holds you to emphasize his points. "Some of these guys think they want hot food, stand-up bar, sit-down toilet, lie-down couch, walk-around headroom, everything up to and including hot and cold running bidets in an airplane. Who the hell needs it? In my plane it takes one hour from Detroit to New York, two hours from New York to Miami. Well, let me tell you about these big, slow scows. After two hours even wall-to-wall girls is no substitute for getting there."

By royal-scow standards, Lear's sleek eight-passenger jet is small—no walk-around room. ("You can't stand up in a Cadillac, either," snaps Lear. "An average-size man sitting in my jet has twenty-eight inches of headroom. Anybody with more than a twenty-eight-inch head should buy some other kind of airplane.") There are no options in equipment. It's available in one color, white. Where most plane makers let customers "design the panel"—that is, pick which instruments, radio and navigation equipment, and so on, they want installed—Lear offers no choice at all. The plane comes with one integrated electronics system, made up largely of Lear developments.

But its small size and Spartan accommodations give it two outstanding advantages. First, cruising at 570 miles an hour (it's been flown at 630 in level flight), it easily outflies the competition and will outclimb an F-100 Super Sabre to 10,000 feet. And second, compared to the planes it competes with, it's cheap—[the price in the mid-1960s was] $595,000 complete. Similar planes from other makers often [were] much more than a million dollars.

When Lear announced [in 1963] that he would build a new jet airplane, aviation experts were scornful. The business-plane field was already crowded and competition tough, they pointed out. Almost the only firms marketing successful business planes were the old, established airframe makers such as North American, Lockheed and Beech. Furthermore, Lear was going about it all wrong with his "hot rod" approach. "They said I'd never build it," Lear recalls, "that if I built it, it wouldn't fly; that if it flew, I couldn't sell it. Well, I did, and it did, and I could."

In the early 1960s market surveys by leading aircraft companies showed that 300 business jets would be sold by 1970. Lear predicted 3000. "They don't ask the right questions when they make surveys," he says. "The trick is to discern a market—before there is any proof that one exists. If you had said in 1925 that we would build nine million automobiles a year by 1965, some statistician would have pointed out that they would fill up every road in the United States and, lined up end to end, would go across the country 11 times. Surveys are no good. I make my surveys in my mind."

On the basis of his mental surveys or some other undisclosed source, Lear predicted that his jet would be a runaway best seller. "We'll sell 'em like bananas—in bunches," he said. Today the quip is turning into fact. One company recently ordered ten, another four; still others bought two and three each. "I think those qualify as bunches," says Lear. One of the company's recent sales was to Frank Sinatra, who hasn't bought a bunch as yet but is seriously considering buying another.

Lear's habitual success doesn't just happen. He's a doer, not a theoretician. He has absolute faith that he will succeed at anything he does. He doesn't rely on faith to do the job, however. Lear works seven days a week ("Even Christmas," says Mrs. Lear plaintively).

He spends his days moving from one department to another (frequently with his favorite dog, a small black poodle named Jet, trotting after him) checking every detail of the plane's manufacture and design, ordering changes, making improvements. "This plane is going to be just like the Volkswagen," he says. "Ten years from now it will look just the same. But it will fly faster, land slower, use less fuel and be more reliable."

In an airplane, weight equals performance; a lighter plane (for a given power) can fly faster, carry more, go farther. Weight, consequently, is Lear's passion. Automatically, as he passes an engineer's desk, he grabs a part and hefts it to judge weight. "How much?" he asks.

"Three grandmothers."

"Get rid of one," he barks and moves on.

Grandmother is Learese for pound. It started one day when an engineer was trying to get Lear to approve the design for a part and protested that it weighed only four pounds. "Don't you know," shouted Lear, "that I'd sell my grandmother to save just *one* pound?" The name stuck.

Lear has cut hundreds of pounds from his jet after the engineers had squeezed it down as far as they could. One afternoon he strode into the seat-manufacturing division of the plant and asked to see the aluminum shell around which the pilot's seat is built. "Why couldn't we cut a square foot right out of the back here?" he asked, drawing a square on the aluminum. "This part doesn't support anything." The engineer working on the seat grinned sheepishly. "Another grandmother and a half," said Lear happily.

Lear hates paper work and rarely writes memos or letters. He prefers more direct methods. Not long ago he thought of a better way to connect a rod in a control system to give better action. In most companies such an idea would go to engineering for evaluation, where the plan would be debated and finally approved. Specifications would be set and plans drawn. Eventually prototypes would be made for testing. Months after the original idea, the change might be ordered, new drawings would be made, and the altered part would go into production.

But not at Lear Jet. When Lear thought of the change, he walked across to the area making the control rod, grabbed the nearest production worker and the part he wanted to modify, drew several lines directly on the part with his pencil and explained how he wanted the new system put together. "Call me when you have it finished," he said and walked off. An hour later, Lear looked over the control mechanism, approved it and sent it to the engineering department with instructions that all drawings be changed to conform. The next day the new part was being installed in airplanes. "Patience," says Lear, "was never one of my virtues. When I make a change, I want every drawing in the plant to be changed within an hour."

He applies the same technique to almost any problem. When his first prototype jet was in its flight-test program, Lear and his engineers decided to change the shape of the wing's leading edge to give better stall characteristics. In most aircraft plants such a major overhaul would be a six-month job, starting with complete redesign and retooling. It would cost hundreds of thousands of dollars.

Lear decided to make the change late one Friday afternoon and had templates made to indicate the new shape. He called one of Wichita's best auto body-and-fender men, told him to get his tools and come on out. Lear had the body man spread hard-drying fender compound on the leading edge, then file and grind it to the proper shape. It was finished early the next morning and cost $48 in labor. The airplane flew with the new wing before noon on Saturday. It proved the point, and subsequent production wings were changed to conform.

The day I first met Lear was a holiday. One of Lear's executives met me at Wichita airport and drove me to the plant on the other side of the field. We found Lear in the engineering department. Most lights were off; the scores of drawing boards, arranged in neat lines, were covered. Lear was alone in the vast room, hunched over a board, making changes on a drawing. He had flown a Lear Jet in from Los Angeles a few minutes earlier and during the flight had thought of an improvement in the locking device to hold the pilot's seat in place. He explained the idea to me—it was a way to do the job with fewer, lighter parts—and finished the drawing. Then he scrawled, "See me about this. WPL," and put the cover back on the board. We went downstairs, where he gathered several executives who were working despite the holiday and got reports on what had happened while he was away. Lear stopped by the electronics department, personally checked out an automatic direction finder that had failed on his flight and that he had had removed from the airplane. Before the day was over, he went through a half-dozen other departments, gave an interview to a reporter from an aviation magazine and glanced through a stack of papers on his desk. It was eight o'clock when Mrs. Lear met us at the plant and we went out for dinner.

Later that night, as Lear's car turned into the driveway of his home, we were surrounded by a pack of leaping, barking dogs. Lear jumped from the car with a bag of meat scraps he had brought home from the restaurant. Laughing and talking to his five dogs, he began throwing scraps of meat.

Lear lives in a well-to-do, tree-shaded suburb of Wichita. His home, large and pleasant but definitely not in the mansion category, could be owned by any moderately successful doctor or small businessman. There is one servant, a combination cook and housekeeper. Mrs. Lear serves dinner—even company meals—herself. A roomy patio graces the back of the house, but there is no olympic-sized swimming pool or other sign of unusual wealth.

Lear, in fact, definitely seems to prefer a relatively simple life. When he and his family were living in Europe a few years ago, he got fed up with the baronial splendor of the mansion outside of Geneva he had rented. He bought a piece of property and had a modest American-type house, which he named Le Ranch, built on it.

When the dogs had been fed after our homecoming, Lear went into the den, poured himself a nightcap and indulged in what may be his only hobby, organ playing. He decided to take up organ about a year ago. He bought an organ and an instruction book. Today, despite the fact that he's never taken a lesson, he plays as though he's been at it for years.

Lear's day started the next morning at 7:30, when he took his place at the head of the breakfast table. Within a minute or two his bacon and poached eggs were in front of him— Lear is served first in his household, other men next, women last—and he had glanced through the paper. As he dug into an egg, he reached for the phone beside his plate. The first of several calls was a 20-minute chat with the manager of a factory he recently opened in Detroit to build stereo-tape playback units for automobiles.

After breakfast we climbed into his Cadillac, and Lear started the engine. Lear always drives, I found later. Even when we were met at the airport in other cities, he always drove, no matter who owned the car.

At the plant Lear strode directly from his car to the electronics department to see how work was progressing on the direction finder he had tested the night before, then headed for his office. As he took off his jacket, he yelled to his secretary to get the president of the electronics company that made the direction finder on the phone. "Put it on my private line," he said and walked into the executive washroom. "I don't waste a minute," he grinned as he closed the booth door and began his conversation.

When Lear returned from the washroom, two executives had spread a flock of proposed ads out on a large conference table for his approval. An official of one of the country's largest brokerage firms was on the phone waiting to talk. He glanced at the ads for 30 seconds. "Don't we have some more pictures?" he growled and picked up the phone as an adman scurried out to get more photographs. Lear stood simultaneously talking on the phone, scratching out lines of copy on one of the ads and writing in new copy. By the time he cradled the phone, he had rewritten the copy, shortening it severely, and picked a new picture. "An ad isn't a brochure," he lectured his ad people. "Anybody who's got time to read all those words has got too much time. I'm not interested in the bastard.

"I'm no artist," he told me as his assistants left with the approved ad, "but I can see what stinks. What it amounts to is that I write the ads and work on the layout, too."

Lear similarly handles details of sales, finance, purchasing, production, electronics, engines, interiors and a dozen other areas involved in making and selling airplanes. Throughout the next hour a steady stream of employees crowded through the office to talk with the boss about details in these areas and others. He held a dozen phone conversations, one haggling with a San Francisco surplus dealer over the price of some electric motors. He sounded as though he had taken his training in a Cairo bazaar.

Lear runs a one-man show and seldom lets anyone else make a decision. "I tell them," he snaps, "that if they put up half the money, they can make half the decisions." Despite his tendency to dominate his surroundings, however, Lear exudes charm. He's totally guileless and straightforward. When pleased, he shows it. But he can be completely intolerant, too, and doesn't mind, as one put it, "bloodying his employees in front of witnesses." An engineer came by Lear's office one day to discuss a problem for which he had no solution. Normally Lear likes nothing better than solving problems that have stumped his engineers. But this day he didn't want to be bothered. "If I've got to go up there and solve it myself," Lear shouted, "then what the hell do I need you for?"

An executive sitting in the office attempted to ease the situation. "Don't get excited, Bill," he said.

"Who's excited?" Lear yelled in a voice that could be heard in neighboring states and brought secretaries out of their chairs throughout the plant.

"What's the problem, Bill?" asked a passing employee attracted by the noise.

"The problem," answered Lear in his window-rattling tones, "is that there is an overabundance of idiocy around here."

Engineers unable to put up with Lear's temper and his insistence on approving every detail have left in droves. "When you work for Bill Lear," snapped one, "you work for fifty cents a day and all you can take."

"All he's got around him now," growls another, "is a bunch of yes-men."

Whether that judgment is correct or not, there's no arguing with the fact that Lear isn't the easiest man in the world to get along with. Blunt as a battering ram and roughly as insistent, he has made his share of enemies. Most of his business rivals refuse to comment on him, even privately. "Well, the son of a bitch is unique," growled one, who refused to be quoted by name or comment further.

Even Lear's top executives have their troubles. Back when Lear was still chairman of the board of Lear, Inc., the $100-million-a-year electronics company he sold to start Lear Jet, he decided he needed some freedom from everyday managerial duties to work on projects that particularly interested him. So he installed as president an executive named Richard Mock. It wasn't a totally happy situation. "He was always bursting out of his lab with some new idea he wanted to get into production right away," complained a frustrated Mock. "No sooner would we get some new item into the works than he'd want to improve it. Or else he'd start pulling engineers from their jobs to help him work out something else. I spent lots of my time trying to keep him from sidetracking the company."

Lear seems to have a talent for making people mad. Back in the late 1950s he took off for Europe to set up several new plants and to establish the Lear line of electronic equipment there. While he was away from home base, one division of his company developed a new aircraft instrument called the LTRA-7, a combination transmitter, receiver and navigation device. Lear got back, tried it out, decided it was no good and canceled the whole program. Since the production line was already set up, the company took a bad financial licking. "The only thing wrong with the LTRA-7," said one bitter engineer, "was that Bill Lear didn't invent it. He couldn't stand the idea of us doing something successful without him."

In earlier years Lear split his time between his plant, then on Long Island, and New York's Stork Club. There, at his regular table (which he called his "night office"), he became known for the clutch of beautiful show girls who usually surrounded him. Lear has been married four times. His present wife is Moya Olsen, daughter of comedian Ole Olsen of Olsen and Johnson fame. He has three children by earlier marriages; he and Moya have four. In his younger days Lear enjoyed the reputation of a roué and still likes to play the part. "This guy's writing the story of my love life," he told people while I was with him. "Only trouble is that they can't find any asbestos paper to print it on."

Despite such statements, Lear seems to have simmered down into a moderately doting family man. He frequently takes his wife and children still living at home (most are grown now) along on his many trips. He is obviously proud of his children and likes to work into the conversation that Bill, Jr., is a test pilot.

Lear's offbeat, flamboyant style isn't new; in fact, it's his

lifelong trademark. A half century ago he played hooky
from school in Chicago to ride around on his bike and search
for stalled motorists. Lear would offer to help. "Most
troubles were in the electrical system in those days," he
recalls. "Usually the carbons in the distributor would break
down. I would carry a piece of battery carbon in my pocket.
When I found a stalled car, I'd take it out, saw off a piece
to fit and get them going." Lear learned an important lesson
from these encounters. "Invariably they'd pat me on the head
and say, 'Thank you,' and away they'd go. Then I got smart.
When the engine was running, I'd say, 'Just a minute. I want
to adjust that a little more.' Then I'd take the carbon out and
start to walk away. I'd insist on getting paid before I put
it back in." From that point on, Lear put a price on every
job.

His first full-time employment came at the age of 13. He
got a job as an auto mechanic at six dollars a week but soon
became fascinated with flying and radio, the two fields that
were to remain lifelong interests. Eventually he quit his paid
job to take an unpaid one as a mechanic at Chicago's Grant
Park Airport.

Lear's flying career didn't begin auspiciously. On his first
hop the antiquated biplane he was flying flipped when landing and pitched Lear out on his head.

Lear, however, was also becoming something of an expert
in the fledgling field of radio. "I worked as a radio engineer,"
he says. "In those days that was a radio repairman fifty miles
from home." He soon found himself hired by a company
that built battery eliminators, rectifying circuits that would
allow radios to operate on house current. The dynamic loud-
speaker, essentially the same device found in radios today,
was just coming into use, replacing the gooseneck horn
speakers then common. Lear suggested to the company that
it should build a new kind of radio using the dynamic
speaker. The company followed his suggestion and came out
with the Majestic. Millions were sold, and radio became
common in American homes.

A short time later Lear figured out a way to build radio
coils a fraction of the size they had been before and formed
the Radio Coil and Wire Company to turn them out. As a
by-product, he built a compact, for its day, radio to run on
an automobile battery and installed it in a car. He took the

idea to Paul Galvin, president of a small Chicago firm. After expressing doubt as to whether radios in cars would ever be practical, Galvin decided to manufacture a trial batch of the units. A short time later the company's name was changed to Motorola.

Lear, now known as radio's "boy wonder," quickly tired of the automobile-radio business and sold out his interest in Motorola. "I wanted to be in some business that would justify my flying airplanes," he recalls. "So I moved out to Curtis Reynolds Airport in Chicago and started making aircraft radios. Then, around Christmas 1933, I and my little crew of six or seven people left for New York. On January 1, 1934, we set up business there. And by Friday, April 13, I was busted."

"The most amazing thing about Bill Lear," says one of his old friends, veteran aviation writer Devon Francis, "is that he has absolute confidence that he will succeed in whatever he does. So, when he went broke, he didn't sit around worrying about it. He just decided to get some money. He said to himself, 'What does someone need?' " What he came up with was an idea for building a multiband radio in a simpler way than had been done before. He took the idea to RCA and sold it for $250,000. "It didn't surprise him in the least when RCA bought it," says Francis. "After all, that's what he thought it up for."

Perhaps Lear's biggest triumph was the F-5 autopilot, which he designed and built in 1949 for U.S. jet fighters. Prior to the F-5, autopilots were too big for fighters, although they were widely used in bombers. Fighter pilots, consequently, frequently arrived at the target area exhausted from hours of precision flying and navigating. In addition, many planes and pilots were lost in World War Two when weather closed in and pilots were unable to find their way back home.

Lear's device, hardly bigger than a bread box, not only could fly the plane to its destination, but could lock on to ground signals and land a returning plane in zero-zero weather. For his trouble he got a big government contract to produce the units and also won the 1950 Collier Trophy, an award held in previous years by such aviation greats as Orville Wright, Glenn Curtis and General Hap Arnold.

The FAA, incidentally, has never approved any blind-landing system, including Lear's, for use on U.S. airliners.

Military pilots have been using the Lear blind-landing system for 15 years. In the early 1960s Air France equipped its Caravelles with Lear autopilots and has made more than 1200 hands-off landings in zero-visibility weather with passengers aboard. "The FAA," says Lear with characteristic bluntness, "is a scourge on the progress of aviation."

By the late 1950s Lear, Inc., had grown to one of the major aircraft-electronics manufacturers in the country, and Lear moved to Europe to start production there and drum up business for Lear products. It was there that he first learned of the P-16, a Swiss-designed ground-support jet. Two prototypes had crashed, and the project was abandoned. Lear, however, was convinced that the plane was basically sound and the trouble had been in malfunctioning systems. He hired the same firm of engineers to do the basic aerodynamic work on a business jet and set about developing for this purpose a slight modification of the P-16.

Although Lear was anxious to swing into production, the board of directors of Lear, Inc., was strongly against getting into what aircraft makers call "the tin-bending business." Lear, with the blessing of the board, sold out his 23-percent ownership and charged into the jet business alone. (Lear's stock was bought by the Siegler Company, and the two companies shortly after merged into the Lear-Siegler Corporation, still a giant in the aircraft-electronics business.) He set up a plant in Switzerland but quickly became frustrated by Europe's refusal to move at the Lear pace and by difficulties in getting American-made parts. In early 1963 he packed up the entire plant and shipped it to Wichita. "We didn't know what to take," he says, "so we took everything." With the benefit of the Lear top-speed treatment, the first plane rolled off the assembly line in October.

Generally, aircraft companies handmake the first model of a new plane and don't build the expensive jigs and tooling for mass production until tests have confirmed the adequacy of the design. Lear was so confident that he built the jigs first. Then he launched into production before FAA certification, another risky procedure. Had major changes been necessary, he could have been ruined. But changes weren't necessary, and the gamble paid off. Lear was selling planes several years earlier than would have been possible with conventional construction techniques. "With this approach, you're either very right or very wrong," says Lear. "I was right."

The most serious crisis came in June 1964. An FAA inspector, test-flying the airplane, set the controls improperly and cracked up Lear's first plane on takeoff. The two pilots crawled out safely, but the plane was totally destroyed by fire. "We didn't have another plane instrumented," says Lear, "so we lost valuable time." Had he not already been in production and thus another plane ready to be fitted out with instruments, the delay could have been fatal.

Even with the second plane already built, it was a tight squeeze for a while. Since Lear, despite his reputation in electronics, had never built airplanes before and since the design he had chosen was offbeat, banks refused to lend him money. He poured his entire personal fortune—some $11 million—into the project, borrowed against family trusts and even hocked his personal airplane. Finally he worked out a financing plan to keep operating.

Despite the financial problems, Lear performed the impossible. He stunned his competitors and critics by winning FAA certification an incredible 18 months after he set up shop in Wichita.

Today, with Lear Jet production moderately well in hand, Lear has begun to look around for other things to occupy his time. He decided to build stereo-tape playback units for automobiles and set up a factory in Detroit. "With the Lear Jet coming along OK," he said, "I had to find something to do on the second shift." Mrs. Lear smiled. "The real trouble," she said, "was that he was getting to the point where he had a little spare time."

Whatever the reason, the amazing Lear confidence came into view again when he ordered the plant into production on 100,000 of the new tape units without having received a single order for them. "Tape playback in automobiles is going to be the next big thing," says Lear. "I'm going to be in the position of a man with a boat full of life jackets following a ship he knows is going to sink. He won't have any trouble selling them."

Business, to Lear, is life and breath. He goes at it with great zest. Not fully occupied with his jet, his tape player and his oil wells, he recently bought half interest in New York's fledgling community TV antenna system.

Lear is one of the last of the swashbuckling 100-percent

entrepreneurs, a vanishing breed in today's team-play corporate life. "Lear's a loner," says a friend. "He's a screwball, an inventive genius." He's also, and this is pointed out less often, a happy man. Lear has his life arranged precisely as he wants it. "There's nothing I'd rather be doing than exactly what I'm doing now," he says contentedly. "If someone offered me $160 million for my company—about what it's worth now—with the provision that I would have to retire, I'd spit in his eye. For me the best of life is the exercise of ingenuity—in design, in finance, in flying, in business. And that's what I'm doing."

He's doing it successfully, too. Despite the opinions of the aircraft industry that he was going about it all wrong, the Lear Jet is now clearly the front-runner in the highly competitive executive-jet field.

Paradoxically, though, as the financial and other troubles that once threatened to swamp Lear's young company recede and his operation seems certain to become a gold-plated success, Lear shows the old, familiar signs of restlessness. For him the game is in the playing. When it's won, he's bored.

As soon as his original executive jet was firmly established, Lear decided that it was time to design a new one. Which he did. The new plane, called Model 40, was . . . a real "royal scow" in its executive version, but the plane is also designed for airline use. It will compete with the Douglas DC-9, the Boeing 737 and similar small jets. Lear's new jet is designed to seat 28 in the airline version and sell for $1,500,000 completely equipped, about half the price his competition is charging.

So Lear has a new project, plenty of headaches and no spare time. He's happy again. The money piles up but Lear couldn't be less interested. "Hell," he says, "I can only use one coffin."

● ● ●

Not long after reporter C. P. Gilmore turned in the lively account you've just read, the mercurial and unpredictable Lear was off on a new tack: steam-powered cars.

It seemed to him that steam power, which had once looked highly promising but had lost its place to gasoline in the early 1900s, might help solve the air-pollution problem that arose to plague auto makers in the late 1960s. So he put ten million dollars or so into a new venture named Lear Motors and gave a small group of engineers the assignment of developing a cheap, efficient, powerful, lightweight, pollution-free steam engine for automobiles.

As of this writing they're still at work. They have an old Dodge sedan with a boiler in the trunk, plus a number of other experimental conversions. They're also working on a still newer automobile power system that, in some respects, looks still more promising. This is the so-called vapor-turbine drive, in which a special fluid is heated to produce gas at high pressure and the gas spurts through jet nozzles to spin a turbine wheel. This type of engine, like the steam engine, has the inherent advantage of producing fewer noxious exhaust gases and other emissions than a standard gasoline-powered piston engine.

Today, in his late 60s, Bill Lear shows no more signs of slowing down than he did when reporter Gilmore visited him. He still presses for perfection. He still barks at people who move too slowly for his liking. He still shows the inclination to build a thing today and try it out tomorrow, rather than spending half a year sending blueprints up and down the engineering chain of command.

"I wouldn't be surprised," a Detroit executive remarked not long ago, "if Lear Motors grew up one day to rival General Motors."

12

The Technology Route: The Specialist's Approach

If you had bought the stock of Polaroid Corporation at the right time in the late 1930s and sold it at the right time in the late 1960s, you would have multiplied your money by more than 2000. To put it another way, every $100 you invested would have grown in some 30 years to over $200,000.

That is the kind of company Wall Street's dreams are made on. Speculators continually comb the new-issues market to find a company that will repeat that monumental performance. They hunt eternally for a scruffy little company somewhere out in the boondocks, a company nobody loves today but everybody will love in the 1990s. Some highly knowledgeable hunters who have been engaged in this search over the years say the way to go about it is to look for a man, not a company. Look for a technical innovator, a man with an idea. Then invest in him, no matter how uninviting his company's balance sheet may look at the moment.

The first wave of investors who put their money into Polaroid were doing just that. The infant company had little to offer in the way of immediate cash returns. But it did have Edwin H. Land.

Unlike Bill Lear, Land is a specialist. He has spent his adult life studying light, how it affects materials, how they affect it, how the eye reacts to it, how these effects can be put to use. This has been his absorbing passion ever since he left college. It was so large a passion, in fact, that he left college without graduating. Like Bill Lear (and like many other men in our gallery), he was so impatient to get started that he couldn't bear to spend any more time in formal education. The thought-provoking result is that Edwin Land, acknowledged the world over to be among its most brilliant living scientists,

169

doesn't even have a college diploma.

One of the most comprehensive studies of this brilliant, complex and enormously rich man was written a little more than a decade ago by *Fortune* reporter Francis Bello. Bello's story covers the most interesting parts of Land's life, from Polaroid's infancy in 1937 to its glorious adulthood as one of the hottest growth companies in Wall Street's history. After Bello has finished, we'll briefly update Land's fortunes to the present time.

Edwin Land:
Five Hundred Million Dollars*
by Francis Bello

If a man of the Renaissance were alive today, he might find running an American corporation the most rewarding outlet for his prodigious and manifold talents. In it he could be scientist, artist, inventor, builder and statesman, and through it he might gain the ear of the princes of the state. It would be an exciting company. It might not be the world's largest, for size alone would mean nothing to him. But it would probably be the fastest-growing company that a man still in the prime of life could have created from scratch. (He would, of course, disdain buying up the work of other men.) It would be a company created in a man's image, molded by him in every significant detail, building a product—the embodiment of his genius—that would be unique in all the world. He would gather around him extraordinary associates, selected with meticulous care, who would share his passions and his enthusiasms, who would create and build with him.

Such a man, as it happens, does exist. He is Edwin H. Land; his company is Polaroid Corporation of Cambridge, Massachusetts, which makes the famous 60-second camera.

First, the man: A superbly gifted inventor and scientist, holder of 240 patents (at last count), Land has been Polaroid's president, chairman and research director since he created the company, in 1937. The company was founded on Land's invention of the world's first polarizing sheet material—a type of light filter—soon familiar to almost

*Reprinted from the April 1959 issue of *Fortune* magazine by special permission. Copyright © 1959 by Time Inc.

everyone in the form of sunglasses. On polarizers and their applications, Land has been awarded 96 patents, and in the polarizing business Polaroid still has no substantial competitors. Land's broad scholarship, his iconoclastic and provocative theories of education and his wide-ranging scientific competence have earned him an appointment as institute professor (visiting) at MIT's School for Advanced Study.

The product: Polaroid has built most of its present reputation, and 96.6 percent of its sales, around the 60-second camera that Land invented and announced in 1947. No one has yet devised a competitive instrument or process. Evidently Polaroid's 238 U.S. patents in "one-step" photography—122 of them the work of Land himself—have blanketed not only the process commercialized by Polaroid but all other practical embodiments as well.

The company: From sales of $1,500,000 in 1948, the year Land camera was introduced, Polaroid vaulted to $65 million [in 1958 (and to nearly $400 million in 1968). In 1956] Polaroid stock sold for $12 a share (adjusted for stock distributions). [By 1959 it cost] about $100—or some 50 times 1958 earnings—to buy a piece of the revolution that Polaroid created in photography. [By the end of the 1960s that same stock, adjusting for splits, was worth over $600.]

Polaroid has moved up with amazing speed in the photographic industry. It has overtaken Bell and Howell, which had 1958 sales of $59 million. Eastman Kodak, of course, is in first place, with sales of a little over $800 million (67 percent photographic), and General Aniline and Film (Ansco) is in second place with about $140 million. If General Aniline's nonphotographic sales were to be excluded—and they can only be estimated—Polaroid would almost certainly emerge as second in the industry. [These rankings have undergone several changes since this article was written.]

Land's revolution was at first derided by all the experts, the people who always know why a revolution cannot succeed. These experts included virtually every camera dealer in the country, every "advanced" amateur photographer and nearly everyone on Wall Street. What the experts—and the industry itself—failed to appreciate in 1948 was the fact that photography was far from realizing its full market potential. At that time approximately a third of all American families did not own a camera; many more did not use the one they had. The reason should have been obvious. All other modern technical products—from automobiles to television sets—are essentially self-sufficient once they have been supplied with energy or a signal to run on. And they produce their results immediately. But when people used a camera, they had to wait anywhere from a few hours to a few days to see the results. This was a serious postponement of gratification. As a result, photography was actively pursued by only a few million hobbyists, who very often derived more pleasure from the mechanical elegance of their instruments than from the results they could produce.

The satisfaction of getting results quickly makes Land-camera owners heavy buyers of film. The typical owner of an ordinary camera may buy three or four rolls of film per year. It is not uncommon for owners of the Land camera to buy ten rolls or more. Thus, Polaroid probably sold 15 million to 18 million rolls of film [in 1958], worth $20 million to $25 million to the company. [By the late 1960s Polaroid's film sales were running to more than $200 million a year.]

Land's associates cannot recall his ever having given an order. He guides his company sensitively, thoughtfully—and with immense and obvious enjoyment of what he is doing. He manages by persuasion and delegation, believing that men perform best the jobs they create for themselves. His deepest concern is that all Polaroid employees do not yet have such jobs, and he has promised them that this will be changed as swiftly as possible.

While Land has a pervasive knowledge of every aspect of Polaroid's business, from research and production through marketing and finance, he has no hesitation in seeking counsel wherever he can find it. He counts as friends and advisors some of the country's leading academic scientists and some of the most perspicacious minds on Wall Street (several are on Polaroid's board). It is characteristic of him that when he began working on one-step photography, he turned to Ansel Adams, both a great photographer and a great technician, for help in selecting the qualities that would make Polaroid film outstanding.

Land works in a cheerful book-lined room on the ground floor of a drab three-story building—one of nine scattered around Cambridge that Polaroid occupies in whole or part. (It owns only one of them, plus three new manufacturing buildings in Waltham.) One door of Land's office leads to a room containing rows of tables piled with neat stacks of current periodicals, business records and correspondence; on the walls are charts showing Polaroid's production, sales and profit figures. Another door leads directly to Land's own laboratory.

Throughout the day Land's research associates stream in and out to bring him results of experiments, to discuss a problem or to delight him with the report of an unexpected finding. Frequently Land slips back to a large projection room behind the laboratory, where he is carrying on experiments designed to show how the eye sees color. (This work has thrown astonishing new light on color vision, which seems to overturn many of the fundamental concepts dating back to Newton.)

Land is acutely aware that his role as Polaroid's creator, head and research director is a difficult one—and it would be easy for his brilliance to dazzle, outshine and discourage his associates. Instead, he has a rare gift for inspiring them to high achievements of their own. He is careful, moreover, not to spoil anyone else's joy in creating. "Any intelligent man," says Land, "can finish another man's sentence. We are all careful never to do that." He is convinced that the ability to create and invent is not rare; in his opinion it is common but generally uncultivated.

When Polaroid was founded in 1937, it was one of the most exciting little venture-capital companies of its day, but it contained no hint of a camera. Polaroid's original product was a transparent plastic sheet capable of polarizing light, that is, of blocking all light waves except those vibrating in a single plane. When two polarizing filters are placed against each other and rotated, they act as a light "valve," controlling the amount of light passing through, from almost full transmission to virtual extinction.

Land's interest in polarization began one night, he recalls, when he was walking along Broadway in New York City. The year was 1926; Land was 17 and a freshman at Harvard. It suddenly struck him that polarizing filters could eliminate headlight glare and thus decrease the hazard of night driving. Taking a leave of absence from college, he began spending eight to ten hours a day in the New York Public Library reading everything that seemed pertinent to his new interest. At night he carried out experiments in a small laboratory he had set up in a rented room on 55th Street off Broadway. To further his work, he gained secret access—also at night, via a corridor and an unlocked window on the ninth floor—to a physics laboratory at Columbia University.

By 1928 Land had perfected his first polarizing sheets and sought advice on patents from a young attorney friend named Julius Silver. Silver referred Land to Donald Brown, then in a New York patent firm and now vice-president and patent counsel of Polaroid. Land had no difficulty obtaining a basic patent on his sheet polarizers (which was issued in 1934), but his idea of preventing headlight glare had been anticipated by at least four other inventors whose applications dated back as far as 1920. In 1928 the Patent Office still hadn't decided which of the various applications to honor, and Land's claim was added to the four others, pending final adjudication.

While natural crystals capable of polarizing light had been known since the early 1800s, the first practical polarizing materials, in sheet form, were announced by Land at a special Harvard physics colloquium in 1932.

Land's relationship with Harvard has been unusual as well as fruitful. When the inspiration to work on polarizers came to him in 1926, he left college for three years. When he returned in 1929, he brought with him his rudimentary polarizer (patent pending) and also a wife, Terre. Harvard welcomed him by providing a large laboratory where he and Terre worked for about three years. (Mrs. Land subsequently gave up research, devoting herself to raising their two daughters.) At the end of the three years it seemed to Land so urgent to start making his new and much-improved polarizers that after giving the colloquium on his invention, he applied for another leave from Harvard, even though only a few courses stood between him and his B.A. He never did take his bachelor's degree. In 1957, however, Harvard awarded him an honorary Sc.D.

In 1932 Land and a young Harvard physics instructor, George W. Wheelwright III, formed Land-Wheelwright Laboratories to make polarizers and to carry on research. In 1937 Land organized the present Polaroid Corporation. The financial arrangement he negotiated could be the envy of any young inventor—or old inventor, for that matter. Land was introduced to a number of influential Wall Streeters, including James P. Warburg, W. Averill Harriman, Lewis Strauss and his partners in Kuhn, Loeb, and members of Schroder Rockefeller. The 28-year-old Land made such an impression on this group that they provided an initial $375,000 in capital, left Land with a majority of the voting stock and placed him in complete control of the company for ten years.

Polaroid's original board of directors included, among others, Harriman, Strauss, Warburg and Silver. . . . Another of Polaroid's original backers and board members, Carlton Fuller, took a leave of absence from his job as president of Schroder Rockefeller in 1941 to help out as financial officer. He never went back to banking. Investment analysts who have been busily "discovering" Polaroid in the last couple of years are often surprised to find such seasoned hands as Fuller and Silver in key positions.

In the prewar period 1937–41, Polaroid sales climbed from $142,000 to one million dollars. Polaroid sunglasses became increasingly popular at $1.95 a pair; Polaroid filters enjoyed a steady sale to scientific laboratories and photographers; a glare-free Polaroid study lamp was marketed and sold well. In 1939, at the New York World's Fair, Polaroid demonstrated full-color three-dimensional movies—viewed through Polaroid glasses.

Meanwhile, in the laboratory, Land and his associates had developed a new and ingenious 3-D system—called Vectography—in which the two images of a stereo picture are printed in perfect register one on top of the other on a single frame. As in the conventional 3-D system, Polaroid glasses [were] needed to see the two images properly.

When Hollywood desperately jumped into 3-D movies in 1953, it adopted the old stereo system requiring two projectors, which were almost impossible to keep in register. As a result, customers usually saw a wretched picture, and the 3-D boom collapsed in little more than a year. In that brief period, however, Polaroid sold almost 100 million viewing glasses for some six million dollars.

What originally enticed the New York bankers into financing Polaroid, and the company's primary goal from 1937 to 1947, was the dream of putting its polarizing filters on every automobile headlight and every windshield in America.

When two cars suitably equipped approached each other at night, neither driver would be blinded by the other's headlights; yet for each the road ahead would be clearly illuminated by his own lights. Obviously, this would greatly reduce the hazard of night driving. While Land had failed to win a patent on this concept, Polaroid bought up the patent rights in 1938 from the man who had been adjudged the inventor but who had no practical polarizing filter to do the job.

There had not been enough time before World War Two for Polaroid to persuade Detroit to put Polaroid filters on all its new cars. Then, during the war, the idea had to be dropped while Polaroid turned out military optics. In 1945 Polaroid's sales reached nearly $17 million. A year later they had toppled below five million, and Polaroid was counting heavily on Detroit's adoption of headlight and windshield polarizers. Finally, in 1947, extensive tests of the Polaroid system were conducted at the General Motors proving ground. The system passed all the engineering requirements.

Nevertheless, Detroit turned Polaroid down. Chief reason: The industry said it saw no practical way to provide the new system for 33 million motor vehicles then on the highways, and it believed that drivers of these vehicles would be handicapped by the somewhat brighter headlights that would have to be used on filter-equipped cars.

This was a serious blow to Land, especially since General Electric had shown that the added brightness did not increase the already existing hazard. It should have been obvious in any case that very few of the 33 million vehicles on the road in 1947 (most of them built before the war) would be in use for very long.

Detroit has been content to let the matter drop—but not Land. He has continued research on the project, and there is no doubt that he will seek another hearing in Detroit when he feels he is ready to beat down all possible opposition.

During 1947 Polaroid's sales were $1,500,000, its operating loss two million dollars. Fortunately, a tax credit, based on the loss-carryback provision, cut the net loss to just under a million dollars.

Nineteen forty-seven would have been dismal indeed except that in February Land had disclosed his 60-second photographic process. Land could thank his daughter for the inspiration to invent the process. One day during World War

Two, when he was taking pictures of her, she asked impatiently how soon she could see them. As Land explained that it took time to get them developed, he suddenly realized that there was something basically wrong with photography. Why should anyone have to wait hours, or even days, to see a picture?

During 1944, when he could steal time from a crowded schedule, Land began experimenting with ways to get a finished picture directly out of the camera that took it. If he had troubled to ask experts what they thought of his objective, they would have been happy to tell him to stop wasting his time.

What, exactly, was the problem that Land faced? It would have been a neat trick just to develop an exposed negative inside a camera, within a minute or two, when the temperature might range from freezing to 110 degrees, with a reagent that could be incorporated in the roll of film and could be handled cleanly as an essentially dry material. But this would have had scant commercial value. Land had to find a way to do all this and simultaneously to provide chemicals that would pick out the unexposed silver grains in the negative, transport them through the active reagent and deposit them unscathed on a facing sheet of paper. On reaching this paper, the inert and invisible silver had to be released from chemical bondage and converted into metallic silver, thereby producing an exact positive counterpart of the negative image. Finally, when lifted out of the camera, the positive print had to be essentially dry and long-lasting—and it had to compete in quality with conventional photographs on which scientists the world over had spent more than 100 years of research.

In view of all this, the statement made by one of Land's close associates does not seem farfetched. "I would be willing to bet," he says, "that a hundred Ph.D.'s would not have been able to duplicate Land's feat in ten years of uninterrupted work."

Land moved ahead with unbelievable speed. Within six months he had essentially worked out all the basic physical elements of the commercial process.

Land himself can provide no explanation for the inventive process as he has experienced it. He believes that the ability to create may be the fundamental distinction between the human animal and all others. "Can you imagine," he asks, "an ape inventing an arrowhead?" He is impatient with the widespread notion that modern man has found, in science, some brand-new tool that "makes" discoveries and inventions. Instead, he believes the ability to discover and invent is something extremely ancient in man and something we know nothing about.

"I find it very important," says Land, "to work intensively for long hours when I am beginning to see solutions to a problem. At such times atavistic competences seem to come welling up. You are handling so many variables at a barely conscious level that you can't afford to be interrupted. If you are, it may take a year to cover the same ground you could cover otherwise in sixty hours."

Up until 1946—after years of part-time work on the camera and film—Land had never had more than a handful of assistants. Because of the war, these were young girls, bright, untrained in science and almost all of them, as it happened, graduates of Smith. Since 1948 his closest associate in developing and improving the 60-second process has been a Smith arts major named Meroë Morse. A daughter of Marston Morse, professor of mathematics at the Institute for Advanced Study in Princeton, Miss Morse [later became] head of black-and-white film research at Polaroid. Land credits her with many important contributions, especially those leading to Polaroid's present impressive line of films.

The chemistry and technology of preparing the positive sheet, which yields the finished Polaroid picture, is a tightly held commercial secret. In the well-guarded building where the positive sheet is coated and where the film developer is mixed, all drums and bottles of chemicals carry only coded labels. (The negative material, which differs from conventional negative chiefly in having a paper base, is made for Polaroid by Kodak and du Pont.)

With the 60-second camera and its original sepia film substantially worked out in 1947, Land moved to get them to the market as quickly as possible. The job of designing the camera and the special machinery needed to make the camera's film was directed by William J. McCune, now vice-president for engineering. McCune and a few indefatigable associates—including a gifted mechanical engineer, Otto Wolff—contributed a whole new series of inventions to support Land's fundamental work. One example: A study of shutters revealed that the timing of even the best on the market was accurate only to ± 25 percent; McCune's group invented a new shutter that is accurate to ± 10 percent.

Since Polaroid, back in 1947, did not have $350,000 to spend on tools for the camera, it searched for a subcontractor who would bear the cost in return for a contract to build the camera. A small Rochester firm, now defunct, needed work desperately enough to take the gamble, in return for an order of 10,000 cameras. This was the beginning of Polaroid's policy of not making anything it can buy outside at an acceptable price. . . .

While confident of ultimate success, Polaroid was coldly objective about the problem of introducing a wholly new and untried camera costing $80 to $90. Land and his associates held long sessions with marketing experts at Harvard Business School and elsewhere and at one point gave serious thought to developing a nationwide door-to-door sales organization.

Ultimately it was clear that the normal retail outlets would have to be used. So as to make the best possible impression on photographic dealers, Polaroid set out to hire someone who had an outstanding reputation in the industry. The man Polaroid found was J. Harold Booth, a vice-president of Bell and Howell who had had 20 years of broad experience in engineering, manufacturing and sales.

Booth was enthusiastic about the Land camera from the moment he saw it. When he joined Polaroid in 1948 as executive vice-president and general manager, he brought to the firm not only his reputation but a great gift for promotion. His job was to sell the camera without any sales organization whatever and with an advertising budget so small that it seemed scarcely adequate to launch the camera in the Boston area alone.

Booth and his sales manager, Robert C. Casselman, conceived the plan of offering one department store in each major city an exclusive on the new camera for 30 days, provided the store would advertise prominently in newspapers—with only modest help from Polaroid—and would give the camera an intense promotional play throughout the store.

The Land camera went on sale for the first time on November 26, 1948, at Jordan Marsh, the big Boston department store. Demand was so great that frantic salesmen inadvertently sold display models from which parts were missing.

Polaroid paused to build up its depleted inventory. Then, in January 1949, Booth opened a dazzling promotion in Miami. He figured that cameras sold to well-heeled Miami vacationers would soon be scattered all over America, with every owner a Polaroid salesman. As part of his promotion, Booth supplied a squad of pretty girls and a batch of life-guards with Land cameras to snap pictures at pools and beaches and give them away to gape-mouthed tourists. Within a few weeks most Miami stores had sold out their stock of Land cameras.

So the promotion moved from city to city. And while the great majority of dealers received the camera coldly, Polaroid's 1949 sales soared to $6,680,000, of which over five million came from the new camera and film.

The first and only real crisis in 60-second photography arose in 1950, when Polaroid shifted from its original sepia picture to one that was black and white. In laboratory tests the new pictures seemed at least as lasting as the sepia, but six months after the new film reached dealers it was obvious that serious color fading took place under certain conditions.

Land concluded that the silver image was being attacked from both top and bottom by humidity and atmospheric contaminants. He set up two teams to tackle the problem. He and Meroë Morse headed one team to rebuild the positive sheet from the base up. A second team, headed by Elkan R. Blout, general manager of research . . . began looking for a plastic—to be used as a print coating—that would be practically odorless, would dry quickly into an insoluble, flexible, transparent coating and would not yellow with age. More than 200 new polymers were synthesized before the requirements were met. The plastic and new film were merged, and today Polaroid asserts that its prints will last fully as well as conventional prints. (Such teamwork between what Land calls the "photographic scientists" and the "chemical scientists" is an old story at Polaroid. In the current color-film program the chemists are dreaming up and synthesizing scores of new molecules, which the photographic team under Howard Rogers incorporates in experimental color film.)

Many dealers who had predicted a short commercial life

for the Land camera thought their judgment confirmed during the print-fading period. And, indeed, in 1954 and 1955 there was a definite decline in Polaroid's growth rate. But [after] 1955 Polaroid . . . had three booming years with sales growth of 31, 41 and 36 percent. Much of the credit for this upturn must go to Robert Casselman, promoted to sales vice-president in 1956.

Polaroid's meteoric growth since 1955 can also be credited, in part, to new films whose speed (equivalent to ASA 200 and 400) compared favorably with the fastest conventional films then on the market. This year, or early next, Polaroid expects to introduce films roughly ten times faster (ASA 3000). Simultaneously it will offer a new "electric eye" shutter that can be clamped on the front of its present cameras and will automatically provide correct exposures for all outdoor lighting conditions. . . .

Land keeps challenging his design staff to come up with a camera so light and compact that no one will want to be without one. He foresees the day when 100 million Americans will carry Land cameras as regularly as they now carry wallets and wristwatches. He believes that when 60-second cameras are this handy, every owner will snap the shutter at least once a day—in his business, on trips or at home. This exuberant vision implies film sales 200 times Polaroid's present rate.

The vest-pocket Land camera is not yet in sight, but Polaroid is working on new models that will take pictures comparable in size to those made by its present large cameras but will be significantly smaller and more convenient to use. The present large models weigh about four and a half pounds and are relatively bulky. [Models weighing less than a pound were introduced in the 1960s, but there is still no pocket Polaroid.]

Land has no doubt that Polaroid is going to get at least five or ten times as big as it is today. But what he passionately wants is for Polaroid to be known as the first manufacturer in the world that recognized the human dignity of every employee all day long. . . . [One day in 1958] Land called his top associates and supervisors together. He said, "I think we are going to be magnificently successful and in a very short time . . . [but] if after we succeed in *just* doing that, we are just another large company, we will have contributed further to the hazard of the degradation of American culture. . . .

"A country without a mission cannot survive as a country. There may be many ways of creating that mission, and many groups will play their role, but I want to talk about the proper role of industry. Its proper role, I believe, is to make a new kind of product—something people have not thought of as a product at all. When you've reached a standard of living high enough for most people, where do you turn next? It seems to me there is only one place to turn. Industry should address itself now to the production of a worthwhile, highly rewarding, highly creative, inspiring daily job for every one of a hundred million Americans."

So that management would know it had a promise to keep, Land also outlined his aspirations at a company Christmas party.

"We are going to make our new factories," he promised, "the first factories in the world that are designed so that machines work for people instead of people for machines. What we are after in America is an industrial society where a person maintains at work the full dignity that he has at home. Now, I don't mean anything silly—I don't mean you're all going to be happy. You'll be unhappy—but in new, exciting and important ways. You'll fix that by doing something worthwhile, and then you'll be happy for a few hours. Alternately happy and unhappy, you will build something new, just as you do at home in the family.

"You are often unhappy about your children. But you are proud of them. You wouldn't give up the splendid years of misery involved in raising a child. Well, building a job should be like raising a child."

* * *

Edwin Land was dreaming a number of dreams when reporter Bello talked to him in 1959. Most of the dreams have since come true.

The most important dream was that of developing a cheap, simple, workable system for instant color photography. Polaroid did that in the early 1960s. By backing up the invention with an aggressive marketing program, the company moved up to run neck and neck with its giant rival, Kodak, in yearly sales.

Kodak is no longer the undisputed leader in the industry. As this book goes to press, both companies' sales and earnings are suffering from recession ailments, and both their stocks are trading on the Big Board at prices well below their highs in the bull markets of the late 1960s. Nobody on Wall Street cares to predict which company will forge ahead faster when the next bull market moves in. As one broker says, "They're both number one."

At the height of the bull market in 1968 and 1969, Land's and his family's holdings of Polaroid stock were worth over half a billion dollars. The stock's price dropped sharply from its peak, but not nearly so sharply as the prices of some other glamour stocks such as Ling-Temco-Vought (chapter 15). At the lowest ebb of the 1970 bear market Polaroid was down from the neighborhood of $140 per share to the neighborhood of $80. Considering that many glamour stocks were smashed down to a quarter or even a tenth of their bull highs, Polaroid's performance wasn't bad at all.

Edwin Land, today in his early 60s, is still fantastically rich. His amazing company is still growing. It is entirely conceivable that by the time Land elects to retire, his fortune will have risen to more than a billion dollars.

13

Who Says It Can't Be Done?

There is a recurrent theme in the lives of the very, very rich. You must have noticed it, and will go on noticing it, on our tour through the gallery. Almost every one of these immoderately wealthy men began his career against a background of loud jeers. Whatever he was trying to do, said all the experts with great confidence, couldn't be done.

Edwin Land was assured that it was perfectly ridiculous to think of making a camera that would develop its own pictures. James Ling's nutty idea that he could sell his little contracting company's stock to the public gave rise to guffaws all over Texas. Hollywood laughed uproariously at Howard Hughes's foolish investments in movies. And on and on it goes.

Evidently it takes a peculiarly stubborn kind of mind to become one of the great rich. You not only need to have an idea; you also need to have supreme faith in that idea. The faith must be strong enough to stand up for years against jeers, guffaws and pessimistic head shakings.

It is almost a certainty that there are unknown men walking the streets today who, but for a lack of that stubborn faith, might have become hundred-millionaires. Such a man might have had a grand fortune-building idea last year or last decade. He allowed experts and nonexperts to talk or laugh him out of it, and now nobody knows his name. A day will probably come when some other man will be clobbered by that same idea, will maintain his faith in it and will rise to earn a place in some future list of the very, very rich.

This will be an interesting point for you to ponder if you ever conceive a fortune-building idea. The point is made neatly and concisely by writer-philosopher John L. Kent in the following article from *Success Unlimited* magazine. This magazine, you may recall, is published by that grand old success teacher, Clement Stone.

They Wish They'd Never Said It*
by John L. Kent

If you've sometimes made a hasty judgment or expressed an opinion that later turned out wrong, and if you've wished you never said it, don't feel bad. The world's biggest thinkers, scientists and industrialists have similarly said things for publication they later wished they could erase from the printed page. The comments were usually pessimistic.

Of course, there is a logical explanation. Psychologists and other social scientists say that anything new upsets our routine thinking. So we unconsciously reject new ideas and new devices.

There is no doubt that the caveman who first invented the wheel was met with a derisive "It won't work!" from his fellow cavemen.

Most inventors and other creative people expect some negative reaction. But they are always shocked to meet opposition from experts.

When the invention works successfully or the discovery is proved out in practical application, these experts—often respected scientists and important businessmen—wish they had never said anything. But it is too late. Because of their position and prestige, their words had been recorded. In the black print of newspapers and science journals, their statements are available for all to see forever in the future.

For example, Dr. Vannevar Bush, a leading American engineer-scientist, testified before a congressional committee in 1945 that the proposed 3000-mile, high-angle rocket equipped with a nuclear warhead should be "left out of our thinking." Ten years later the intercontinental ballistics missile made its appearance. It has a nuclear warhead.

Possibly the greatest number of wrong statements were made by important people about the airplane. Some said it

*Reprinted with permission from the September 1970 issue of *Success Unlimited*, America's Leading Success Magazine, 6355 Broadway, Chicago, Illinois 60660. Copyright © 1970. Further reprint rights reserved.

would never fly. Others, who later conceded that it could fly, still thought it would be of little use. For example:

In 1870 Bishop Milton Wright declared that "flight is reserved for angels. To think anything else is blasphemy." If that name rings a bell, it should. Bishop Wright was the father of Orville and Wilbur.

At about the time the Wright brothers were experimenting with their primitive airplane, a noted American astronomer-mathematician, Professor Simon Newcomb, expounded on the impossibility of flight. In a major technical essay he wrote, "The demonstration that no possible combination of known substances, known forms of machinery and known forms of force can be united in a practical machine by which man shall fly long distances through the air seems to the writer as complete as it is possible for the demonstration of any physical fact to be."

In 1910, after watching an air show, Marshal Ferdinand Foch, the French military leader, said, "All very fine for sport, you know. But the airplane is of no use to the army."

In 1922 Assistant Secretary of the Navy Franklin D. Roosevelt said that "it is highly unlikely that an airplane, or even a fleet of them, could ever successfully sink a fleet of navy vessels under battle conditions."

As late as 1939 Rear Admiral Clark Woodward said that "as for sinking a ship with a bomb, you just can't do it." Two years later: Pearl Harbor. . . .

The long road traveled by Thomas Edison in perfecting and making practical electric light was strewn with often caustic comments by the experts who saw only failure. One editor of a large metropolitan paper, upon learning that his paper had published an optimistic article on Edison's experiments, reprimanded the feature writer with "Don't you know it has been absolutely demonstrated that that kind of light is against the laws of nature?"

Perhaps the editor had little faith in the future, but one would think that a fellow scientist would be more optimistic. But such, alas, was not the case with Professor Henry Morton, president of the prestigious Stevens Institute of Technology. In 1897 he protested against the enthusiasm shown by other scientists in Edison's efforts, saying, "everyone acquainted with the subject will recognize it as a conspicuous failure."

The development that has done most to change our way of living—the automobile—has been ridiculed as much as the airplane, which was being developed at about the same time. The mere idea of a self-powered vehicle was laughed at—even by presumably knowledgeable people:

Alexander Dow, president of the Detroit Edison Company, for whom Henry Ford was chief engineer at the time he started his experiments with the auto, offered Ford a promotion to plant superintendent if he would cease tinkering with the automobile. Said he, "I don't object to experiments with electricity; electricity is the coming thing. But gasoline—no!"

Chauncey Depew, a leading railroad executive and head of the New York Central System from 1899 to 1928, warned a relative not to invest $5000 in Ford stock because "nothing has come along to beat the horse."

The experts who doubted the auto and the airplane have their counterparts in more recent experts who doubted that space travel would be possible. Consider, for example:

A top English astronomer (who shall remain nameless, as he is still with us) predicted in the summer of 1956 that man may never get into space and that "space travel is utter bilge." Soviet Russia rocketed *Sputnik One* into the sky a year later.

Just as the Soviets were getting *Sputnik One* ready for its daily 15 orbits around the earth, a top executive of one of the largest aeronautical firms in the United States (who shall also remain nameless, as he is still living) predicted that manned space flight would not be achieved before the year 1990. Five years later John Glenn orbited the earth in a spacecraft made by—you guessed it, the executive's own firm!

So if there are times when you could have . . . [bitten] your tongue over a few badly chosen words, you may take solace in the fact that others in high places have made similar mistakes. What you will never know, however, is how many opportunities you missed because you reacted in such a manner. Reflect on this and you'll no doubt think back to times when "you wish you'd never said it!"

14

The Magic of "OPM": 1. The Borrowing Route

You hear the same conversation over and over again in bars clear around the world. Somebody tells an anecdote about a rich man in whose wake he has been tossed, or the TV set in the corner reveals some trivial intelligence about a tycoon and his yacht and his expensive lady friends. The men hunched over their drinks begin to speculate about how it would feel to be rich. Then they laugh at each other for entertaining such grandiose and fantastic thoughts. Finally they sink softly into comforting platitudes. They assure each other that it would be foolish for *them* to strive or hope for wealth.

"You gotta have money to make money," says the guy at the end of the bar.

"Yep," says somebody else glumly, "them as has gets."

Everybody else murmurs and nods. It is agreed unanimously that sage words have been spoken.

The fact is, of course, that these comfortable old bits of folk wisdom are sheer nonsense. They are mainly an excuse for not trying. With few exceptions, the immoderately rich men we're visiting in this book started with nothing or next to nothing—started in conditions of poverty in some cases. Their lives amply disprove the ancient wisdoms. The truth is that monumental piles of money can be made by any man, whether he has money to start with or not.

It is undeniably true that money begets money—or can be made to beget it, given sound management and a pinch of luck. But it need not be one's own money. If you have but a little of your own, you can use other people's.

The technique of using other people's money is so common and so well thought of among the very rich that it has been

dignified with capital initials: Other People's Money—OPM
for short. Most of the men you're meeting in this golden gallery have used OPM at one time or another in their lives.
Many of them used it in the very beginning to lift themselves
out of poverty or lowly employee status, to launch themselves
on the first mile of the long, hard climb. You'll find OPM
cropping up again and again, in various forms and with
various applications, as we saunter about the gallery. But
the man who best illustrates the technique is the man we're
now about to meet, one of the very, very richest of the rich,
Daniel Keith Ludwig.

Ludwig began as an ordinary paycheck earner like you
and me. He ended with a fortune that has been estimated
as high as three billion dollars. My own calculations put him
in the neighborhood of one billion dollars. (Somehow there
doesn't seem to be much difference between the two figures.
Both make the mind reel.) He did it mainly by using OPM.

We can illustrate the value of OPM with a simple and familiar example. Let's say you have $10,000 to invest in real
estate. You find a spot somewhere on the edge of an expanding town, an area where real-estate values are rising by,
let's say, 25 percent every couple of years.

All right, how do you put your money to work? You can
take the cash route: You find a plot of land that is on the
market for $10,000, and you plunk your money into it. Two
years later you sell out for $12,500. You've made 25 percent
on your money.

That's pretty good, but it could be a lot better. Instead of
taking the cash route, you use OPM. Instead of a $10,000
plot of land, you find a $40,000 house. You put your ten
grand in as a down payment on the house and borrow
the remaining 30 grand from a bank under a standard mortgage arrangement.

Now let's see where you end. After two years the house
has appreciated in value by 25 percent, just as the plot of land
did. The house is now worth $50,000. You sell out, pay off
the bank and walk away with $20,000. Instead of making a
mere 25 percent, you've doubled your money by using OPM.

The illustration is oversimplified, of course. It omits con-
siderations such as interest, taxes and brokerage fees. But no
matter how you cut it, the OPM route clearly carries you
farther than the cash route.

The disadvantage of the OPM route, of course, is that it involves a greater degree of risk. If the bottom drops out of the local real-estate market while you're in the midst of your gambit, the OPM route leaves you saddled with a burden of debt. Either you carry this debt until the market improves or you sell out at a loss. With the cash route you escape this kind of problem. But, as we've already noted and will note many more times in this book, it is virtually impossible to grow rich without taking risks.

The stock market's so-called margin system is another familiar illustration of the use of OPM. Under certain conditions, in buying listed stocks, you're allowed to borrow part of the purchase price from your broker. The stock market's margin rules are strict, and not for decades has it been legal to borrow as big a percentage of a stock's price as you can borrow to buy real estate. Still millions of investors habitually buy on margin. They obviously believe even a little OPM is better than none.

Daniel Ludwig is a man who would agree with their philosophy. Let's look at his remarkable career.

Daniel Ludwig: One Billion Dollars

He is a highly secretive man, this Daniel Ludwig. He lives quietly in a Manhattan penthouse, from which he generally walks to his office a few blocks away. He is in his middle 70s, somewhat crippled by an old back injury, and as he makes his slow and painful way along the sidewalk, all alone, he might be taken for an elderly pensioner out for a breath of air. He seldom talks to anybody on his daily jaunt and is particularly curt with reporters who occasionally try to accost him along his route. He hasn't talked to reporters for years.

Even when he does talk to them, his habitual secrecy keeps him from revealing everything. He fails to mention, or perhaps deliberately hides, all kinds of information, from the important to the relatively trivial. Back in 1957 he granted to *Fortune* reporter Dero Saunders what the magazine said was the first press interview in Ludwig's whole career—and even then he seems not to have abandoned his lifelong reticence. Saunders reported, for example, that the twice-married Ludwig had no children of his own. In fact, he had a daughter by his first marriage. Important? Hardly. Yet the peculiar little inaccuracy illustrates Ludwig's temperament. As Dero Saunders himself wrote somewhat wryly in the 1957 report, "Ludwig's most notable characteristic . . . is a life-long penchant for keeping his mouth shut."

He still keeps it shut today, and so do his aides. A reporter phoning Ludwig's New York headquarters will be airily told by the operator that there is no Daniel Ludwig in the company—at least not on her list of telephone extensions. Further inquiry will reveal that a shadowy figure answering to that name does occasionally drop in, but nobody admits to knowing exactly who he is, what he does or how he can be reached.

Yet Dan Ludwig patently does exist. His footprints can be found all over the world.

He owns what is probably the world's biggest private shipping fleet—bigger than those of either Stavros Niarchos or Aristotle Onassis. The fabulous Greek shipping tycoons make considerably more splash than Ludwig and are far more colorful, but in sheer fortune building Ludwig towers high above them. His fleet approximates five million deadweight tons and includes the five or six biggest oil tankers ever built.

Ludwig also owns outright, or is the major shareholder in, a string of savings-and-loan companies; a large collection of hotels, office buildings and other real-estate ventures in the U.S. and overseas; coal and iron and other natural-resource developments from Australia to Mexico; petroleum and petro-chemical refineries in Florida and Panama.

He has amassed this huge collection of businesses in an atmosphere of eerie silence. For many years he and his second wife lived in an unostentatious house in the commuter town of Darien, Connecticut. "We almost never saw them," says a neighbor. "They never came to cocktail parties around town or anything like that. Nobody knew exactly who they were. I always thought he was some kind of bank executive—you know, a salary guy, maybe forty grand, nobody very important."

Ludwig in his prime was a tall, lean, ruggedly handsome man. He was born in June 1897 in South Haven, Michigan, a small lakeside community. His father was a real-estate broker and speculator, comfortably successful but not rich.

Young Daniel was fascinated by boats and ships. At the age of nine he found a sunken 26-foot diesel boat that had been abandoned as not worth the salvage costs. He bought it from the owner for $25, which he amassed by working and by borrowing from his father. He raised the boat and spent an entire winter repairing it. The following summer he earned some $50 by chartering the boat. This was his first experience in the shipping business, and he enjoyed every minute of it— particularly the knowledge that he had come out with a profit.

His father and mother separated when he was in his early teens, and he went with his father to Port Arthur, Texas, a shipping town in which the father had found some real-estate opportunities. Still intrigued by ships, young Dan dropped out of high school to go to work on the waterfront. He drifted around for a few years, ending at a marine-engine plant from which he was sent out to help install ship engines in various ports around the country. He liked the work, discovered he was good at it and began moonlighting, installing and repairing engines on his own. At the age of 19 he had more private contracts than he could handle; so he quit his job. It was the last job he would ever have.

Over the next 20 years there were many months when he wished he did have a job. Unlike some of the other men we'll meet in this gilded gallery, Dan Ludwig did not enjoy high success at an early age. He bounced from one waterborne venture to another, buying and repairing and selling and chartering ships, and sometimes he made money and sometimes he lost. He seldom had much cash to spare, was almost always in debt and on several occasions teetered on the edge of bankruptcy. His problems were aggravated when, at the age of 29, he was injured by a gasoline explosion in the cargo hold of an aging tanker. "The reason he was down in the hold," says a former executive of one of Ludwig's companies, "is that two crewmen had been overcome by fumes and Dan went down to haul them out. For the rest of his life after that explosion he was tormented by pain in his back. But if you asked him how he got hurt, he'd just say, 'Oh, I was in an accident.' A lot of people assumed it was an automobile crash. That was the kind of guy Dan always was—never said much about himself."

It was in the mid-1930s, when the late-blooming Ludwig was nearing the age of 40, that he finally began building the foundation of his present monumental fortune. That was when he discovered OPM.

He had borrowed money often before, of course, starting with his first ship-salvage venture at age nine. "But," says a Chase Manhattan Bank officer, "it hadn't been what you could call creative borrowing. He hadn't learned how to use other people's money as a lever to increase his own economic horsepower."

Ludwig arrived at his success formula in two main steps. The first step came when he wanted to borrow some money to buy an old general-cargo ship and convert it into an oil tanker. (Oil transport paid more than dry cargo.) He went to various banks in New York. They looked at his frayed shirt collar and asked what he proposed to put up as collateral. He had to admit he owned but little in the way of worldly goods. He did have one elderly tanker afloat, however—the one in which his back had been hurt—and it occurred to him that he might be able to make a deal involving this ship.

"He came to this bank," says the Chase man, "and told us he had his tanker chartered out to some oil company. The monthly charter fees he received were just about equal to the monthly payments he'd have to make on the loan he wanted. So he proposed to assign the charter to the bank. The bank would then collect the charter fees directly from the oil company, and that money would go toward paying off Ludwig's loan."

To many bankers it seemed like a crazy setup. Yet it was in reality as safe for the bank as almost any small-business loan. Ludwig alone might not have been a four-A credit risk, but the oil company's credit was good. The bank could assume that, barring unforeseen economic catastrophes, the oil company would faithfully keep up its charter payments on the tanker. Even if Ludwig's new ship-converting venture sank, as had some of his others, the bank would still keep getting its money as long as the old tanker and the oil company stayed afloat. In effect, Ludwig was boosting his own feeble credit rating by using the oil company's.

The bank made the loan on that basis. Ludwig bought the old general-cargo ship he wanted, converted her to an oil tanker, chartered her out, used her to get another loan on the same basis and converted still another dry-cargo ship to oil.

This went on for a few years. As each loan was paid off, Ludwig came out with free and clear title to a ship. The charter fees for that ship stopped flowing to a bank and began flowing into his pocket. His cash position, his credit rating and his shirt collars improved rapidly.

And now he was struck by a still more intriguing idea. If he could borrow money on an existing ship, why couldn't he also borrow on a ship not yet built?

This was his second giant step in learning the uses of OPM.

Ludwig's new proposition went something like this: He would design a tanker or some other ship for a specialized purpose. Before the keel was even laid, he would find a customer to charter her when she was completed. Waving the charter contract, he would walk into a bank and ask for a loan with which to build the ship. The loan was to be of the deferred-payment variety, under which the bank expected little or none of its money back until the ship was actually afloat. Once she was afloat, the charter fees would be assigned to the bank, and the loan would be paid off as before. Eventually, when the entire years-long transaction was completed, Ludwig would sail away as owner of a ship in which he had invested barely a dime of his own money.

Once again the proposition startled the banks. But once again it made sense when examined closely. Ludwig's own credit rating was now quite acceptable—and, as before, he was backed up by the credit of his charter customers. "A loan arrangement of this kind," says the Chase officer, "is what we call 'two-name paper'—meaning, in effect, that payment is guaranteed by two different companies or men who are more or less independent of each other economically. That is, if one gets into trouble and defaults, the other won't necessarily be in the same trouble and, if all goes well, will honor the obligation. The bank, you see, gets an extra measure of safety for its money."

Ludwig was now well launched on his great fortune-building odyssey. He had started by renting space in other people's docks and shipyards. Now he began building his own facilities—using OPM, of course. His small ship-building company prospered and grew explosively during World War Two, when the U.S. government was a greedy customer for every tanker he could build.

An impressive postwar boom began to show itself in the

late 1940s, and Ludwig looked for ways to expand. He decided (as did many other shipbuilders and shipping operators) that the United States had become one of the world's worst places in which to base a business of his kind. Labor costs, materials prices and taxes were all too high, and the entire shipping industry was bogged in a vast, tangled seaweed bed of tariff problems and other governmental restrictions. It was time, Ludwig thought, to look around the world.

In the early 1950s he found an enticing deal in Japan. The Japanese, losers of the war and at that time economic losers, too, had a huge naval shipyard at Kure—birthplace of battleships, aircraft carriers and other giant craft. The war's end had closed it down, throwing thousands out of work and plunging the region into a severe, long-lasting and seemingly incurable depression. The Japanese government was anxious to get something started there but was treading warily for fear that Kure might be turned into an American naval yard and permanent military base. When Ludwig came around—a private American citizen with lots of cash and even more credit—the Japanese welcomed him joyfully. (One local official, it is said, literally had tears of happiness streaming down his cheeks as he signed some contracts later.) The Japanese quickly made a deal with the taciturn American. In return for certain easy concessions on his part— he had to hire Japanese labor and use Japanese steel, for instance, which he wanted to do, anyway—they gave him a cheap, long-term lease of the Kure shipyard plus an attractive assortment of tax and tariff deals and other pot sweeteners.

Ludwig built tankers, iron-ore carriers and other ships at Kure from then until the present time. He built bigger and bigger ships; each succeeding generation could carry more cargo at a cheaper rate per ton. He sold some, kept others. As his fleet expanded, he set up new companies around the world to operate the ships—companies incorporated in nations such as Liberia and Panama, which offer a shipper all kinds of advantages in terms of taxes, labor laws and ship-registration expenses. In time he began to fit new pieces into the structure of his global empire. He acquired mining and petroleum properties whose transportation needs could be served by his ships. He set up banking-and-loan companies that could participate in the financial flow his empire generated. He amassed what must surely be one of the highest piles of wealth ever shoveled together by one man.

One man? That is almost literally true. Ludwig owns many of his ventures and properties outright; he is majority owner of most of the others. Unlike some other men we'll meet here (see particularly the story of Jim Ling, chapter 15), Ludwig has never been attracted by the idea of equity financing, in which you raise money for a venture by selling some or most of the ownership and future profits to other people. Ludwig hasn't wanted a horde of stockholders telling him what to do. He has always preferred to move ahead by borrowing other people's money and keeping the ownership for himself. Except in a private deal, it has never been possible to buy stock in any Ludwig venture.

Ludwig, today well past the age when most men retire, may at last regret having run a one-man show so long. There seems to be no natural successor to take over the huge, complicated empire and keep it running. There are some trusted friends and aides, but no one man among them emerges clearly as the heir apparent. In fact, Ludwig's lifelong obsession with secrecy has been such that most of his own executives know less about the corporate complex than they could wish. "Each executive is in charge of his own little section," says one insider, "and each man is given to understand that anything beyond his own section is none of his damned business. Ludwig may be the only man in the company who really knows everything there is to know about it."

Ludwig's successors, whoever they turn out to be, may wish in the end that the great borrower had engineered the colossal structure in a different way. But at the moment one achievement stands out starkly: Daniel Keith Ludwig came from nowhere and made himself one of the richest men on earth. Contrary to the old barroom platitudes, them as ain't got can get.

15

The Magic of "OPM": 2. The Equity Route

As we've seen in the case of Daniel Ludwig, one way to make other people's money work for you is to borrow it. There is another way, and the man we're about to study— James Joseph Ling—is a man who until a few years ago was acknowledged to have mastered it. His fortunes have recently fallen and the business community has abandoned the tone of awestruck wonder with which it once flattered him. Today he's "Hard-Luck Ling." Still, his achievement cannot be denied.

Ling used OPM to climb from nowhere to enormous prominence as chief of perhaps the fastest-growing major company Wall Street ever saw. The huge, complex venture fell ill in 1969 and is still not off the critical list as this book goes to press. All the same, some Wall Streeters believe that what Jim Ling could do once, he can do again. Next time, perhaps, he will do it a little more carefully.

Ling used OPM mainly in the form of equity money. He borrowed, too, but it was the equity route that made him famous. Let's see what this route is all about.

Suppose, to construct a simple example, you stumble onto a business idea that seems to offer some promise. You need money to get the venture started. You have little or no spare cash of your own. What do you do?

As we've noted, you can borrow what you need. Or you can take the equity route. You go to a few well-heeled friends—five, let's say—and you outline your idea and ask them if they'd like to risk some money in it as coventurers. You stress the word *risk*. You aren't asking to borrow the money; nor are you contracting to pay it back. The five friends are to become co-owners of the business along with you—in other words, stockholders in an informal sense. If the business succeeds, each will reap his proportionate share of the profits. If the business fails, each will sadly kiss his money good-bye.

Let's suppose your idea is a sound one and you're a good talker. Each friend puts up $5000; so the infant company is capitalized at $25,000. Each friend gets (informally) one share of the stock. You also get one share, though you've put up no money yourself. The agreement is that you will earn your share by doing all the work—in fact, have already earned a substantial part of it by having developed the idea in the first place. You are the idea man and the chief (perhaps only) operating executive. Your five friends, having full-time jobs of their own, will take little or no part in the day-to-day management of the business. They are simply the venture capitalists.

Thus, you're launched in business through the use of OPM. Your little company has six shareholders. From now on you will collect one-sixth of the net profits, if any.

From here on, if the venture succeeds, you can go in many different directions. You can keep the company closely held if you and the other shareholders don't want outside interference. Or, if a time comes when you or they want to reap some capital gains in cash, you can widen the circle of shareholders or even go public. You can split the original six shares into dozens or hundreds or thousands having equivalent value, and you can sell off some of the stock at whatever price the market will bear. (If the venture is truly successful, the original investors will, of course, sell their stock for much more than their original $5000.) Under the right conditions you can create new stock, sell it to the public and bring new working capital in to help the company grow. Or you can hold some shares as treasury stock and use that stock in place of money to pay for other, smaller companies your growing enterprise may want to buy.

You can build an empire this way—build it all, or almost all, on other people's money.

Meet a man who did.

James Ling:
One Hundred Million Dollars

Two things about James Ling impress visitors immediately —his size and his nervous energy. He is a big, dark man, six feet two and somewhere over 200 pounds, and though he is in his late 40s, he still looks fairly trim and athletic. There is only a faint suggestion of middle-aged heaviness. He might be a recently retired football player. No doubt his lack of fat results partly from his constant jittery activity. He seldom sits still; he sleeps few hours, often waking in the middle of the night to find his brain churning with magnificent ideas. *Signature* magazine once suggested he has an "incurable overdose of productive adrenaline." Others have put it in other ways. "He's savagely competitive," says a New York stockbroker. "He loves a fight for its own sake. He hardly ever drinks, but I've seen him almost drunk with the joy of competing. He makes business into something close to a body-contact sport."

In 1968, the year of a superheated bull market, Ling was chief executive and major stockholder of perhaps the hottest company on the Big Board: Ling-Temco-Vought (LTV, for short). The company was only seven years old. It had been created in 1961. In those seven years it had risen to become one of the 15 biggest companies in the United States, and its common stock's trading price had screamed upward from less than $20 per share to the range of $135. Ling was a Wall Street legend in his own lifetime. His name was linked with those of other legendary company builders and stock jugglers such as Samuel Insull and Andrew Carnegie.

Two years later LTV common was trading below ten dollars, and the party was over. Investors who had been foolish or unlucky enough to hold the stock during that swift downhill journey were calling Ling various names, none of them kind. They may have been consoled somewhat by the knowledge that Ling, the biggest LTV stockholder of all, had ridden down with them. At the height of his glory, his net worth was in the neighborhood of $100 million. He is still a multimillionaire today, but not nearly as multi as he used to be.

In some ways Ling's career parallels that of Bernard Cornfeld (chapter 7), another man who reached the top in the late 1960s but failed to hang tight. Both men were mauled by the 1969 bear market. Both—who knows?—may ride back to glory on the back of the next bull. It will be interesting to watch them.

It has been interesting to watch Ling in the past. The spectacle has often been dazzling. James Joseph Ling (the name is Bavarian, not Chinese as many seem to think) was born humbly in Oklahoma early in the 1920s. His father was an oil-field laborer. His mother died when he was in grade school, and he eventually went to live with an aunt. At the age of 14, feeling he was big enough and smart enough to hack it on his own, he quit school and ran away from the aunt. He never completed his high-school education. He spent some years bumming around the country and at age 19 landed in Dallas, where he found a job with an electrical contractor—and also, incidentally, got married.

World War Two had begun. Young Ling, supplementing his daytime pay by working nights in an aircraft plant, made enough money to put a down payment on a small house. Then, in 1944, he enlisted in the U.S. Navy. The navy put him to work as an electrician.

Back from the war in 1946, Ling decided he was tired of working for other people. It was time, he felt, to start his own business. He sold his house to raise capital, added the profit to some saved navy pay and put together a miniature wad of some $3000. With this money he started a little electrical-contracting outfit called Ling Electric. The main assets were Ling himself, a rented office and a used truck.

At first he made his living solely by wiring homes. Residential construction, which had been stifled by shortages of materials and labor during the war, was beginning to boom as the pent-up demand was released in the late 1940s. The home-building boom was to continue almost unabated, in fact, through the entire decade of the 1950s. But the young contractor kept his eyes and ears open, and after a while he thought he saw a still bigger world to conquer: the world of office and industrial construction—which was also starting to boom. In the residential business he worked for a few hundred dollars here and a few hundred there. But in the office and industrial business, he observed with interest, an electrician's contracts were measured in the thousands of dollars.

He hustled hard, won some nonresidential wiring contracts, learned to improve his profits by buying cheap military-surplus wire and other supplies. His little outfit prospered. By the early 1950s Ling Electric was riding high above the million-dollar mark in gross annual sales.

But the young contractor wasn't altogether satisfied. For

one thing, income taxes were eating him alive. As a sole proprietorship, Ling Electric paid the full personal tax rates. Despite his large gross sales, Jim Ling's take-home pay was merely that of a medium-high salary earner. This irritated him. The itch was intensified by the fact that some grandiose expansion plans were beginning to ferment in his head, and he lacked capital with which to put the plans into effect.

The way to go, he figured, was to incorporate. This would alleviate the tax problem, to begin with. Corporate rates are lower than personal rates, and a corporation has more opportunities for legal money juggling than does a lone individual taxpayer. Moreover, incorporation would pave the way for expansion. As a corporation, Ling Electric would be able to raise capital by selling stock to the public.

A minor electrical contractor going public? It was unheard of. When Ling approached Texas brokers and investment bankers with the notion, they found it quite amusing. He couldn't find anybody in the investment community who was willing to help him float the proposed stock issue.

So he did it himself. Neither Texas nor any other state has a law saying an electrical contractor can't issue stock. The notion may have been funny, but it was perfectly allowable as far as the law was concerned. Ling went through the required legal steps, turned Ling Electric into Ling Electric Inc. and obtained authorization to issue 800,000 shares of common stock and sell some of them to the public.

The new corporation's internal equity setup was engineered so that Ling personally kept exactly half the stock. The rest—400,000 shares—were to be offered to the public at $2.25 per share. Ling rounded up a small group of friends to help him do the selling. While the Texas financial community looked on in popeyed amazement, they went out and sold the stock door-to-door and by telephone—exactly as the brash young Bernard Cornfeld was then peddling mutual funds in Europe. To the horror of conservative local financiers, Ling's group even handed out prospectuses at the Texas State Fair. They sold the entire stock issue in a few months. Deducting the salesmen's commissions and other costs, Ling Electric ended with about three-quarters of a million dollars in new working capital.

And not only that—in this one nervy maneuver, Ling had established a new, high market value for his company and for his own equity in it. Previously it had been just a small outfit of doubtful worth—in fact, of no known market value. If Ling had wanted to sell it, he might have had trouble finding a buyer. The buyer, looking at Ling's tax-riddled personal earnings, would not likely have offered more than $250,000 for it, if even that. But now Ling owned 400,000 shares that were valued on the local over-the-counter market at nearly one million dollars—and, in subsequent market fluctuations, were to rise well over that figure in some months. He could now sell out anytime he liked and walk away a millionaire.

He had no plan to sell out, however. His plan was to build an empire.

First he bought another electrical-contracting firm, paying cash. This doubled the size of Ling Electric; the stock's market price rose, and Ling thus moved into a favorable position for buying other companies without cash. The stock, having an established and growing market value, could be used instead of money. In a stock-swap deal that used very little of his own or his company's cash, Ling now bought an electronics-manufacturing firm and changed the name to Ling Electronics. The stock price rose higher. Next, in a similar stock deal, he acquired another electronics outfit called Altec and changed his company's name to Ling-Altec Electronics.

By the late 1950s he was more than just a Texas phenomenon. The national business community was beginning to take note of him. The *Wall Street Journal*, which monitors national trends from its lofty post inside Dow Jones and Company, around the corner from Wall Street, felt Ling might be a national trend in 1960 and devoted a front-page story to him. In that year his net worth was pegged at ten million dollars.

He had only just started. Late in 1960, in another exchange of stock, he acquired the assets of a large Dallas-based company called Temco Electronics and Missiles Company and once again changed his own company's name, this time to Ling-Temco Electronics.

No longer could he be considered a small businessman. His new, merged company had sales of nearly $150 million in 1960. Now he was able to go to Wall Street itself for help in raising capital and working out stock gambits. This helped his next deal: the acquisition of Chance Vought Corporation, major aircraft and missile manufacturer.

The deal wasn't easy to bring off, for Chance Vought

didn't really want to be acquired. Its management fought Ling off bitterly and noisily—but this only made Ling enjoy it more (and, as a dividend, brought his company some valuable publicity). Unluckily for Chance Vought's managers, they owned very little of their company's stock. Ling didn't need to buy 51 percent of it to nail down a controlling interest. He managed to get hold of roughly two-fifths of it—by buying on the open market and by making a tender offer to existing shareholders—and that was enough. In the spring of 1961 Ling's company once more changed its name: Ling-Temco-Vought, Inc.

It was at about this time that the word *conglomerate* first began to be used in Wall Street. The word refers to a company that grows by acquiring other companies in diverse lines of business. A few such companies had existed before—notably the old American-Marietta Company, today part of Martin Marietta. But it wasn't until the early 1960s that this breed of company was recognized and talked about as a separate and noteworthy category. It was to become one of the hottest categories in the seething stock market of the 1960s—and LTV, raised to fame by the noisy squabble with Chance Vought, became the archetype.

Jim Ling was now a financial wheeler and dealer of nationwide repute. He didn't let matters rest there, however. His fertile brain had conceived a grand new way of using OPM.

He wanted to acquire other companies on which his eye had alighted—big, wealthy companies, some of them bigger at that time than LTV itself. He planned to buy them, as usual, either by offering his own company's stock as payment or by putting up that stock as collateral for loans. The stock, of course, was worth what the market said it was worth. The higher the market price went, the more valuable the stock would be for Ling's purposes—the more buying he could do with it. The problem, therefore, was to raise the market price.

He recalled the day when his original contracting outfit had gone public. Simply by selling stock, by getting the market to place a value on the little company, he had vastly increased its apparent worth. Now he wondered, Might it not be possible to do the same with some of LTV's component parts?

Over the years, in acquiring other companies, the Ling

parent company had simply absorbed them into itself. They kept operating as before, but they vanished as independent equities. Their stock disappeared from the marketplace. As each was absorbed, the original shareholders turned in their stock and were given the stock of Ling's parent company in return. You could no longer buy stock separately in Altec, Chance Vought or the others; you could only buy the stock of LTV, the big basket that held them all.

These once-independent companies were being represented in LTV's financial statements at what is called their "book value." The book value of a company is essentially an accountant's assessment of the company's worth. It is naturally a very conservative assessment. Ling thought he saw room for improvement.

In boom times, as Ling well knew, the stock market almost always values any sound company at more than its book value. That is, if you take the going market price of the company's stock—the price investors are willing to pay for it—and then multiply that price by the total number of shares outstanding, the resulting figure is likely to be far higher than the book value calculated by company accountants. The reason is that the stock market usually pours a heady dose of hope into the calculations. The stock price is based not only on the current, perceptible, tangible worth of the company but also on what investors think or hope or pray it will be worth in the future. This element of hope is absent, of course, from the severe and somber book-value calculations.

Mulling over these thoughts, Ling asked some questions that few conglomerate builders before had ever thought to ask. Why carry acquired companies at their mere book value? Why not set them up as independent equities, create stock for them, sell some of that stock to the public and let the market pump up their value?

And that is what Ling did in 1965. First he divided LTV's principal operating divisions into three separate corporations named LTV Aerospace, LTV Electrosystems and LTV Ling-Altec. Each of the three issued its own stock. The parent company, LTV, Inc., kept roughly 75 to 80 percent of that stock in each case. The rest was offered to the public.

The public did what Ling had figured it would do. Investors bid up the stock prices of the three newly formed corporations. LTV, Inc., the parent, holding more than three-quarters of that stock, was now able to represent its acquired companies in terms of the market value rather than the stodgy old book value. The parent company's apparent worth shot upward as a result, and so did its own stock's market price.

It was a gorgeous example of the clever use of OPM. Ling had obtained something for nothing. The whole dazzling deal cost him hardly anything beyond the purely clerical and procedural expenses involved in the stock issues.

Many another man would have stopped right there. Ling personally owned hundreds of thousands of LTV, Inc., shares, plus thousands upon thousands of warrants to buy more shares at prices below the market price. With LTV's stock price skipping upward so joyfully, he was growing richer by the day. In some weeks he found he was more than a million dollars richer at the close of trading on Friday than he had been when he woke up on Monday. Many another man would have rested.

But it seems to be characteristic of the very, very rich that money alone doesn't make them happy. Ling, in the middle 1960s, was quite wealthy enough to retire to some peaceful Eden of his choosing. He had no real need to do any more work ever again.

"But anybody who thought he'd quit," says one of his financial publicity men, "didn't know the man. To Ling money is only the way you keep score. What he likes is the game itself. He's two hundred pounds of pure aggression. If he were ever forced to retire, he'd shrivel up like flowers in November."

Instead of retiring, Ling went after Wilson and Company.

Wilson was a huge old company, a sort of conglomerate in its own conservative way, with about a billion dollars in annual sales derived from three main businesses: meatpacking, sporting goods and drugs. In terms of sales it was twice LTV's size. The irrepressible Jim Ling determined to acquire it.

How on each? By using OPM, of course.

Wilson was what Wall Streeters call undervalued—meaning that in relation to its earnings and in relation to other companies in similar lines of business, its stock was trading at a low price. The reasons were manifold, but notable among them was the fact that Wilson had always been a quiet company. It didn't ballyhoo itself or its stock as much as did most of its competitors. Investors weren't paying much attention to it.

Wilson's stock price was low enough so that Ling figured he could buy a controlling interest for only $80 million. (*Only* is a relative term, of course.) Where would he get the $80 million? By borrowing, using LTV's own soaring stock to back up his credit.

He borrowed, bought some of the Wilson stock on the open market, got the rest through a tender offer to existing shareholders. Wilson thus became part of LTV. But LTV was now in debt to the tune of $80 million, and Ling's next problem was to get out from under that burden. His approach to the problem took Wall Street's breath away. It was perhaps the cleverest of all Ling's clever uses of OPM.

He transferred the major portion of the debt into Wilson's books. That is, he engineered the situation so that, technically speaking, the money was owed by Wilson rather than by the parent company. Then, as he had done before with LTV itself, he split Wilson into three separate corporations along the company's natural product lines—Wilson and Company Meat Processors, Wilson Sporting Goods and Wilson Pharmaceuticals. (Wall Street promptly dubbed these three companies Meatball, Golfball and Goofball.) Each of the three new companies was authorized to issue its own stock. The bulk of the new stock became the property of the parent company, LTV, Inc., and the rest was sold to the public. The money brought in by the public sale was enough to pay off almost all the debt that had originally been transferred to Wilson's books.

Wall Street was stunned by the brilliance of the maneuver. Ling had managed to acquire a giant company without using, in the end, more than a few spoonfuls of his own company's money.

But the best was yet to come. Investors bid up the prices of Meatball, Golfball and Goofball stock, motivated partly by the knowledge that Ling was at the helm. LTV, Inc., held more than three-fourths of the three Wilson companies' shares, and as the stock prices went up, so did the companies' value as entered in the parent's financial statements. In the end LTV's holdings in the three companies, in terms of market price, were worth nearly twice what the old Wilson and Company had been worth before the takeover. And once again, of course, the trading price of LTV shot up.

Jim Ling, the onetime teen-age bum, was a Wall Street legend in his mid-40s. Around the stock exchanges and in the bankers' clubs they were predicting he would next try to buy Bell Telephone. He planned to split it into several separate companies, so the story went. The first would be called Ting-a-Ling, the second Ting-a-Ling-a-Ling. . . .

That story wasn't accurate, but Ling was preparing other moves that were nearly as stunning. Throughout the late 1960s, using OPM as cleverly as before, he took one company after another into the amazing LTV family. One was Greatameria Corporation, which in turn owned Braniff Airways, National Car Rental and a string of insurance companies. Another was Jones and Laughlin Steel.

And then came 1969 and 1970, the years of the bear. It was almost to be expected that a company such as LTV, built on a complex framework of equity financing, would experience trouble when the equity markets turned sour. LTV did more than experience trouble. It nearly collapsed.

Ling was in the midst of various new gambits when the markets crashed. Stock prices of the parent company and all its children fell like winged ducks. Ling-style moves that depended on high stock prices had to be abandoned. Debts that were to be paid off through these moves could no longer be paid. Interest costs mounted. Meanwhile, the day-to-day operating earnings of the subsidiary companies were dwindling in the general business slowdown. Braniff fell into a pit of black despair along with most other airlines. Wilson Sporting Goods watched its customers vanish in droves. The structure Ling had built was crumpling beneath him.

LTV's stock price had reached the dizzy height of $135 in the glorious days of 1968. Now it went down, down, down as though it would never stop. Finally, in 1971, it crunched to a shuddering halt at a fraction above $9. As this book goes to press, it is wavering about in the general area of $10 to $20. Nobody seems to want it anymore. It almost never makes the "most active" list and on many days could compete successfully for inclusion among the least active. In the opinion of some, it is a dog.

The ride is over.

For the time being, at least.

16

Real Estate:
Building Big

About 20 years ago a writer named Thomas Ewing Dabney completed a biography of hotel magnate Conrad Hilton. Since Hilton was then 60 years old, Dabney had every right to guess he had pinned down his subject at or near the end of the story. After all, reasoned Dabney, a man who reaches his 60s with millions of dollars in his bank account can be expected to slow down and coast toward retirement, right?

Wrong. The title Dabney originally picked for his biography was *The Man Who Bought the Plaza,* referring to New York's Plaza Hotel, one of the world's leading society hangouts. The book was all ready to go to press when Hilton pulled off a still bigger coup, the biggest in his career up to then: He bought New York's Waldorf-Astoria Hotel. If the Plaza was a queen among hotels, the Waldorf was the empress. Dabney and his publisher hastily pulled their book off the press, added a new chapter and changed the title to *The Man Who Bought the Waldorf.*

Not long after the book was published, Conrad Hilton obsoleted his harried biographer again. This time he bought the entire Statler chain of hotels. He paid $110 million. As far as anybody knew, it was the biggest single real-estate transaction in history.

Conrad Hilton, today past 80, still doesn't seem ready to retire as this book goes to press. He may yet obsolete us as he did Dabney.

Hilton is a man who obviously loves his work. Like others we've met and are to meet in this gallery, he is not attracted by the idea of idle luxury. He long ago accumulated more money than he could conceivably spend. He could have retired in the 1940s and lived ever after in kingly comfort, never again stirring from poolside or armchair. But he couldn't stay out of the game.

His game was real estate—specifically hotels. He bought them, built them, ran them, tinkered with them, sold them, manipulated them like gigantic chess pieces. He did all this mainly through the clever use of other people's money—a technique we studied in the two previous chapters.

The story that follows doesn't say where he came from or how he got his start; so we'll sketch his seedling period briefly here. Conrad Nicholson ("Connie") Hilton was born in New Mexico on Christmas Day 1887. His father ran a variety of small-town businesses, including a rickety little hotel. These businesses had their ups and downs. They were on the downward leg of a cycle when the senior Hilton died, and young Conrad's inheritance was a couple of thousand dollars. Putting this inheritance together with a small wad of cash he'd gathered on his own, the young man set out to seek his fortune with about $5000 to his name.

He was interested in small-town banks. He and his father had been fellow stockholders in a tiny bank (capitalization: $30,000) that they had organized in their own town. Having a thorough knowledge of banking and an acquaintanceship with several old New Mexico bankers, young Hilton knew he could make his little bundle of seed capital go a long way. He could use it as a basis for borrowing. If he found a business property he wanted to buy, he could offer his $5000 as a down payment and go to the banks for tens of thousands more.

And so he went out looking for a small bank to buy. As it turned out, he didn't buy a bank. He bought a hotel.

The folksy tones that follow are those of Hilton himself, recalling his career for a *Nation's Business* interviewer.

Conrad Hilton:
One Hundred Million Dollars*

When the Puerto Rican government wrote a half-dozen hotel executives back in the Forties asking if they were interested in building a hotel in San Juan, Conrad Hilton began his reply, *"Mi estimado amigo."* He enthusiastically outlined

*Copyright © *Nation's Business*—the Chamber of Commerce of the United States. Reprinted by permission.

his conditions in the language spoken on the island.

Writing in Spanish struck just the right note and helped persuade the Puerto Rican agency that he should operate the hotel. He also shrewdly laid down terms that would set the pattern for what is now a richly rewarding international hotel network.

Conrad N. Hilton is a dreamer who makes his dreams come true. In 1919, with his limited funds pinned inside his coat, he went to Texas and made his first hotel purchase.

Today . . . Mr. Hilton is chairman of Hilton Hotels Corporation and president and chairman of Hilton International Company. Some 67 hotels, from Trinidad to Tel Aviv, currently fly the Hilton flag. He now has more hotels abroad than in the United States. Domestic operations grossed $187 million last year, while the International Company took in $94 million.

Conrad Hilton had been known as the man who bought the Waldorf—the ultimate symbol of the stature of a hotelman. Then, in 1954, he acquired the Statler hotels in a dazzling real-estate deal that cost seven times the price of the Louisiana Purchase.

An example of his ingenuity in making the best use of his assets was his creation of the 9000-square-foot Williford Room in the huge Conrad Hilton Hotel in Chicago. He got the room by dividing another room in half—horizontally. By building a new floor halfway between the original floor and the extra-high ceiling, he produced another badly needed room literally out of thin air.

Still the tall, erect, gracious host, Conrad Hilton reviewed his remarkable success saga in an interview with *Nation's Business* in his elegant office in Beverly Hills. Here is his story:

Your first experience in the hotel business goes back to when your father had a boardinghouse-type hotel in the New Mexico Territory, doesn't it?

That was a rather limited experience. There were eight children in the family, and my father kept adding on rooms as the family grew. Then, as we went off to school, he found some rooms on hand and established this hotel. But the first hotel that I had was in Cisco, Texas—the Mobley Hotel.

My father was a pioneer settler in this little town of San

Antonio, New Mexico. I think, when he started off, his merchandise consisted of a jug of whiskey. Maybe he had a bolt of calico to go with it. Anyway, he was a very industrious man, and with what he earned, he grubstaked this fellow who hit coal.

So he had this coal mine, and gradually, in this little community, my father was giving employment to virtually everybody: people in the coal mines, people to haul the coal. He bought the farmers' produce, he had the store, he had the post office, and eventually we had a little bank and this little hotel.

I personally established the bank. That was my idea.

This was one of your first dreams—to be a banker—is that right?

Yes, but after the First World War was over, my father had died, and I didn't know what I wanted to do.

An old friend, Emmett Vaughey, was very ill in Albuquerque, and I went up to see him. I remember his words very well. He said, "I am not long for this world. The good Lord is going to take me soon, but if you will go to Texas, you will make your fortune."

Now, this advice—almost an order—from a man about to die so impressed me, I decided to do it.

So I did—still not knowing what I wanted to do, whether I wanted to go into banking or what. I stopped off first at Wichita Falls, Texas, and I went in to see a bank, and the owner said, "I wouldn't sell you this bank at any price."

Now, when I speak about buying a bank, it had to be a small bank, you see. I didn't have a lot of money; in fact, I had about $5000. But I had credit.

The fellow in Wichita Falls said, "Why don't you go down to these southern oil fields? There is a booming town there, and I think you could find a bank down there."

So I landed in Cisco, Texas, in the midst of an oil boom, and I found a bank for sale for $75,000.

So I thought, "Well, this is just about my size." I checked with a banker over there that I had known before. He was in El Paso, and I did most of my banking with him.

He said, "You damn fool! Go ahead and buy the bank. That is a good deal. Draw on me for all the money you haven't got."

So I went back to Cisco, and I sent this fellow a telegram: "WILL TAKE BANK." I was dreaming big. This would be the cornerstone on a banking empire in Texas. I was even too impatient to bargain. He sent me back a telegram: "PRICE RAISED. WILL NOT ACCEPT LESS THAN $80,000." I was furious. Here, against all my instinct and years of experience haggling and trading when working for my father, I had met his asking price, and he had raised it.

That night I went over to this little hotel—the Mobley Hotel—and what a lot of bustle: everything busy and people waiting to get a bed for eight hours. They'd turn over three times in 24 hours. I introduced myself to the owner of it, and I said, "You seem to be doing a good business."

He said, "I am doing a fine business, but I could make more money out in the oil fields."

I said, "Would you sell this hotel?" trying not to appear too anxious. He said, "I might sell it a little bit later."

So I said to myself, I am going to buy this hotel. And I did.

Now, that is how I started.

So it was a bustling town, they were turning over those beds pretty fast, and you looked at the books and decided this was a good proposition, right?

I saw that it was much better than banking. I hadn't taken over the hotel 24 hours before I decided, This is what I am going to do. This is my life.

It was set right there?

Right there I made up my mind I didn't want anything else. That was in 1919. Certainly, the banker raising the price $5000 steered me off banking. But what really did it was going over there and seeing the bustle, having the owner tell me about all the business that he was doing, how the trains were coming in there at night and the money that he was making. When he showed me his books, I figured that I could get all of my money back in one year.

We didn't have any income tax then; so what a deal that was!

Imagine getting our money back today in a year. Today you have to figure on getting it back in 20 years. That is what it takes us with taxes and labor costs. So the hotel business is not as lucrative today as it was in those days.

I hit on a couple of major principles for operating hotels at the old Mobley.

What were they?

I saw, around the hotel, we were not getting what we should out of the space. So I changed it, and I have kept that as a rule throughout my life, to find out what is the best use I could make of space. You see, you can either lose your money or you can make it, depending upon whether you know what the public wants. You have to know that and give them the most in the space available.

I figured out that customers at the Mobley could get food someplace else and that they didn't need the hotel dining room. So we put beds in there. We were making no money on the food, and the rooms were in terrific demand. Today you might find that the best use of space is in a restaurant.

Another thing was building *esprit de corps* among the help. We got all the employees together and told them that they were largely responsible for whether the guests of the hotel were pleased and would ever come back. I have done that throughout my life.

What do you feel is your greatest accomplishment in your career? Getting the Waldorf?

Well, I would say that the important things that I did in my life, insofar as the hotel business is concerned, were the purchase of the Waldorf and the Statler hotels and the inauguration of the international hotels. I felt, from the knowledge I had, that we had certain advantages in the international field that we did not have here. For instance, we had lower labor costs than we have here, as you know.

Then, there was a great demand. For instance, in Paris we just built the Paris Hilton, the first hotel built in Paris in 33 years. Figure that, a city that size and it has not had a new hotel in 33 years.

Why had nobody else built a hotel?

The hotel people in Paris didn't want another hotel; they liked it as it was. And it is not easy to build a hotel today, what with high taxes and high labor. But what we have wanted to do was to build hotels in the principal cities of the world.

We believe that we are helping out world peace by having these hotels. We have found out that although people may be mad at each other, once they come into our hotel, they are no longer mad.

Mr. Hilton, owning the Waldorf was one of your big dreams for many years. But the Hilton Corporation directors were pretty uncertain about it, weren't they?

That is right.

Why was the Waldorf, in your mind, such a huge target?

I saw it as the greatest hotel in the world. Its elegant rooms had housed the royalty of the world. When someone would call up asking for "the king," the telephone operator at the Waldorf would have to ask, "Which king, please?" But the hotel had gone broke. I remember one director who was very much opposed to it. I had bought bonds on the Waldorf in 1942 for four and a half cents on the dollar. That is how bad it was. Now it was 1949.

This director even called me up on the phone from Los Angeles to tell me of a warning. He said, "I just had a call from so-and-so. He said, 'For God's sake, don't let Connie buy the Waldorf.' "

But that didn't stop you?

It didn't stop me at all, because I knew the intrinsic and great value and prestige it would give our company to have a hotel like that.

This director, when the meeting came, said, "I will never vote against you when the voting starts, but I am against your doing this."

So my board of directors couldn't share my enthusiasm. And as president of the Hilton Hotels Corporation I couldn't buy without their approval.

But as Connie Hilton I could do as I had done 30 years before in Cisco, Texas. I could buy it myself and raise the money by selling the idea to backers who could see it as I did.

So I set things in motion in the old familiar way I had done in years past. I had leased old hotels in Texas. Then I had built that hotel in Dallas—and raised my first million dollars doing it. And I had bought hotels cheaply after the depression and nursed them back to health. Now I called the man I considered the leader of the Wall Street crowd that held the Waldorf stock. I had been flirting with "The Queen" long enough.

"I'm ready to make you an offer today," I said. "What time should I come by?"

That afternoon I walked into his office and offered to buy 249,042 shares—a controlling number—at $12 a share.

"The offer is good for twenty-four hours," I said. Then I handed him my own check for $100,000 to bind the bargain. He said, "Give me forty-eight hours." I agreed. The offer was accepted, and all that stood between me and the Waldorf was three million dollars.

I went to some outside fellows. I said, "Look, would you put in two hundred and fifty thousand dollars in a deal with me on the Waldorf? I don't offer it to you, but I may want to offer it to you." They said yes. So I figured I could raise enough to buy it.

I tried to stick to my practice of stopping work at 6:00 P.M. and dancing every night and playing golf. But final negotiations to get the money cut into my recreation. In fact, the only thing I didn't miss was mass each morning at St. Patrick's Cathedral.

Now that the money was being raised, the Hilton board of directors said, "No, you don't, either. As long as you have gone this far, this hotel is going to belong to the Hilton Hotels Corporation."

So then the corporation did put up the money that was still needed?

Yes, they did.

You had an even greater struggle getting the money to build your first hotel, the Dallas Hilton, didn't you?

Yes, I did. I almost went broke on that one. It was in 1925 and was the first hotel that I had built.

I told the owner of the land that I wanted to build a million-dollar hotel. I told him that instead of buying his land, I wanted to lease it for 99 years.

He shot back, "I'm not Methuselah. I won't live for ninety-nine years."

But I told him, "If I don't pay, you get not only the land but the building." When he had agreed to that and the amount of the lease, then I let him have the big charge: "And I'd also like the lease to have a clause saying I could float a loan on the real estate." Did he yelp! But I finally got it.

But I just didn't have the experience or the knowledge. There are a lot of things you have got to think about. And though I raised the million, it wasn't enough. So I ran out of money.

Then, to get out of that jam, I went back to the owner and said, "Look, if you finish the building and take over, I'll give you much more and lease it back from you."

He was quite well-to-do, but he was against it. So I talked and I sold. Finally he said, "All right." That is how I got out of that one.

Do you think you have an intuition about the good locations for hotels?

I think I have sufficient knowledge that I can decide where is a good location and where not to build a hotel. Now, this one [pointing to the nearby Beverly Hilton] I knew was a good location. It would make me so damn mad, later, thinking of it. That used to be a cabbage patch there. And I kept saying to myself, "There is where you should build a hotel. Why don't you get busy and do it?" And I finally did it, but almost too late.

I was almost too late because somebody else was about to grab the land. You know, somebody else could see things, too.

But you moved more quickly?

I just went and said, "I want to make a deal," and I made a deal.

Didn't you have a similar type of problem with the Statler chain? Hadn't William Zeckendorf of Webb and Knapp already made a bid on it?

Yes, he had.

How did you swing that one?

I had been thinking about the Statler hotels because I knew that they were not getting along very well internally, that there was a lot of friction. I had a friend who was vice-president—God rest his soul, he is gone now—Jimmie McCabe, a wonderful man.

One day a number of citizens were invited on a trip over the Grand Canyon on a new plane of United Air Lines. I said, "I believe I will sit with Jimmie McCabe." During the trip he said to me, "Why don't you go ahead and buy the Statler hotels?"

Mr. Zeckendorf had already entered into negotiations for it?

Yes. They had put up a million dollars. Mrs. Statler was trustee for quite a few shares in the corporation that Mr. Statler had left Cornell University. And she was also trustee for a couple of the children.

So—I think it wasn't any later than the next day—I got on the phone to Joe Binns in New York, who at that time was our vice-president. I said, "Where is Mrs. Statler?"

"Well," he said, "she is here, but she is getting ready to leave."

I said, "Hold her there; I want to see her. I will leave immediately." I was in California.

He called back and said, "She will wait here for you."

There were three trustees, as I recall, and I figured, "Well, you can't fool around here. If you want these hotels, you have got to act quick."

I said to Mrs. Statler, "Will you support me on a bid? I will give you a bid that will be much better than the bid you have now for the hotels." She said, "I will," just like that, very sweet.

She was ready to listen to another hotelman?

Yes. She had a feeling for the tradition of the hotels, and she wanted to see a hotelman running those hotels.

Zeckendorf had offered a good price for them, but he had put up only one million of the $110 million offered.

So, instead of putting up one million, I put up seven million.

They had to take my offer. As trustees they couldn't take a one-million-dollar offer when they had a seven-million-dollar offer.

This was the earnest-money part of it, right?

This was a cash deposit guaranteeing that I would go through with the deal, but I offered the same total price.

The total deal was $110 million, all cash?

Yes. It was the biggest real-estate deal, I believe, ever made.

Mr. Hilton, I know you had a terribly rough time during the depression. You lost one hotel after another. You borrowed to the hilt. What made you continue?

I wouldn't give up. In the first place, I wouldn't give up because that isn't the way I am constituted. And I figured that I would be able to work this situation out sooner or later. At that time hotels were going broke all over. In fact, I think the record shows that about 80 percent of all hotels in America went broke.

And at one time I was $500,000 in debt and nothing coming in. But I worked out of it.

What are some of the principles that you have employed in operating hotels besides looking for waste space and building esprit de corps?

One of the principles that I insist on—which I think works, judging from the letters that I get—I must have my hotels in first-class condition. I want the guest, when he comes in there, to see a nice room, a clean bathroom; so I insist on that.

I have found that you will not complain about what I charge you for your room if I give you something that is pleasing to you when you enter that hotel. But if I give you an old, worn-out carpet, for example, you are not going to like it, and you are going to be unhappy.

I have learned, also, that each hotel must have a personality geared to its location, that you must be accurate in forecasting demand, that you can save with mass purchasing, that you need promotion and selling and training.

I gather from reading your book, Be My Guest, *that your family, particularly your mother, had considerable influence on you.*

Yes. I recall that every now and then, when I was particularly successful, somebody in the family would kind of knock the air out a bit. I came home one time and told my mother, "You are looking at a man with hotels now valued at forty-one million dollars."

She retorted, "You don't look a bit different to me, except you have got a spot on your tie."

It was apparent in reading your book that three touch-stones in your life have been your faith, hard work and vision. What personal qualities do you think are essential to success in any line of endeavor?

Well, I'll tell you. Something that I have strictly adhered to is to have integrity, never under any circumstances to deceive anybody, to have your word good.

Under no circumstances deviate from that.

In operating internationally, what procedure do you think is best to follow? Or does it vary with each particular country? I know you have some partnership arrangements with governments.

We like to make deals where we have the government in with us; then we don't have any trouble. We have tried, insofar as our international hotels are concerned, to say, "We will operate this hotel. You build it, you furnish it; we will provide the operating capital, we will provide the staff, and from then on you won't have any work. And we will divide up the profits, two-thirds to you—one-third to us." That is what we try to do.

How did you arrive at that two-thirds–one-third?

We just figured it was a fair deal, and it has turned out fine for them and for us.

17

Real Estate: Building Small

Conrad Hilton made his name known by decorating the world with huge buildings, great dazzling structures whose gloss and glitter made them stark monuments to money. Merely strolling into a Hilton hotel for a humble glass of beer somehow makes one feel richer, as though the effluvium of wealth exuding from the walls is somehow absorbed into one's wallet by osmosis. Now we'll look at a family group that achieved similar fame and similar wealth by an entirely different route.

The Levitts—a father and two sons—erected buildings that were precisely the opposite of Hilton's. The Levitts specialized in small, single-family houses that were deliberately designed to be as inexpensive as possible. They invented ways of doing this more effectively than any builder in the world had ever done it before. Their family name—and the associated name "Levittown"—became famous throughout the United States and through much of the Western world.

There are architects, sociologists and others who complain that the Levitts created aesthetic and social monstrosities, caricatures of suburbia, great, bleak, barrackslike tracts of look-alike homes that came to be inhabited by think-alike people. There have been congressmen who grumbled that the Levitts got their start as shameless war profiteers, launching their fabulous business largely on a cushion of the taxpayers' money. The Levitts have never lacked for critics. But whether or not these criticisms are valid, two facts can hardly be argued with: The Levitts built houses for people who could not otherwise have afforded to live in neighborhoods half so pleasant. And, giving sound value for money received every inch of the way, they made themselves very, very rich.

The Levitts:
One Hundred Million Dollars

The only member of the fabulous trio who still survives is the older son, William, a short man with a faint resemblance to actor William Powell. He sold the business in 1968 for some $92 million worth of ITT stock and today, in his middle 60s, enjoys the life of an elderly international playboy, equipped with a 237-foot oceangoing yacht and a glamorous French wife. But all the world's pleasures tend to bore him from time to time, and once in a while he comes back to see how things are going at Levitt and Sons. He can't keep his hand out of the building business. He dreams of grandiose new ventures. His biggest dream—perhaps the biggest ever dreamed by any man, anywhere—is that of going out into the wilderness somewhere and building a complete, self-contained, perfectly organized city from the ground up. —

He might actually do it. The very, very rich tend to find themselves restless in retirement. Their money itself doesn't bring them total enjoyment. What they enjoy is the game of getting it.

The Levitt empire was founded in 1929 on New York's Long Island. Abraham Levitt, an obscure middle-class citizen, had started a career as a lawyer but had found that profession not to his taste. Looking for something else to do, he became aware that some Long Island home builders were growing moderately rich. New York City was growing rapidly, and Long Island's bedroom communities were filling up with people. Each town was expanding centrifugally. As the central area filled, builders would buy cheap land out on the fringe and put up new houses. That fringe would fill, and the builders would extract their profits and move out to the next fringe.

Abraham Levitt decided to build a house. His older son, William, was just then graduating from New York University with business and economics courses under his belt. Father and son went into the building business together. They built a house, quickly sold it for a good profit, thereby improved their credit rating, borrowed bank money and bought several more fringe-area lots. Levitt and Sons was on its way.

Abraham's other son, Alfred, four years younger than

William, was just starting college. The family building business intrigued him so much that he wanted to quit college and plunge in with his father and brother. But Abraham insisted that he complete his formal education. Alfred consoled himself by studying architecture.

The family business grew slowly and erratically through the depression. There was nothing particularly noteworthy about Levitt and Sons at this stage. It was just one of thousands of small building outfits scattered all over the United States. It was basically similar to all the others. As *Fortune* was later to remark, the building business in those days was "the shame of American capitalism." It was the only major industry that hadn't figured out how to gain the economies of mass production or big-scale corporate organization. All home builders in America were small builders, putting up one or two houses at a time.

As early as 1935 Abraham and his two sons were talking about this "shame" without seeing any clear way to do anything about it. Abraham was the social thinker of the trio. He liked to talk about inexpensive housing as a kind of moral debt that capitalism owed to the people. Bill was the aggressive, driving businessman and the risk taker. He believed it would be possible to build homes on a mass-production basis, sell them for about one-third less than comparable homes built in the conventional way and still come out with a pleasing profit. Alfred, the architect, worried about the possible shoddiness of mass housing. He concluded in the end that excellence of design could be built into mass housing very cheaply, since the architect's and landscaper's fees could be divided among many houses instead of being reflected in the price of just one.

But money was tight in the mid-1930s, and the Levitts' credit standing was shaky—as was almost every builder's—and all the talk about cheap housing was only talk.

Levitt and Sons built many houses in the 1930s—but built them in the standard way, one by one. They were sound houses, and they were cleverly situated in neighborhoods where land values are still rising today. Some early Levitt homes cost $10,000 when new and today fetch prices in the range of $70,000 to $80,000. But those were not the homes that made the Levitts rich.

Early in World War Two the Levitts suddenly got a chance

to try what they had been dreaming about. The U.S. government wanted somebody to build 1600 houses at Norfolk, Virginia, for war workers. The houses had to be cheap, and they had to go up fast. The government put the project up for competitive bidding.

Few other builders in the country, if any, had been dreaming the same mad dreams as the Levitts. Most builders, in bidding on the Norfolk contract, based cost and time estimates on their previous experience in putting up one or a few houses at a time. Levitt and Sons, instead, took a wild gamble. For years Abraham and his sons had been talking about mass production, and they had arrived at some vague notions of the amount of money that might be saved by this method. The method had never been seriously tried, certainly never on the scale of 1600 houses. There was no past experience to draw on. For all anybody knew, the Levitts' dreams were pure nonsense. All the same, Levitt and Sons submitted a bid based on the idea of mass production. It was the low bid—so far below the second-place bid, in fact, that government procurement officers at first thought it must be a typographical error.

"No," said Abraham when one of the officers phoned, "it's no error. That's our bid."

There was a long pause while the officer collected his thoughts. Finally he said quietly, "Good God, man, you're going to go bankrupt." And he hung up.

The Levitts did not go bankrupt. To their delight, the reality turned out to be even better than the dream. They bought lumber and other materials in huge volume at low prices. They cut the lumber by machine, all at once, instead of having individual carpenters saw it by hand. They signed up electrical and plumbing contractors at low rates because of the enormous volume of work involved. And in the end they not only walked away from Norfolk with a tidy profit, but they finished the project several months earlier than they or anyone else had thought possible.

The firm of Levitt and Sons had at last found itself.

After the war, as other builders watched popeyed, the first mass-produced Levittown arose on Long Island. The Levitts started by buying several thousand acres of potato fields. Then they duplicated their Norfolk trick on a scale about ten times as big. In the five years 1947 to 1951 they built 17,450 assembly-line homes on that vast tract, plus some 2000 other homes on smaller tracts elsewhere. The staggering five-year total of nearly 20,000 houses had a value of something like $170 million.

The Levittown homes sold in the price range of $8000 to $10,000. (Resale values today: around $35,000). These prices were so ridiculously low that Levitt and Sons hardly had to do any selling. Buyers literally lined up to sign contracts. In the end Levittown, New York, became a community of 75,000 people.

It was a feat that dazzled the construction industry. For centuries builders had been laboriously erecting houses one by one. And now, suddenly, a builder had come along and erected an entire town.

There were many critics who didn't like what the Levitts had done. Some didn't like the way Levittown looked. "It's a huge suburban slum and will get slummier as it gets older," grumped one prominent architect. It didn't. The fact that most of the homes have quadrupled in value since they were built indicates Levittown is still considered a desirable address.

Other critics didn't like the huge amounts of money Levitt and Sons piled up. Some congressmen were particularly unhappy over the fact that most Levittown homes were sold—and the Levitts' profits made—on the basis of government-guaranteed mortgages.

This wasn't the result of any chicanery by the Levitts. After the war the national shortage of housing had been so severe that the Federal Housing Administration, the Veterans Administration and other agencies went to great lengths in efforts to help builders build and buyers buy. The government offered to shoulder some of the builders' risk, supply some of their needed capital and absorb some of the buyers' interest payments in various attractive deals. The Levitts, like other builders, simply took advantage of these gifts from Washington. Later the same Congress that had authorized the gifts took Levitt and others to task for accepting those gifts.

In a Senate hearing in 1954 Bill Levitt shyly admitted that his company had made a gross profit of about five million dollars on the first 4028 Levittown houses. The senators gasped with pious horror. But Levitt and Sons had not in fact done anything that any smart businessman wouldn't do.

Old Abraham Levitt died in the late 1950s. The two sons carried their company to new heights. They built other Levittowns, in Pennsylvania and New Jersey. When Alfred died in the middle 1960s, Bill became sole owner of the giant company and enlarged it still more. The public seemed to be shying away from large tracts of look-alike houses; so he now spread his operations into smaller tracts scattered all over the country and overseas. By the late 1960s he was operating on two new Long Island sites, three in New Jersey, three in the area of Washington, D.C., and others in Florida, Puerto Rico, the Chicago area and the suburbs of Paris.

The assembly-line techniques were still paying off. While the national housing industry sank morosely into its own private depression in the late 1960s, Levitt and Sons built and sold more dollars' worth of houses every year. By 1968 the company's sales were running at a rate of about $150 million a year—roughly the value of the original Levittown.

Levitt and Sons was now a large, juicy company. It attracted the hungry eye of Harold S. Geneen, a conglomerate builder in the style of Jim Ling. Geneen was chairman and president of International Telephone and Telegraph, and it seemed to him Levitt and Sons might be a lively addition to ITT's diverse and growing family. He made an offer.

To Bill Levitt, the sole owner, ITT's proposal offered an ideal way to change his huge but nonliquid equity into cash. He accepted and walked away with some 898,000 shares of ITT's common stock, then worth about $92 million on the New York Stock Exchange. Putting this stock together with his other investments and properties, he was worth considerably more than $100 million at the age of 61.

U.S. antitrust lawyers later decided the ITT-Levitt merger had not been such a good idea. ITT was given until August 1974 to divest itself of the building company. Nobody inside or outside the company seems quite sure how the divestiture will be accomplished or where Levitt and Sons will go afterward. There is some guessing around Wall Street that Bill Levitt, still in robust health and full of energy and perhaps bored by his retirement, might want to buy back a controlling interest in the company he helped bring into the world. He might want to use it as the vehicle for some of his grandiose city-building dreams.

"He hasn't told us what he wants to do, and as far as I

know, he hasn't told anybody," said an executive recently at the company's modern headquarters at Lake Success, New York. "We don't know where we're headed. The company will stay alive whether Bill Levitt comes back or not, of course. But I hope he comes back. It might be exciting to ride through the 1970s chasing his visions."

18

The Psychology
of the Rich

The question has fascinated psychologists for at least a century: Why do only certain men grow rich?

The question has irritated the rich for almost as long. Why do psychologists come around asking such nutty questions?

The fact is that nobody, including the rich themselves, knows for sure what internal aches and itches operate in a man to lift him above the great sea of the unrich. Clement Stone and other fortune teachers believe they know some of the answers, but most observers feel these can't be all the answers and probably aren't even the main ones. Not only are the psychological causes of wealth unknown; there is a strong suspicion that all attempts to elucidate them have been a solemn and scholarly waste of time.

Some highly respected observers say flatly that the rich, as a group, have no special personality traits that mark them as different from anybody else. One such observer is Dr. Frederick Herzberg, a psychology professor at Case Western Reserve University who acts as a consultant to corporations and government agencies. His specialty is "work motivation." He is, in a sense, a fortune teacher. But he candidly admits he doesn't know what drives and hang-ups make one man rise to wealth while another man, starting at the same gate, shambles down to oblivion. "There is no communality among highly successful men," says Dr. Herzberg. "Their personality types are as varied as all other people's."

Another observer is Dr. Eugene Emerson Jennings, psychologist at Michigan State's Graduate School of Business Administration and also a consultant to several corporations —among them IBM. "I did a fantastic amount of testing back in the 1950s," he says, "trying to isolate personality traits by which we could predict how far a man might rise in or out of the company. But we've stopped testing at IBM. We found we couldn't predict anything reliably."

Dr. Jennings remarks sourly that the business world teems with psychological-test peddlers who claim they can predict employees' future success—can spot one young man as a future entrepreneur and another as doomed to failure. "A fellow from Kansas called me up a while back and said he had a foolproof test. I told him OK, fine, we'll give the test to the next thousand candidates who turn up at IBM. And I told him that just to make things interesting, he was to put up a thousand-dollar performance bond to show his faith. If the majority of the candidates did what he predicted over the next ten years, he was to get his thousand bucks back. Fair enough? Well, he hung up, and I never heard from him again."

The very, very rich tend to share this view that it is futile to probe for wealth-making personality traits. One man with strong opinions on the subject was Joseph P. Kennedy, father of the noted political clan. He was worth something like a third of a billion dollars (main route: the stock market) when he died a few years ago. A Princeton University psychology student once sent him a long questionnaire purporting to probe his psyche to its darkest depths. Kennedy shot the questionnaire back unanswered, along with a curt note: "Dear Mr. ———: I am rich because I have a lot of money."

Old Joe Kennedy's answer may be the only reliable one there is. All the same, let's see what other answers have been proposed. If you and I hope to grow rich, it might be interesting—it might even be useful—to see whether our personalities resemble those of the wealthy. We may discover ourselves to be totally unlike these unusual men in emotional makeup. If that turns out to be so, perhaps we can then save ourselves a lot of time and needless misery. We may decide we aren't of the capital-gathering breed after all. Our indicated course will then be simply to relax and enjoy what paltry income we've got.

● ● ●

The psychoanalytic theories of moneymaking are so weird that, although they presumably make sense to psychoanalysts, they sound like utter gibberish to nearly everybody else. To attempt an analysis of these theories here would be to step into a quicksand of verbiage from which we might never reach firm land again. So let's steer clear. A quick look from a safe distance ought to satisfy us.

Sigmund Freud addressed himself to the subject of money in a 1908 paper called *Character and Anal Eroticism*. By a bewilderingly circuitous route, he arrived at the notion that money is to an adult what feces are to a child. Evidently (so goes the Freudian reasoning), a child conceives feces to be part of his body and fears to lose them. If he becomes obsessed with this fear for one reason or another, later in life he may be obsessed with a thundering drive to collect material possessions.

Well, all right. To each his own theory. It must be remembered that Freud had a huge love of language, and one can suspect that he sometimes invented emotional hang-ups for the sheer joy of making up phrases about them.

Later generations of psychoanalysts have arrived at other theories, also by long and winding routes. Writing in the *Psychoanalytic Quarterly* years ago, Dr. Otto Fenichel of Prague and Los Angeles said that "the drive to amass wealth seems to be a special form of the instinct of possession." Clear enough so far. This instinct, however, is "a special form of bodily narcissism and an expression of the fear of bodily injury." The most important form of this fear is "the fear of genital injury." Therefore, says Dr. Fenichel, obsessive wealth gatherers are that way because they suffer from "castration anxiety."

The wealthy men we've visited in this gallery would no doubt be interested to learn these odd things about themselves. Some might feel inclined to argue. The problem with psychoanalytic theory is that it can be argued about all night long and no firm conclusions can ever be reached. So let's now step onto firmer ground. Let's look at some traits of the rich that various researchers believe can be demonstrated— and that show up in a tangible way among the men in our gallery.

Sex: male. It is not a statistical accident that all the very, very rich individuals in this gallery are men. The fact is, there are no women now living in the United States—at least none known to *Fortune,* to Ferdinand *(Super-Rich)* Lundberg or to me—who have started from scratch and amassed as much as $100 million on their own.

There are some women who have almost made it. The late cosmetics tycoon Helena Rubinstein was very rich. Actress-entrepreneur Lucille Ball may be the richest self-made woman now living. Her net worth is in the $50-million range. She could conceivably reach the level of $100 million some day, but she hasn't done it yet. There are no women among the great self-made rich.

Why not?

I was afraid you'd ask that.

The women's liberation movement would, of course, argue that women don't become very, very rich because our cultural and economic setup denies them the opportunity to do so. Some psychologists (mostly male) think, on the other hand, that women simply don't have the great capital-accumulating drives—that few or none would become immoderately rich even if all the sex barriers were removed.

"Women tend to be somewhat more sensible about this than men are," says one psychiatrist, earnestly begging not to be identified. "A woman wants enough money to make herself and her family comfortable—enough, perhaps, to enable her to live in luxury. But once she reaches that level of wealth, she usually quits striving for more. Many men, on the other hand, go on furiously piling up wealth long after they've got more than they can possibly spend. It's hard to imagine a female Howard Hughes."

This may be so. In the career of the typical American family, the wife starts out by helping her husband increase his income and maybe even goading him to try harder. But when they reach middle age and a comfortable degree of wealth, she performs an about-face. He goes on driving himself while she, worried about ulcers and heart attacks, faces in the opposite direction and tries to slow him down.

It's hard to say for sure whether these differences are brought on by social and cultural forces or are part of the two sexes' built-in equipment. You can get an argument on the subject at any cocktail party. But let's not argue here. Let's simply say that if you want to be very, very rich, your chances are best if you start out male.

Child-parent problems. Looking over our gilded gallery, it's remarkable how many of these stupendously successful men lost one or both parents early in life through death or divorce. More than half of them, in fact, went through that wounding experience. Is this a statistical accident, or does it mean something?

It is apparently no accident. Researchers working with far larger samples than ours have been struck by the high incidence of parental death or divorce in the lives of the self-made rich. One such sampling was made in the 1960s under a research grant from the Small Business Administration. Three college professors—David Moore of Cornell, Orvis Collins and Darab Unwalla of Michigan State—went out and interviewed the "founding entrepreneurs" of 110 companies. "The theme of parental death crops up repeatedly," they reported in their book, *The Enterprising Man.* "The picture that comes through from the interviews is one of the lonely child, grubby fists in tear-filled eyes, accepting the loss and facing a dangerous future. . . ."

Why does the death or going away of a parent make a youngster start out to become wealthy? The three researchers suggest a couple of possibilities. One is that the bereaved child from then on has a massive sense of insecurity. He sets out to get so much money that he can never be left stranded again. Another possibility is that the loss of a parent makes him more than usually self-reliant. In trying to heal his emotional wound, he convinces himself that he doesn't really need the parent; he can hack it on his own. While most of us meekly bumble through life working for other people (the company becomes the parent), an orphaned or half-orphaned youngster may try instead to climb the economic ladder by himself, as head of his own business.

School problems. Another remarkable fact about the men in the gallery is that fully half of them are high-school dropouts, and only a third bothered to finish college. This tendency of capital gatherers to scorn formal education, or to find it unpalatable for some reason or other, has baffled and fascinated researchers ever since the phenomenon of wealth first became a subject of academic study. In a classic statistical study of 600 millionaires in 1925, sociologist Pitirim Sorokin found to his surprise that only 11.7 percent had college degrees. Sorokin mused, "This means that perhaps Andrew Carnegie was right when he said, 'College education is not necessary to business success.' " It wasn't necessary in Carnegie's day, and it wasn't in Sorokin's day, and it still doesn't seem to be today.

The tendency of the great rich to be late bloomers—to be misfits in school, to seem earmarked for failure in their early years—is intriguing to those of us who haven't yet made our first $100 million. We, too, must be late bloomers. The subject is interesting enough to deserve a chapter all to itself. We'll probe it in more detail in chapter 22.

Marital problems. Pitirim Sorokin was also struck by the fact that, among his 600 millionaires, divorce was statistically twice as common as in the general U.S. population. In Sorokin's era as today, the divorces and other marital scrapes and scandals of the very rich made good reading and sold newspapers. The rich seemed to have more marriage and sex problems than other people, but most scholarly observers guessed this was simply because the rich were more visible. It was startling to have Sorokin come along and prove statistically what the public had long accepted as dogma: The richer you are, the more likely you are to be divorced.

The men in our gallery faithfully follow the trend. Half have been divorced at least once.

Why? Money is one obvious answer. Divorce is expensive. For the average middle-income salary earner it is so expensive as to be, in many cases, financially crippling. The very rich often find divorce expenses acutely painful but never crippling. The simple fact is that it is easier for a rich man to get divorced than a middle-income man.

But there seems to be more to it than that. One psychologist who has made a years-long study of the self-made rich is Dr. Alfred E. Messer, a professor at Emory University in Atlanta and chief of the Georgia Mental Health Institute's Family Studies Laboratory. Dr. Messer, along with many other students of the American family, finds that self-made rich men often have a peculiar lack of warmth, an inability to form a close, lasting relationship with man, woman or child.

This lack stems from the same forces that make such a man into a capital gatherer in the first place. "The man's childhood is likely to have been rough," says Dr. Messer. "The typical story is that of a parent dying or going away or—what amounts to the same thing—rejecting the child, abandoning him emotionally. The child grows up with the understandable feeling that he can't rely on other people, he must prove himself worthy *by himself*. He seeks to prove it with money. In one typical case I had a patient who habitually carried four thousand dollars around in his pocket, his way of showing he'd made it on his own, he didn't need anybody."

An emotional setup such as this doesn't make for a warm and loving marriage, Dr. Messer points out. "The typical self-made man often thinks of his wife the way he thinks of his money. She is a jewel, a bauble. He has married her to increase his apparent worth. He wants the world to judge him by the prettiness of this jewel."

Two things can go wrong with such an arrangement, of course. The first possibility is that the jewel will fade, and the man must then go out to find a new one. The second possibility is that the jewel will prefer to be a woman. "She will make emotional demands on the man—demands that he isn't prepared to meet. She wants him to confide in her; she wants to share his problems and his life. This is exactly what he doesn't want."

Dr. Messer finds all this rather sad. "This country needs the self-made man, the enterpriser," he says. "Obviously, somebody has to start and run the businesses that produce the national income and provide the jobs. But our entrepreneurs often achieve these ends at great cost to themselves."

Dr. Messer seems to be stating a peculiarly baffling paradox. The type of man most likely to grow very, very rich is the type of man least likely to enjoy it.

Conversely, those of us who might enjoy it may not make it.

Work worship. On the other hand, perhaps the rich enjoy their lives after all. It makes no sense for one man to say what another man is supposed to enjoy. It might be that the very, very rich derive as much pleasure from their work as most ordinary men derive from their marriages, children, sports, hobbies and TV sets.

For a worship of work, an absolute love of it, is notable among the shared traits of the great self-made rich. It is a commonly accepted item of public dogma that the rich spend lives of idle and sometimes deliciously sinful luxury, but this is an illusion arising from the fact that stories of the rich at play make better copy than stories of the rich at work. A tycoon might work 30 straight 14-hour days, but no newspaper would consider the fact worth mentioning. But let the poor fellow seek a day of rest, let him be discovered crocked at a party, let him be seen chasing bird and bunny, and the garishly embellished story will appear in the next day's society columns.

The rich work—either because they enjoy it or because they feel driven to do it. Many of them (Joe Hirshhorn, for instance) admit quite frankly that their compulsion to work has destroyed their marriages and hurt their relationships with their children and perhaps damaged other components of their personal lives. They sometimes talk about this in a sad and apologetic way, but they always end with a shrug. There's nothing they can do about it. Work is part of their being. They can no more easily change their work habits than they can change the color of their eyes.

The *Chicago Tribune* once asked reporter Richard Gosswiller to roam around the city, talk to a lot of rich men and ask what advice they'd give to a man seeking wealth today. Gosswiller's report appears in chapter 23, but there was an odd little fact that he didn't include in the report, an apt demonstration of the compulsion to work that exists among the rich.

"One of the things I still find hardest to believe," says Gosswiller, "is that almost all these men were in their offices when I called. You'd think, with all that money, they'd be off somewhere relaxing and enjoying it. But, no, they were all hard at work. It occurred to me that maybe this was the real secret of getting rich, even though none of them mentioned it: Be compulsive."

19

The Promoters:
Of Ideas

We've contemplated the career of Clement Stone, salesman. Now let's look at two men who are Stone-plus-something. Not only salesmen—promoters.

What is a promoter? *Webster's New International Dictionary* defines him as somebody who ". . . sets on foot and takes the preliminary steps in a scheme or undertaking. . . ." Well, yes, that's true as far as it goes. An initiator, in other words.

But that definition could be applied with perfect accuracy to almost everybody you'll meet in this book. Something must be lacking from the dictionary definition, for the word fits only a few, even stretched as far as it will stretch.

The truth is, the word *promoter*, as Americans use it, has a strong emotional element, an element of attitude and approach that is very hard to define with an acceptable degree of precision. A promoter is something like a salesman only more so. He sells, yes. As *Webster's* tells us, he also initiates. But he does more. He follows through. He tends and nurtures. He inseminates, he raises to maturity, he harvests. And he does all this in a brash, aggressive, unembarrassed, brassy, pushy way that is believed around the world to be, in some obscure way, peculiarly American. (The accuracy of this belief would be an intriguing subject of inquiry for some other book, not for this one. My personal observation is that the average healthy Swiss or Frenchman, with a good head of steam behind him and a large magnetic pile of money in front of him, can outbrass the average American without even trying. But no matter. What's important is that the belief exists: All promoters are Americans. As a matter of fact there is no word in either French or German that has precisely the same meaning, with the same connotations and emotional overtones, as *promoter* in English.)

A promoter tends to shock people by his way of doing things. Sometimes—as in the first case you'll read below—he is accused of behaving dishonestly, of breaking or bending the law. In fact, the word carries with it a faint aroma of shady dealings. Yet it often appears, when his deals are examined closely, that they are neither unlawful nor even shady. They are only clever. This, plus the cheerful brassiness with which they are carried out, can startle and irritate those who are watching from the sidelines. "Why, the gall of the man!" the sideliners gasp. And, deep inside, each sideliner asks himself, "Why don't I ever have the guts to do something like that?" The promoter's reputation for trickiness springs from the observers' jealousy more often than from any moral failing in the promoter himself.

Perhaps it could be said, in the end, that the promoter's key character trait is impatience. He wants to make things happen *fast*. Driven by this urge, he hustles twice as fast as other men. He refuses to be stopped by things that other men would meekly accept as barriers. If he can't go around a barrier, he kicks it down. He makes a lot of noise and doesn't seem to care. And people keep saying, "Why, the gall. . . ."

The gall of Glenn W. Turner, the first of this breed we'll visit, cannot be doubted. Turner began life as the son of a dirt-poor farmer in South Carolina. He tried being a salesman of other people's products but didn't make a go of it— indicating that a salesman and a promoter are not quite the same thing. Then he borrowed $5000 and, by sheer promotion, multiplied it in three short years to a fortune of more than $100 million. In the process he made many people very angry—including a number of law-enforcement officials.

As reporter Thomas Thompson tells us below in his witty and somewhat startled way, Glenn Turner is essentially a promoter of ideas, not things. It's true that his original small company was formed to sell cosmetics, and it's true that cosmetics are things. But it was the *idea* of beauty rather than the *thing* of cosmetics that Turner really set out to promote, and from that base he branched out into a bewildering variety of other ventures, pyramiding one idea on top of another.

One of Turner's newest ideas is a success course similar to those of Clement Stone and Paul Meyer, the Waco fortune teacher. You'll note that some of Turner's success formulas resemble Stone's and Meyer's quite closely, and some of Turner's self-needling phrases and course titles ("Do it now"; "Positive mental attitude") are pure Stone. But the main title of Turner's course is pure Turner: "Dare to Be Great!"

The word *dare* and the exclamation mark, these are pure promoter.

Glenn Turner:
One Hundred Million Dollars*
by Thomas Thompson

One's first few moments around Glenn W. Turner are spent in accommodating to his appearance, as a man might bite on a gold coin to see if it is real. The first time I laid eyes on the fellow, he was wearing a double-knit suit whose green hue seemed copied from a neon sign, elevated boots constructed of ivory-colored unborn calf, a toupee carefully sculpted to his head and a new pair of mesh underwear briefs. I am privy to the latter fact because Turner was so enthusiastic as to style and stride that when descriptive words failed him, he quickly unfastened his trousers and let them down momentarily so that all his office—astonished visitors and nonplussed aides alike—could see.

The office itself takes *some* getting used to. It has eggshell carpet deep enough to hide in, a massive desk on which rests an open Bible and a silver Rolls-Royce toy (when one twists the spare tire, it becomes a music box and tinkles *The Impossible Dream*), furniture of snowy vinyl and suede appropriate to a high roller's suite in any good Las Vegas hotel, a wide-screen picture window of bulletproof glass whose view is of an interior business corridor, and two dominant oil paintings. One painting is directly behind Turner's chair and represents a sharecropper trudging behind a mule. "This is Mr. Turner's yesterday," explains an aide, referring to her employer's birth and childhood on a South Carolina farm. The second painting, which Turner faces as

*Originally published under the title *Dare to Be Great*, by Thomas Thompson, *Life* magazine, May 28, 1971. Copyright © Time Inc. Reprinted with permission.

he does business, shows a rocket ship streaking through the cosmos, onward and upward through a shower of comets and exploding stars. "This," says the assistant with an almost reverent prophecy in her voice, "is Mr. Turner's tomorrow."

It is today, the here and now, that makes Turner, who is only 36, of interest, an only-in-America phenomenon. A little more than three years back he was broke and bankrupt—a familiar condition for the eighth-grade dropout whose lack of education is matched by the fact that he was born with a harelip and still speaks with that unfortunate handicap. But, as he tells the story, he borrowed $5000 in 1967 to start a cosmetics company, "the field with the highest profit potential in business—they powder 'em when they come into the world and paint 'em when they go out"—and set up shop in a one-room office in Orlando, Florida, so chosen because that city was near both Cape Kennedy and the then-just-announced Disney World. He named it Koscot Interplanetary, Inc.

Using unorthodox business techniques, so unorthodox that at least 20 state attorneys general have investigated him and several were moved to file various court actions against him, Turner claims nonetheless to have built an empire that has swept the country from sea to sea, moved into at least nine foreign countries on four continents, branched out into helicopter manufacturing and sales, a wig company, a mink house that markets everything from fur-covered golf tees to $5000 maxicoats, a music-recording firm and several other enterprises that at last count consisted of 37 corporations employing some 200,000 people (mostly salesmen) and valued —by Turner's own estimate, since he owns 100 percent of the stock—at somewhere between $100 million and $200 million.

His latest endeavor, a self-motivation course called "Dare to Be Great," will someday become, predicts Turner, "the international language of the world." Turner dreamed up the course as a way to spread his personal philosophy, i.e., that within every human being lies a great pool of resources largely untapped, doomed to grow stagnant. He originally planned to call his course "Dare to Be Big," but he feared that women, particularly plump women, would not want to be any bigger. Now he has grandiose plans to install it as a course in every high school in America ("If we could start each day with 'Dare to Be Great,' then there'd be no more student protest"), to build colleges around its philosophy, to translate it into the languages of the world. Already linguists are converting the lessons into German and Italian.

"Dare to Be Great" comes in a large, fat black briefcase that, when opened, contains 20 tape cassettes, a tape recorder and a white plastic notebook that repeats—in print—the same material on the tapes. There are 20 chapters, called "orbits" in deference to Turner's enchantment with outer space. The introduction page offers advice to the student who wishes to become great:

"Congratulations! You have just decided to change your life. You are now in the process of becoming a new man. William James, the father of American philosophy, said, 'The greatest discovery of my generation is that we have learned we can alter our lives by altering our attitudes of mind.'

"Play the cassette tapes over and over again. The power of timed repetition is immeasurable. For example, tell a person something repeatedly and this is what happens: The first time he says, 'I don't believe it.' The second time he says, 'Well, maybe so.' The third time he says, 'Well, it kind of makes sense.' The fourth time, 'I believe I'll try that.' The fifth time, 'That's great, I used it today!' "

When one browses through the textbook and listens to the cassettes, the material seems innocuous, familiar, sometimes naïve, hardly destined to wake up a sick and weary world. It is Dale Carnegie, Émile Coué and all the other self-improvement wheezes all over again. There are quotations from Disraeli, Goethe, Chesterfield, Seneca, Emerson, even Napoleon—"Imagination rules the world." Mostly it is a potpourri of salesman patter and a coach's pep talk: "Develop a Positive Mental Attitude! Remember Everybody's Name! Do It Now! Don't Put It Off Until Tomorrow! If you have the intelligence to lean down and tie your shoestrings, you can reach up and lace the stars!"

But when one learns that it can cost up to $5000 to take the complete course—four "adventures" that will eventually consist of some 40 tapes and a dozen seminars—one realizes that the amount of money Turner could make off his philosophy might someday approximate the budget of an emerging, if not developing, country.

Turner approaches each day as if he had just been shot out of the Zacchini Brothers circus cannon. He comes on like a hurricane boring across central Florida. He shakes hands with a grip that could rip a telephone book in half. "I love to lift weights," he explains. "It makes you feel you can pick up the side of a house. You can't, of course; so instead you go out and do something *great!*" *Great* is the key word. It pops up in the man's every fourth sentence, paired with an equal number of *Fan-tas-tics!* He travels more than a presidential candidate does the week before elections. One day's schedule might read, "Breakfast meeting, San Francisco; lunch address, Reno; dinner speech, Phoenix; 10:00 P.M. conference, El Pasó." The schedule could just as easily read Singapore or London or Sydney, because he has been to all of them in the past few months, spreading the word, selling "Dare to Be Great."

"In London three hundred people came to the airport in a rain and cried when I left. They begged me to stay there and help them," said Turner, who seemed totally amazed at the reaction. Fifteen years earlier, in the U.S. Army, his sergeant had detailed him to scrubbing toilets to keep him and his harelip out of sight.

He travels four days out of five. There is scant time for his wife, Alice, a tall, gentle, blue-eyed Tennessee blonde who affects complicated hairdos and who could command the front line in any theatrical production where a certain remote sexiness was required. When he does find an off afternoon, Turner gathers up Alice, their three sons and baby daughter, and they set off on a houseboat, meandering up the St. Johns River, past cypress, past suspicious-looking logs that *might* be alligators, into the quiet and the stillness. Turner pulls his engine back to its most gentle speed when passing an old black fisherman asleep on a bank. "I commit myself so totally to my family on these days," he says, "that there can be no doubt in their minds as to my love. They understand why I can't be with them more."

Nor is there time for a social or intellectual life. The last book Turner remembers reading and liking was *The Carpetbaggers.* "I'm gonna be bigger than Howard Hughes someday," he said as he shut its cover. When he dines, he does not look at his food or, quite probably, even taste it. He went to see *Love Story* and four days later could not remember being there, because his mind had been racing throughout; his own dreams and schemes were more vivid than anything he could see on the screen.

On a very recent day, while scuttling across the country 40,000 feet up in his Lear Jet, one of 11 aircraft operated by his personal fleet, Glenn-Aire, Turner was engrossed in plans to (1) buy or start a newspaper, because he is upset with the existing publication in Orlando, which often attacks him or, worse, ignores him, (2) start a panty-hose company, (3) create a cash credit card wherein a customer would get a ten-percent discount at a vast network of stores around the country if he paid in hard money, (4) build a chain of motels called Commuter Inns whose mother house would be a 42-story wonder in Orlando, erected in the shape of a rocket ship and whose guests would endure both countdown and blast-off to reach their rooms.

And, while working his way through an enormous stack of mail, he suddenly looked up and announced, "I'm thinking about starting my own post office. I have the network already. I can deliver anything anywhere in one day."

The fact that Turner was flying at the moment from Orlando to Boston, where he would address a mock United Nations Assembly sponsored by Harvard law students and where he would coincidentally attend a dinner for possible Democratic presidential candidate Senator Harold Hughes, was not lost on me, either. Particularly when a remark that Turner had made a day or two earlier was so fresh in mind. He had been showing me around his now-vast headquarters in Orlando, a blue metallic building that seems to stretch on longer than a Cape Kennedy hangar, and I had asked if he was interested in politics, in running for elective office. "I wouldn't want to be a senator or a president," he had said. "But I wouldn't mind being a king maker." He said that he would never be so presumptuous as to tell his huge number of employees how to vote—"but it certainly wouldn't hurt some candidate if I announced how I *personally* was voting."

Shortly thereafter we passed a chamber of humming computers, and Turner tossed out a remark that seemed to illuminate itself in red lights and a warning siren. "I have the name of every registered voter in Florida on that computer," he said, "and four years from now maybe I'll have every voter in America on there."

"Why would you want that?" I asked.

"You never can tell," Turner said. "Might come in handy someday."

Glenn Turner is, of course, that American classic—super-huckster. He looks like the man you bought your last used car from or the fellow who knocked at your door with that fantastic encyclopedia offer. He is part carnival barker, part fundamentalist faith healer with all the raw sexual force of an Elmer Gantry, part snake-oil salesman. But more than that he is a box of paradoxes packed inside a crate of enigmas and delivered to the center of a sideshow hall of mirrors. Every time I was tempted to yell "flimflam man" and zip up my wallet pocket, I would discover something disarming, like the fact that Turner is one of the largest employers of handicapped and mentally retarded people in the state of Florida. He has taken on sponsorship and distribution for Flame of Hope perfume, that fragrance manufactured by the retarded and chairmaned by Mrs. Rose Kennedy. He has donated one million dollars to build an opportunity center for the handicapped and retarded in his native South Carolina.

On his personal staff are many people to whom fate seemed to have dealt losing hands. A pair of 19-year-old twin dwarfs, orphans, only 33 inches high, joined Turner's company as cosmetics distributors and quickly were promoted to goodwill ambassadors. Now they ride on the Lear Jet, occupying only one seat, and they stand before large audiences and tell how Turner treated them as human beings and changed their lives. A 31-year-old blind man from Maine whose college history degree earned him a job pitting olives in a pizza parlor for $48 a week is now making $30,000 a year for Turner. "Glenn Turner was the spark that set my life on fire," he says.

One recent afternoon a mother brought her mongoloid daughter who painted sunflowers into Turner's building, and though they had no appointment, both were quickly admitted to his private office. "You keep those kind of people away from Turner and that's the quickest way to get fired," said a secretary. Turner interrupted his crowded schedule and spent half an hour talking to the child, buying three of her primitive works for $100 each and sending her home with tears and dignity.

Turner keeps his pockets filled with wads of $100 bills, which he scatters like grass seed on a dying lawn. When he traveled to Mexico City and walked through a peasant slum, he stopped every person he met and bent down and talked in his curious harelipped southern English to people who had no idea what he was saying. But his words seemed to light up their faces even more than the $100 bills he pressed in their hands. He used up all the money he had and ordered his aides to empty their pockets as well.

After his speech at the Harvard convocation, he was invited to Sunday-night supper with a group of students. As he was passing through the cafeteria line, he was abruptly solicited by an SDS member for contributions to a welfare power march on Washington. Turner lectured the hirsute student for several minutes. "If you give a man a fish, you feed him for one day," he said, standing there in a full-length mink coat, "but if you teach him *how* to fish, you feed him for the rest of his life." Then he dropped a $100 bill into the astonished radical's Granger pipe-tobacco can.

While driving down an Orlando boulevard looking for the Florida Citrus Open Invitational golf tournament, of which he was a sponsor, Turner saw a bedraggled-looking man leaning against a bus stop. "See that feller there?" he suddenly cried, thrusting out a gold-clothed arm. "I could make that feller a millionaire in two years!" The man never looked up, unaware that destiny in a blue Cadillac was speeding by. Turner drove on, rattled on. "My teeth may be false," he said, "but my tongue is true. I failed twenty-seven times as a door-to-door sewing-machine salesman. . . . Sometimes I think I'm the reincarnation of Abraham Lincoln, 'cause we think exactly alike. He failed *eighteen* times before he became president!"

At first one assumes that Turner must be a conservative somewhere to the right of Alexander the Great. He is, after all, deeply southern, and he wears on his lapel at all times an American flag—not just any American flag but a bejeweled one cast into ripples that seems almost to furl and unfurl as he speaks of patriotism and respect for the office of the U.S. president. But he turns out to be a moderate Democrat, dovish and disenchanted on Vietnam, outraged when an Orlando landlord refused this spring to lease an apartment to one of his black employees. Eight members of his staff who lived there threatened to move out immediately unless the man was admitted, and Turner threatened to buy the complex himself if all else failed. The black man was accepted.

When Florida's business community rallied massively this year to oppose a corporate tax, Turner went on record as being *for* such a tax, pointing out in speeches that it was only just and proper for business to return part of its good fortune to the state that housed it. And, by his count, Turner has taken several hundred long-haired hippies into his sales organization. "They don't cut their hair for me," he says, "but at least they wash and put on clean clothes. One of them's head of my entire Eye-talian operation."

Morally, Turner says, he conducts himself like Caesar's wife. "I don't drink, smoke or play around," he confided in a speech before the Chicago White Sox, who were interested in signing up for "Dare to Be Great." "In fact, I'm just about perfect."

Turner built his empire on the controversial principle of "multilevel" selling. In essence, he sold distributorships in his cosmetics company that entitled a person not only to sell the Koscot line of beauty aids but to sell subfranchises to others and get a large finder's fee as well. Example: A man purchases a Koscot distributorship for $5000, which theoretically sets him up in business as a cosmetics salesman. But he also earns the right to sign up subdistributors for $2000, and he gets $700 commission on each. When various attorneys general began looking into the fast-growing Koscot operation, it was discovered that a great many distributors were not as interested in selling cosmetics as they were in getting finder's fees.

One attorney general quickly branded it a "pyramid" scheme, another likened it to chain letters, still others cried "lottery" or "fraud" or "sale of unregistered securities." The New York attorney general's office took special note of the fact that Turner's representatives were painting pie-in-the-sky pictures at sales meetings, waving fat checks around and suggesting that Koscot distributors could make $50,000 to $100,000 a year. The New York attorney general calculated that at the end of 1970 there were 1600 distributors in his state alone, and were they all to make the $100,000 by bringing other people into the program, they would have to lure 150,000 more distributors into Koscot within one year, and these would then have to add another 150 million by the end of the second year.

In Pennsylvania, the attorney general noted that each Koscot distributor was encouraged to bring 12 new people into the program a year—only one per month. Surely you can sign up one man a month, the pitch went, perhaps your brother-in-law or your neighbor. But were each of these 12 new people then able to bring another 12, making a total of 144, and were each of these 144 able to bring another 12 in, and so on down the line through 12 tiers, at the bottom of the pyramid would theoretically be 8,916,100,448,256 people —or more than 2000 times the population of the planet earth.

Sales pitches to join Koscot as distributors and subdistributors were made at high-pressure meetings chairmaned by men in silk suits and honeyed voices who spun dreams of Golden Eagles (top salesmen) who made $180,000 a year, Silver Eagles (average salesmen) who made $160,000 and lowly Buzzards (goof-offs, presumably) who managed $120,-000. If a prospect was interested but not interested enough to part with his $2000 or $5000 then and there, he would be invited for a free one-day trip to Orlando, flying on a Turner airplane, in the company of ebullient men who cried out during the journey, "How do you feel?" and roared back to one another, "Grrr-eat!" At Koscot headquarters the prospect would heap his plate with barbecue, watch a color film detailing the history of Glenn Turner's success story, intercut and heavily embroidered with shots of idyllic sunsets on tropical beaches, expensive cars, jet airplanes, spectacular women, of a future on that soft cloud above the dust of everyday life. If the prospect was at last willing but had not sufficient cash, Koscot pitchmen had been known to escort him directly to the bank or loan office, murmuring in his ear all the way.

"The scope of the fraud and misrepresentations and the amounts of money being exacted from unsuspecting citizens . . . is enormous," said the Pennsylvania attorney general in his court proceeding against Koscot. "The social implications are equally enormous when one considers that most of these people who invest in this program will be innocent lambs being led to slaughter by a dream of 'heaven on earth.' Most of these people will go into debt or will convert their life savings, and at least three out of four will be doomed to failure."

When the lawsuits began to mount, Turner announced, "I must be getting successful; I'm told GM is sued eighteen times a day." He sought out famed attorney F. Lee Bailey and said, in introduction, "I have a small problem—me versus the United States." "I always did like a fair fight," answered Bailey.

Bailey remembers listening to the man from Florida for half an hour. "I decided then and there that he was legit," said Bailey. "His business structure was not well set up, but there was nothing wrong with *him*. We shook hands, and I took him on." Bailey has since helped reorganize Turner's domain and brought in more professional eastern accountants and business experts.

Since then Bailey and Turner have pacified most of the complaining states, largely by setting up a distributorship quota in each, one distributor per 7000 people. Specifically, Turner has vowed to deemphasize the "wholesale" aspects of his business, as the selling of subfranchises is called, and emphasize the "retail" end, the selling of cosmetics and allied products. No states have complained about the quality of his cosmetics, and, indeed, some prosecutors have used them and even reordered.

When Turner is introduced at a meeting—he often makes 20 speeches a week, either to sell his products or his philosophies—he does not walk to the podium; he runs! Sometimes he stands up on two folding chairs and rocks back and forth, adding to his remarks the suspense that he could collapse at any moment. He rips off homilies and statistics so rapidly and with such seeming conviction that they begin to sound as gospel: "If you throw dirt, you're bound to lose ground"; "The man who's not running with the ball nobody tries to tackle"; "The only difficulty in climbing the ladder of success is getting through the crowd at the bottom"; "Most people spend more time planning their two-week vacations than they do planning their lives"; "Out of 500 new millionaires in 1966, 52.6 percent never had a high-school degree. I started making my first in 1967 because I knew I had the chance."

Before one speech Turner turned to me and said. "Watch what I can do with these people." The m.c. introduced him as "the establishment's answer to marijuana—he can turn anybody on." Turner was off, seizing the microphone, stalking the stage, stripping off his jacket, loosening his tie. His speech was in three courses—the first uproariously country-boy funny, the second so moving that women wept, the third so inspiring and promising that the audience rose to its feet in standing ovation.

"I hope to be remembered," he told them, "as the fellow who created more millionaires than any other man . . . and by making successes out of people nobody would fool with. In my organization you'll find more losers, more dropouts, more has-beens than anywhere else. I *like* the welfares. I *like* the failures. But there don't have to be any failures! The only failure I'd ever expect to meet is in hell, and I don't plan to go there. I'm going up. . . . The reason I've made it as far as I have is that I'm too dumb to know why it won't work. I may be the biggest liar in the world . . . or the most sincere man you'll ever meet."

When he was finished, he walked down the hall. "What makes me happy is turning on people to their potential," he said. "Life is brainwashing—nothing else! You're brainwashed to think you can or you can't. People can! I'm gonna change the world."

On a gloomy Sunday morning in Boston, Turner was confined to his hotel room waiting for a car to take him to a meeting. He was speaking of some of his new ideas—an orange-flavored mouthwash to make breakfast taste good, the dog-cosmetic market, "mostly untapped—and with five-million-dollar potential each year," and he mentioned the million-dollar castle he is building outside Orlando, with moats and turrets and a boathouse, to entertain 150 people, and suddenly I had had enough.

By making every man think he can drive a Cadillac and live in a castle and wear a gold suit, I wondered, aren't you emphasizing somewhat obnoxious American values? Aren't you negating the unquestionable good work you do with the handicapped and the poor?

Turner looked as if I had shot an arrow into his breast. "I use money as a tool!" he fired back. "People respect money and power. You have to hit money first. I stand up in front of them as an example. How you gonna help people who are poor and handicapped and retarded—if you're the same? What I'm selling is attitude. If a man listens to me, does what I say, then his attitude will change and so will his life. He might go out and buy a Cadillac—or he might write a great poem."

Now he made a fist and pounded his other hand with it.

The energies and juices seemed backed up in him, eager to erupt through his words. He leaped from his chair and swept about the room. "If they ever closed us down—and they won't," he said, *they* referring to state agencies, "that wouldn't matter. I can sell anything." His eyes cased the suite. They fell on the drapes. "I can sell these!" he cried, almost pulling them down. "I can sell those!" he said, snatching up an ashtray. "I can sell Sheraton water glasses! If they put me in jail someday, that won't matter, either. I'd figure I was put there to reform the penal system. I'd start a course for the inmates, teach 'em how to break out." He paused for inspiration, which quickly came: "I'd call it 'Dare to Be Free!'"

20

The Promoters: Of Things

There are some businessmen who wouldn't enjoy being called promoters. But the man we're now about to consider, Jeno Paulucci, doesn't seem to mind at all. He likes the word. He is that kind of man.

It may be a key identifying characteristic of a true promoter, in fact, that he doesn't get mad when people call him a promoter.

In an autobiography that Paulucci wrote a few years ago, he dwells at length on his association with another promoter, Stan Freberg, satirist and TV-commercial maker. Paulucci had hired Freberg to make some commercials touting the products of Paulucci's company, Chun King Corporation. The two of them made a bet: If the sales of Chun King chow mein, chop suey and other products didn't rise appreciably after a certain series of commercials appeared on the air, Freberg would pull Paulucci in a ricksha along Los Angeles's La Cienega Boulevard. If the sales did rise, Paulucci would do the same for Freberg.

The sales rose. Freberg got his free ride in a ricksha. Paulucci was delighted to fulfill the terms of the bet, for the result was a wealth of free publicity for his company.

That was the act of a promoter. It is very hard to imagine other company presidents pulling colleagues along city streets in rickshas. They would be too embarrassed; they would fear for their personal dignity and the company image. But it is characteristic of Paulucci, as of all promoters, that his embarrassment threshold is set very high—if, indeed, he has one at all.

Stan Freberg once called him a "pretty wild promoter." Paulucci took it as a compliment, later recalling it with the same pride he showed in recalling his Horatio Alger Award and other high honors.

Like Glenn Turner, Paulucci was born poor. His route to riches was not that of promoting ideas. Instead, he promoted things—in fact, perhaps the most basic of all commodities: foods.

The food business might seem to outsiders like a quiet, stable, maybe somewhat boring business. The way Jeno Paulucci went at it, it was a grand and wacky adventure.

Jeno Paulucci:
One Hundred Million Dollars

"Pound for pound," an ad-agency executive once said, "Paulucci is the worst son of a bitch in the country to work for."

"Personally I like him," said another. "Only thing is, he's mad."

Jeno Paulucci, the promoter from Minnesota, affects people that way and is absolutely delighted to know it. His feeling is that a man who creeps about the earth without making any waves, without stirring anybody up, cannot be living a very interesting life. This is not only his personal philosophy; it could almost be called the main thrust of his business strategy. "I'm a maverick," he says cheerfully. "I believe that's probably the main reason why I've succeeded. I've done things that everybody said couldn't be done, and I've done them in what everybody said was a crazy way. If any young man comes to me and asks how he's to make his fortune, I tell him to do the same. Don't follow everybody else. Get off the beaten track. Be a little mad."

Paulucci believes this so strongly that in the late 1960s he went so far as to write a book, *How It Was to Make $100,-000,000 in a Hurry,* in which he explains and justifies his maverick's philosophy and urges it upon the new young crop of business venturers now starting the long climb. There can be no doubt that the philosophy has worked in Paulucci's case.

Paulucci is a short man (five feet five), solidly built, with a balding head, a loud voice and an engaging smile. Like some others in this gallery, he started with nothing and came from nowhere—in fact, from conditions close to poverty.

He ended as chief executive and sole owner of the Chun King Corporation, by all measures the most successful mass merchandiser of Chinese foods ever to arise in this country (or, as far as is known, anywhere in the world—including China). And today, in his early 50s, he is worth more than $100 million.

It took a certain amount of audacity for a man named Luigino Paulucci to start a Chinese food company in the first place—especially to start it in Minnesota. It took more audacity to make the mad venture succeed. Let's see how the Minnesota promoter came to be.

Luigino Paulucci (he later changed his first name to Jeno) was born in 1918 in a small iron-mining town of northern Minnesota. His father worked as a miner when he could find work—which, Paulucci recalls, in some years was only one week out of four. Young Luigino helped earn the family's bleak living by going down into the pits and bringing up ore samples, which he sold to tourists. When he was in his early teens, with his father's health failing and most of the mines closed because of the Great Depression, the family decided to seek income by going into the retail grocery business. Young Jeno helped build a combination store and home, making the foundation out of used cedar poles that he wheedled from the telephone company. The store was set up in a front room. It was small, but by working long hours the family managed to squeeze enough profit out of it to stay alive.

At the age of 14 Jeno began working after school for a large store near his home—part of a supermarket chain headquartered in Duluth. He began simply as a clerk and muscle boy, assigned to move crates around and unload trucks and mop the floors and generally sweat for his pay. But when customers asked him questions about the food, he found himself actively selling it instead of giving the curt, surly replies that are traditional with food-market muscle boys. "I couldn't help selling," he recalls. "The food business was beginning to fascinate me, and I wanted to be part of it."

To put it another way, he was beginning to find his medium as a promoter. Looking back on his boyhood later, he realized that the promoter's instinct had probably been lurking inside him for a long time before he began selling food. When he had sold mine-ore samples to tourists, for instance, he had been able to increase the price by arranging ores of various colors in glass bottles or vials. The layered strata of ore inside the glass made a pretty little gewgaw that could be sold for a dollar or more—as much as four times the going rate for the same ore less cleverly packaged. This was a classic promoter's approach: the act of multiplying the value of a thing simply by presenting it in a slightly different way, adding a little extra something, going a half step farther than the competition. But young Jeno didn't realize back then, as he scrabbled around in the iron pits, that he was learning the techniques that were going to make him a hundred-millionaire.

The food-store manager soon became aware of Jeno's qualities as a salesman and shifted his duties so as to bring him into contact with the public more often. In the summer of his senior year in high school he was invited to go to work as a fruit-stand barker outside the market chain's headquarters store in Duluth. The offer included a pay arrangement that was part wage, part commission. The idea of working for a commission delighted the fledgling salesman, and he took the job.

The promoter in him now burst forth in full bloom. One day a shipment of bananas—18 crates of them—got damaged in a refrigeration-plant accident. The bananas were still tasty and perfectly edible, but their skins had turned an unusual and somewhat repellent shade of speckled brown. Young Jeno's boss instructed him to get rid of them at any price.

Bananas back then—undamaged ones, that is—generally sold at around 25 cents for four pounds. Jeno's boss suggested he start selling the damaged shipment at four pounds for 19 cents, then go lower if nobody bought.

But Jeno Paulucci was coming of age as a promoter. A delightfully wicked idea stole into his head. Without telling his boss, he piled the brown bananas outdoors in a huge display. Then he began shouting, "Argentine bananas!"

There is no such thing as an Argentine banana. But the name had an exotic lilt to it, a sound of value. A crowd gathered to look at Paulucci's speckled-brown pile. He convinced his listeners that these loathesome-looking objects were a new type of fruit, never before imported into the United States. Being of generous heart, he was prepared to let them go at the astonishingly low price of ten cents a pound (nearly twice what they would have cost as ordinary, undamaged, non-

Argentine bananas). He sold all 18 crates in three hours.

There was now no doubt in his employer's mind that this short young Italian from the Iron Range was a born food merchandiser and promoter. But there was still a doubt in Paulucci's mind. He was earning enough at the fruit stand to put himself through college, and he enrolled in a law course. High-status professions such as law and medicine often strongly magnetize those who are born in lowly circumstances, and this may have been one reason why a law course seemed good to this youngster whose father had worked himself sick in the iron mines. But after a year and a half Paulucci looked himself in the eye and admitted that what he really wanted was not status but, quite frankly, money.

As he recalls the episode in his book, he drove back to the college campus when it was time to reenroll for his fourth semester. He drove around the campus for three hours trying to decide what to do.

"A good lawyer, I'd heard, might make fifty thousand dollars a year or even a hundred thousand. But a marketing man might, *just might,* make the world his oyster. . . ."

He was at a major fork in the road of his life, and he knew it. The choice was not simply between law and merchandising. It was between safety and risk. One road led to a settled, comfortable profession in which young men moved up established pipelines toward known destinations. The other road led—who could say where?

Paulucci could not know then, of course, that he was going to make a $100 million. But he sensed somehow what all other men in our golden gallery have sensed: that you can't get rich on a salary. Not really rich. You can be safe in a salaried job, but if you want to be rich, you must quit the world of salaried men and step into a world of high, sometimes fearfully high, risk.

Paulucci drove away from the campus without reenrolling. He went to work as a traveling salesman for a wholesale grocery firm. Compensation: straight commission, young Paulucci's favorite deal. Soon he was much more than a run-of-the-road traveling salesman. He rapidly rose to the status of big-time promoter. Instead of selling groceries to one store owner at a time in ten-case lots—a setup that would have satisfied most young salesman—he developed a technique by which he rounded up whole groups of merchants in various localities, convinced them they'd save money by buying co-operatively in volume, ended by selling them the groceries in carload lots.

He increased his sales still more by convincing the merchants they should buy this or that vegetable in volume *now*, not next month, for the price was sure to go up next month. To make this pitch believable, he sent himself telegrams, ostensibly from his employers. Each telegram said something like WARN CUSTOMERS PRICE OF PEAS WILL RISE. By waving the urgent-sounding message at his customers, he was able to make them place much bigger orders than they would have otherwise.

He became so good at doing all this that his employers finally gave him a choice: Go on straight salary or just plain go. Jeno Paulucci, this brash young fellow in his 20s, was making more money than the president of the company.

Salary? The idea was ridiculous. Paulucci walked off the job and went back to Duluth. He had a moderately heavy wad of money in the bank. He was ready to go into his own food business.

He probed various possibilities—among them the garlic business—and then finally stumbled into the venture that was to become the basis of his fortune. It was a strange and esoteric business, not one that most food merchandisers would have envisioned as promising high volume or large profit. In fact, to most Duluth businessmen, it seemed at first more like some obscure, faddist hobby than a business.

Oriental bean sprouts.

By chance, one day, Paulucci heard that a small community of Japanese in Minneapolis had set up some hydroponic gardens to grow this ancient oriental delicacy. World War Two was in progress (Paulucci hadn't been drafted because of a knee disability), and the general disruption of markets and transportation left some regions short of vegetables. The Japanese, Paulucci learned, were able to sell their entire small output of bean sprouts without half trying.

Paulucci talked this over with an older man named David Persha, owner of the first food market for which the young promoter had worked. Old Persha, an immigrant from Austria, was ready to get out of the food-retailing business and put his money into some other venture. The idea of bean sprouts startled him at first, but he had watched young Jeno sell Argentine bananas and was inclined to believe Paulucci could promote anything. Persha agreed to go into partnership with the younger man.

Paulucci put up his savings and borrowed $2500 to round out his share of the capital. The partners converted the back of Persha's Duluth store into a hydroponic garden with rows of water-filled troughs. They hired a few Japanese as consultants and gardeners. They bought the needed mung-bean seeds in Texas and Mexico. Paulucci got in touch with some food processors and cooked up deals under which the processors would buy the Paulucci-Persha output of bean sprouts, pack the sprouts in cans or jars and resell them to retail stores. And so a new business was born.

The betting around Duluth was that it would last six months. But the sprouts sold steadily. Soon it became apparent that more hydroponic troughs would be needed than could fit into the back of Persha's old store. Paulucci, the deal maker, went out and made a new one. He had learned about a syndicate of businessmen who had a contract to dehydrate potatoes for the military services. He approached the syndicate shareholders and asked them if they'd be interested in a contract to grow bean sprouts.

"But we don't know anything about bean sprouts," they said. "We've never even *seen* a mung bean."

"Never mind," said Paulucci. "My partner and I have been watching how it's done. We know the whole process. There's nothing to it."

So the syndicate rented two floors of a Duluth building and set up huge rows of gardens. The output increased enormously, and Paulucci hustled to push sales up in proportion. He had literature printed on the mung bean's rather uninteresting history. He distributed bean-sprout recipes. He sold not only to food processors but also directly to restaurant and other retail outlets.

Then it occurred to him that the partnership could make more money by having its canning done on a contract basis instead of selling sprouts to the middlemen, the food processors. He phoned a Wisconsin food packer and made a deal under which the packer would can bean sprouts for a flat fee per case—provided Paulucci could find any cans. During the war all kinds of metals were preempted for military use, and the civilian supply was severely rationed.

Paulucci brashly went to Washington and talked his way into the War Production Board. He introduced himself with a rather grandiose name that he and Persha had chosen for their partnership: the Bean Sprout Growers Association. To Washington officials this must have sounded like some kind of farmers' cooperative rather than a two-man speculation. WPB let the Minnesota promoter have several million slightly damaged tin cans.

Paulucci had his cans labeled with the oriental name Foo Young, though there was not at that time a single Oriental in the company. The business continued to grow. In time Paulucci and Persha bought an old pea-canning plant, converted it and began doing all their own canning.

Then Paulucci decided it would be a good idea to expand the Foo Young product line. By adding celery and other vegetables to the bean sprouts, he could produce a chop-suey mixture.

"What's this Foo Young outfit?" a General Foods executive once asked his public-relations counsel. "Are they Chinese?"

"No," said the PR man, "it's run by an Italian and an Austrian, and most of the plant workers are Minnesota Swedes."

"You're kidding!" said the executive. "Why, even the goddamn cans are dented, like they were shipped all the way from Pong Ping. Somebody out there has got to be the world's best promoter!"

That may have been the case, indeed.

Once in a while Paulucci outpromoted himself. One year he decided to corner the celery market—quietly buy most of the national crop while it was in season and cheap, then sell it when the season ended and the price went up. Nearly 60 carloads were delivered to Duluth. Only then did Paulucci discover that there wasn't enough refrigeration capacity in the whole city to hold the monumental load. Nearly half of it perished before he could sell it off.

But his business stayed alive despite such setbacks. He dreamed big dreams for it in the postwar boom. In the mid-1940s he borrowed money, bought out his partner and became sole owner of the odd little company. Deciding the name Foo Young lacked something, he picked a new name that had a ring of imperial grandeur: Chun King. He began advertising in newspapers and Sunday supplements. He enhanced his trade promotions with girlie calendars. He expanded the product line to include chow mein and other oriental dishes. He enlisted the help of his mother to experiment with Italian spicing in the often bland oriental foods ("I'd never even *liked* chop suey myself"), and he continued to push sales upward.

He was now selling to such large national market chains as Food Fair. Somehow he managed to convey the impression that Chun King was a huge, solidly capitalized company with a vast expanse of modern plant buildings. The fact was that the company had little cash, partly because of heavy spending on expansion and promotion, partly because of unfortunate events such as the celery speculation. Paulucci's office was a cramped little cubicle sheathed with rejected wallboard to save a few dollars a sheet. The old pea-canning plant had burned down, and Chun King products were now produced in a war-surplus Quonset hut. But the big buyers seemed to envision Paulucci as the master of a great complex of shining new kitchens, a man whose office was furnished in antique leather and probably had enormous picture windows looking out over Lake Superior.

Paulucci was giving them a picture of the company not as it was but as he dreamed it could be—in fact, as he was certain it would one day become. Optimism is certainly a necessary trait in a promoter.

The Chun King image nearly disintegrated one day. Paulucci was in the office of Food Fair's head buyer, trying to convince the buyer that the great supermarket chain should stock Chun King instead of competing products. The buyer was prepared to taste-test several oriental canned foods to see whether Chun King's faint Italian spicing really made a difference. Paulucci pulled out a can opener and pried the lid off a can of chop-suey vegetables.

Lying right on top of the vegetables, hidden from the buyer's view by the raised can lid, was a cooked grasshopper.

It was the kind of accident than can happen to any food-processing company once in a while, even the biggest. Chun King's kitchens, though housed in a Quonset hut, were in fact as clean as anybody else's. But Paulucci was strongly aware, as he gazed horrified at the grasshopper, that his company's grand image was in mortal danger.

He hesitated for half a second. Then he picked up a spoon, smiled broadly and said, "This looks so good that I'm going to take the first mouthful myself." He ate the spoonful, including the grasshopper, with apparent relish.

"It didn't taste bad at all," he reported later. The taste was adequately washed away by the fact that Food Fair opted for Chun King.

Thus did the little company grow bigger. Sales began to climb by more than ten percent per year, then 20 percent. Paulucci paid ever-closer attention to the company's advertising—a natural inclination for any man who made the long climb by the routes of salesmanship and promotion. He made his presence felt so often and so strongly among his ad counselors that many of them couldn't stand him. "He was always right there, looking over my shoulder," said one New York adman. "Hell, I couldn't even write a sentence without having him turn it inside out. He drove me nuts." The Chun King Corporation has changed ad agencies at least a dozen times in its career.

The ad industry's difficulties with Paulucci stemmed not only from his constant and overwhelming presence but also from his fondness for wild and bizarre promotions. It was his idea that, since Chun King wasn't wealthy enough to buy nationwide saturation advertising, the company would have to get the most possible mileage out of what little promotion it could afford. This meant the ads had to be unusual, highly memorable. Many of Paulucci's ad agencies shied away from this notion. They wanted to stick with the safe, the proven.

And so Paulucci flitted from one agency to another, one approach to another, until he met Stan Freberg in the late 1950s. Freberg was a promotor much like Paulucci in many respects: a maverick, a believer in trying the unusual. He had made his name as an entertainer specializing in sharp satires of well-known personalities, songs and ideas. Then he had set up a company to produce humorous, satirical radio and television commercials for any company with the guts to try the approach. It was accepted as dogma in the ad industry that humor doesn't sell products, and Freberg was not inundated with clients. But Jeno Paulucci, the Minnesota promoter, was attracted to Freberg and his zany techniques. Against the earnest advice of most of his ad experts, Paulucci hired Freberg to make some Chun King commercials.

The commercials were decidedly noticed. In fact, they became something of a sensation in their day. Many of them satirized other commercials. In one of them, for instance, an announcer stated that nine out of ten doctors recommended Chun King chow mein. The camera panned in on a group of ten doctors, revealing that nine were Chinese.

The makers of commercials thus satirized were not happy. One large company wrote to Paulucci and demanded that he quit using a commercial that poked fun at its own carefully prepared advertising. Paulucci wrote back airily, "We will stop using this commercial immediately after we're through using it."

But though some big companies weren't happy, radio listeners and TV viewers were. They wrote letters by the thousands praising the fresh, self-satirizing approach. They also bought Chun King products. In some test markets sales rose by nearly one-third after a series of Freberg ads appeared.

And Chun King became a big, wealthy corporation at last.

Several times over the years other companies and individual investors had sought to buy into Paulucci's enterprise. The first offer, back in the 1940s, had been a tender of $25,-000 for a half interest. Paulucci needed the cash badly back then, but the company was his baby, and he wanted it to stay his. He turned the deal down. Somewhat later Chef Boy-Ar-Dee offered four million dollars for the Chun King Corporation. Paulucci turned that down, too. He knew the price could go higher. Finally, in 1966, he was approached by the R. J. Reynolds Tobacco Company.

Like other cigarette makers, Reynolds was diversifying into new fields of business as fast as it could run. It had set up, among other things, a division called Reynolds Foods, which was busily acquiring smaller companies. Reynolds Foods indicated it would be very happy to acquire Chun King.

Jeno Paulucci was 48 years old and by no means ready to retire. He was in no mood to rush into a deal with Reynolds. He proceeded slowly, quite prepared to turn Reynolds down as he had rejected other suitors in years past. But he felt he wouldn't mind selling Chun King if a good enough deal could be hammered out. He had other projects to keep him busy—including a small but growing maker of Italian foods and desserts, Jeno's Inc., which he had set up years before but to which he felt he had never paid enough attention.

He finally sold his baby, Chun King, to Reynolds. The price was $63 million, cash.

Adding that cash to his other business ventures and his personal properties and investments, Paulucci had a net worth comfortably above $100 million. The Minnesota promoter, the kid from the iron mines, had made it into the ranks of the very, very rich.

He had made it by doing what other men said couldn't or shouldn't be done. His way had been the maverick's way, always a little bit off the beaten track.

Once, when Chun King was just beginning to achieve respectable size and status, Paulucci thought it might be a good idea to start acting like a big corporation. In his earlier days he hired employees by hunch, but now he decided to try the more scientific methods preached by business schools. He sent away for a battery of psychological tests. A junior executive was in the process of being hired at Chun King, and Paulucci asked him to take the tests. For fun, Paulucci took the same tests himself, using a false name.

When the results came back from the psychologist, it turned out that the junior executive was a sound man and worthy of being hired. But the other guy who had taken the tests was a washout, unfit for any kind of responsible business position. It was the psychologist's advice that Chun King would do better without him.

21

Other People's Work

We've studied OPM, and now we'll look at OPW—the technique of getting rich on other people's work. This technique, in the latter half of the 20th Century, has reached its fullest and gaudiest flowering in the franchising business.

In a typical franchising operation you begin by developing some product or service that has, or promises to have, a broad popular appeal. You then go out and find men and women to sell it for you. These people become your so-called franchisees, or franchise holders. Each invests money and work to build his own local business based on your product or service. You grant him a license to use your trade name, which you promise will be ballyhooed in a national advertising campaign. You also promise that he will be the exclusive franchisee in his territory. You offer him the benefit of your mass-purchasing power, through which he can get his raw materials or other supplies cheaply. You may also offer him other inducements such as professional help in picking his store or office location.

If this sounds like an elaborate con game, it can indeed be just that. In the middle 1960s, the hot, bright summer of the franchising business, many unwary citizens got suckered into deals that were pure swindle from front to back. Dozens of scruffy little franchising companies sprang up, promising fast and fabulous riches to their lucky franchisees. The only people who got rich were the companies' organizers. Many such companies stayed in business only a couple of years and perhaps never intended to stay longer. They extracted stiff licensing fees from hopeful franchisees, spent a year or so going through businesslike motions, then folded up—with the fees still in the organizers' pockets. Others stayed around a little longer—just long enough to go public and get their stock prices bulled up. With the prices at dizzy levels, the organizers sold out and vanished into the night from which they'd come, leaving everybody else holding an empty bag.

As Phineas T. Barnum once noted, you can't fool all the people all the time. The American public wised up quite rapidly, and by 1970 the franchise fever had cooled. A faint, nasty odor still lingers around the business, but by and large it can be said that most of the companies still surviving are honest. Not all profitable, but at least honest.

A well-run franchising operation does in fact offer a good deal on both sides of the handshake. Franchiser and franchisee alike can make money. The franchisee, as a small-time businessman, can work his way up toward the $100,000-a-year income bracket with luck, sweat and patience. The franchiser, the big-time man with hundreds or thousands of small-timers working on his behalf as well as their own, can, of course, grow a lot richer.

Of all franchising industries now operating in the country, the fast-food business may be the most colorful. It has included some of the shoddiest swindles as well as some of the most egregious succcesses. Among the latter is McDonald's, huge and ubiquitous purveyor of hamburgers.

McDonald's was built by a man named Ray Kroc, whose discouraging early life gave no hint that he would ever make the big time. His own and his company's stories are told here by *New York Times* reporter J. Anthony Lukas.

Ray Kroc:
One Hundred Million Dollars*
by J. Anthony Lukas

As is his custom on Wednesday afternoons, Bob Jennings of Joplin, Missouri, left his McDonald's restaurant . . . early on May 5 and, with five other Joplin businessmen, drove down to Table Rock Lake, where he owns a mobile home. After fishing awhile for bigmouth bass, Bob and his friends put some steaks on the outdoor grill and settled back with

*Copyright © 1971 by the New York Times Company. Reprinted by permission.

drinks to hear the evening news.

Only then did they learn that a few hours after they'd left Joplin a tornado had roared up from the southwest and ripped a path several blocks wide through the heart of town, killing one person, injuring 60 and causing damage later estimated at two million dollars.

Three thoughts raced through Bob Jennings's mind: Were his wife and children all right? Was the restaurant damaged? And was his crew getting free hamburgers and coffee out to the victims and rescue workers (standard operating procedure for a McDonald's restaurant in a disaster area)? A quick phone call set his mind at rest on the first two counts: The Jennings family was fine and the restaurant unscathed. To Bob's mild annoyance, though, his crew couldn't get their food past the police lines.

But the next day brought an unexpected bonanza. Schools were closed and, with little else to do in this slow-paced old mining town, hundreds of schoolchildren streamed down to Joplin's only McDonald's. Moreover, farmers and villagers from miles around flocked into town to inspect the tornado damage, and many of them ended up at McDonald's, too. By the end of the day Bob Jennings counted $500 more than usual in his cash drawers.

In the brisk, upbeat world of McDonald's, every disaster presents an opportunity. If a high-school football star is stricken by cancer—as one was recently in Trenton, New Jersey—name a day in his honor and donate the proceeds toward his hospital bills. If fire destroys a Goodwill Industries clothing warehouse—as it did in St. Petersburg, Florida—designate McDonald's as a collection point for donated clothing. If Frump-Frump the Elephant dies—as he did at the zoo in Roanoke, Virginia—offer to buy another elephant.

And if all else goes wrong, trust in Providence, which somehow seems to smile down on the Golden Arches.

Elsewhere along the frenetic superhighway of fast-food franchising, last year's economic cyclone wreaked havoc. In part this was a natural reaction to the absurd speculation in such enterprises, which dazzled investors in 1968 and 1969. Many of the companies that rode the crest of the bull market had little more than a celebrity's name (Bart Starr, Mickey Mantle, Johnny Carson, Joe Namath, Minnie Pearl). Some reported huge "earnings" before a single outlet was opened by totaling their stiff initial franchise fees. Others made most of their profit by selling franchisees everything from mustard to paper cups—a practice that, recent court rulings suggest, may violate the antitrust laws.

So, when the recession hit, the fast-food market collapsed like a soggy, overloaded paper cup. Lum's, a star performer that sold as high as 33½ on the New York Stock Exchange, was down to 6 in [mid-1971]. Dunkin' Donuts, once at 33¼, was down to 13. Minnie Pearl Fried Chicken (now Performance Systems, Inc.) hit 23, then sank to 12½ cents— less than a bag of its chicken costs.

But McDonald's has proved as invulnerable to recession as it has to tornadoes. Although the cost of its hamburgers has increased only five cents (from 15 cents to 20) in 16 years, its other vital statistics have grown recently by about one-third a year. In 1970 sales reached $587 million, a 33-percent increase over 1969 (1971 first-quarter sales were up a staggering 40 percent over the comparable period last year). In 1970 McDonald's was the nation's seventh largest server of food, trailing only the army, the Agriculture Department, the navy, Kentucky Fried Chicken, the Marriott Corporation and ARA Services, a vending-machine and institutional food-service company. It opened a record 297 restaurants during 1970 and 50 more during the first quarter of 1971, bringing its total outlets to 1642 (most of them franchised, but 397 owned and operated by the company itself). Already operating in Canada, Costa Rica, Puerto Rico and the Virgin Islands, the company [plans new] outlets in Germany, the Netherlands, Japan and Australia. And on May 5 [1971], with its stock selling at 75—compared with 40 [half a year earlier]—it declared a three-for-two stock split.

But the McDonald's statistic that has captured the American imagination is its ever-expanding record for selling hamburgers. Emblazoned across the Golden Arches is the slogan "OVER SEVEN BILLION SOLD." At the current rate of four million a day, that sign . . . [will need to be changed often].

The McDonald's people revel in the sensuous feel of figures that large. Cooper and Golin, their inventive public-relations firm, keeps trying to come up with a graphic expression for billions of hamburgers. In July 1969, when the five-billion mark was reached, Cooper and Golin said that if all those hamburgers were shot into orbit, they'd form almost 13 rings around the earth at its broadest point. When sales passed six billion in May 1970, the public-relations men said that many hamburgers would fill more than 2041 747 jets with all seats and equipment removed. And at seven billion [in] January [1971] they came up with a whole slew of comparisons: If a man ate a hamburger every five minutes, he'd have to live 70,000 years to eat them all; if all the flour for the buns were spread out, it would coat everything east of the Mississippi; and if all seven billion were piled into Illinois, everybody in the state would be ankle-deep in hamburgers.

Traveling the nation's highways these days, one often feels at least hubcap-deep in hamburgers. Some New Yorkers have the strange idea that the hot dog is the all-American food, but franchisers scoff at the weenie. "The hot dog is New York, not American," says one authority. "They're Coney Island or Yankee Stadium. How many places west of the Hudson specialize in them? Dog 'n' Suds, Lum's ('Hot Dogs Steamed in Beer') and maybe a few more. Hell, there are more pizza joints."

But hamburgers are everywhere: Burger Chef, Burger King, Big Boy, Wimpy's, Gino's, White Castle, White Tower, not to mention McDonald's. For the Texas rancher, the Iowa farmer, the Detroit construction worker and the tourist on the road anywhere, it is the all-American snack.

Originally, gastronomes say, hamburger came from the medieval Baltic states, where people liked to eat raw beef shredded with a dull knife. Traders from the Hanseatic League brought it to Hamburg, where it is still a favorite dish under the name "steak tartare." Then, as "hamburger," it was brought to America by German immigrants who settled in St. Louis, Milwaukee and Chicago. The broiled and bunned version we now know was probably first served in 1904 at the Louisiana Purchase Exposition in St. Louis.

But not until the 1920s, when Walter Anderson and Edgar Waldo (Billy) Ingram founded White Castle, did Americans start eating hamburgers in large numbers. Ingram recalled in a 1964 speech that 50 years ago one could ride all day through New York "without seeing a single hamburger sign." White Castle had to "break down a deep-seated prejudice" against chopped beef, he recalls, and "sell the romance of the hamburger." They succeeded beyond their wildest dreams. Modeling their stands after Chicago's water tower, they chose "white for purity" and "castle for strength." Their hamburgers were cute little 2½-inch-square patties so thin they would break if you tried to lift them from the bun; yet there are still those who swear by them and follow the chain's admonition, "Buy 'em by the sack."

But White Castle owns and operates each of its 113 outlets. The mass marketing of hamburgers had to await the application of franchising techniques to the food-service field, which began in earnest in the early Fifties. It was back in those days that Harland Sanders, a dropout from the seventh grade who'd tried his hand without great success at streetcar conducting, piloting a ferry boat, stoking fires on the railroad and selling insurance, began attracting wide attention for the unusually tasty chicken he served in his restaurant in Corbin, Kentucky. Putting a couple of pressure cookers and a bag of seasoning in his car, he hit the road offering to cook up a mess of his chicken for any likely-looking restaurant he came to. Today there are 3100 of Colonel Sanders's Kentucky Fried Chicken outlets in the United States.

Ray Kroc's early career was strangely like the colonel's, suggesting that a genius for fast food may grow best in a man who has knocked about on the road himself, snatching opportunity—a sale, a deal, a job, a meal—where he can. After dropping out of high school as a sophomore, Kroc played piano with several traveling bands, served as musical director of a Chicago radio station, sold real estate in Florida and paper cups in the Midwest. He knew failure. "After the Florida boom collapsed, I was stone-broke," he recalls. "I didn't have an overcoat, a topcoat or a pair of gloves. I drove into Chicago on icy streets. When I got home, I was frozen stiff, disillusioned and broke."

In 1937 Kroc went into business for himself as head of a small Chicago company that distributed Multimixers—machines that could mix five malted milks at one time. In 1954 he discovered that a small restaurant in San Bernardino, California, run by Mac and Dick McDonald, had eight of his machines. Nobody else had that many, and Kroc decided he had to see the McDonald operation for himself. He went to San Bernardino and quickly realized what a gold mine the McDonalds had stumbled on. "They had people standing in line clamoring for those fifteen-cent hamburgers," he recalls, still with wonder in his voice. Kroc asked the McDonalds why they didn't open more restaurants. "I was thinking about Multimixers, not hamburgers then; if every McDonald's had eight Multimixers, I'd soon be rich." But Dick McDonald shook his head and pointed to a nearby hill. "See that house up there?" he said. "That's home to me, and I like it there. If we opened a chain, I'd never be home."

Ray Kroc saw his opportunity and grabbed for it. The McDonalds quickly agreed to let him franchise their outlets anywhere in the country in exchange for one-half of one percent of the gross receipts. Kroc began deliberately. His first McDonald's—which he owned himself—opened in Des Plaines, Illinois, a Chicago suburb, on April 15, 1955. The second, in Fresno, California, opened that September, and the third, in Resada, California, in December. But soon the pace picked up. By 1960 there were 228 McDonald's restaurants, and about 100 were opened each year until 1968, when the rate increased to more than 200 a year.

In 1961 Kroc bought the contract—along with the name, all trademarks, copyrights and formulas—from the McDonalds for $2,700,000. Since then he has had little contact with the brothers whose name his company bears. When I asked him about them recently, Kroc said, "Well, I talked with Dick on the phone about a year ago. But I don't see them. They're younger than I am, but they quit. I can't have any anchor hanging on to me. When you're green, you're growing; when you're ripe, you rot."

Although they started the whole thing, Mac and Dick are clearly not McDonald's kind of people.

McDonald's wants people with a driving ambition. Ray Kroc—who has moved up to board chairman and chief executive officer but at 69 remains as active as ever—puts it this way: "Some people reach their level of expectations pretty quickly. We want someone who will get totally involved in the business. If his ambition is to reach the point where he can play golf four days a week or play gin rummy for a cent a point instead of a tenth, we don't want him in a McDonald's restaurant."

Perhaps not even the younger Ray Kroc—certainly not the Ray Kroc who drove back to Chicago cold, disillusioned and broke—could have qualified for a McDonald's license. Applicants, who must wait their turn on a list several hundred names long, are screened, "and only those who look as if they have potential for success are accepted." But when I asked about the criteria for such selection, a company official said there were none. "Basically, we just look for somebody who's good with people," he explained. "In that sense we'd rather get a salesman than an accountant or even a chef."

The company does boast of such franchise holders as a former undersecretary of labor, a member of the House of Representatives from Virgina, a controller in another successful company, a golf pro, a research chemist, a retired airforce colonel, a navy commander and several lawyers, dentists and advertising executives. These may be the cream, but the average McDonald's owner-operator is older than 35, has worked his way up in another business and has a tidy bank account. The initial cash investment, the company takes pains to point out, is set high "to discourage misfits and those with marginal work records."

A McDonald's franchise (plus the lease, equipment and operating capital required to open it) costs between $110,000 and $125,000, depending on the design of the unit and the "frills" (landscaping, seating) the owner wants. Of this, about $65,000 must be in cash; the remainder can be borrowed on the applicant's credit. The company selects the site and builds the restaurant. When he begins operation, the owner pays McDonald's 11.5 percent of his monthly sales (after deducting any sales tax)—3 percent of that as a service fee and 8.5 percent as rent.

This sounds like an expensive proposition, but the record shows that it can be incredibly lucrative. The company says that a well-run restaurant should pay off its original investment in three to five years, then make an annual profit before taxes of 12 to 15 percent. Since the average store now grosses $430,000 and many make more than $500,000, a moderately good operator should be able to count on $50,000 to $75,000 in annual profits.

Take Bob Jennings, the owner in Joplin, Missouri. Bob grew up in Arkansas and went to Southwest Missouri State College on a football scholarship. After two years in the army he joined the Colonial Baking Company in Springfield, Missouri, working his way up to sales manager in four years.

In 1961 a friend named Tom Tucker got a McDonald's franchise in Springfield and asked Bob to be his manager. When the Joplin franchise became available in 1964, Tom and Bob bought it together. Two years later Bob bought Tom out. Bob has worked hard, serving as his own manager, working about 60 hours a week in the restaurant, building its gross from $100,000 to $500,000 a year. Although he is reluctant to discuss his profits, according to the company's reckoning, this should put him in the $60,000-to-$75,000-a-year range. Not bad for somebody known around Joplin as "just a good old boy from Arkansas."

Others have done much better. One of the prime rewards the company holds out for good operators is the opportunity to buy more outlets when they become available. Some operators own four, six or eight restaurants. And that can really pile up the cash. Ray Kroc estimates that 60 to 70 owner-operators are millionaires.

At a recent owners' convention at the Doral Hotel in Miami Beach, the well-dressed wife of one franchise holder came up to Kroc and began reminiscing about the old days, when she used to help out at the french-fry cooker. Suddenly she held out a finger still scarred from hot grease. "I don't mind *that*, because it made *this* possible," she said, holding out another finger decorated with a huge diamond ring.

McDonald's wants go-getters, all right, but it doesn't want iconoclasts. It wants people who will follow "the system." Occasionally Kroc's rhetoric suggests something different. Several years ago he called franchising "an updated version of the American dream," which gave some people the idea that McDonald's franchisees were largely autonomous entrepreneurs battling their own way toward the rich prizes of American capitalism. But when I asked him about that phrase the other day, he conceded that the stress should be on "updated version."

"Let's face it, things have changed since the old days. The guy whose father had a little grocery store can't go out today and open a store like that. He knows you just can't buck the big supermarket chains. You just can't do it. But this is something you can do. We give people an opportunity to get into business for themselves, without taking the whole risk alone. All we ask is that they follow our way of doing things, the proven way."

As the man says, let's face it: McDonald's isn't selling food so much as it is a system. The food just isn't that good. The vaunted McDonald's hamburger—a machine-stamped 1.6-ounce patty 3.875 inches wide when raw and less when cooked, .221 inches thick, sprinkled with a quarter ounce of onion and covered with splats of mustard and catsup and a pickle slice, all resting on a 4½-inch bun—is precious little meat and a lot of what people in Joplin call "fixin's." Even if you like it that way, it tastes pretty much like a dozen other fast-food hamburgers. Some of McDonald's top officials concede that they don't care much for their own hamburger. "If you don't quote me," said one man, "I never eat 'em."

The french fries are something else. Most operators regard them as their most popular dish. "No question about it, the fry is our ace in the hole," says Bob Jennings. "That little booger, ole buddy, is delicious." I consulted a 15-year-old fast-food freak I know, who partially confirmed the judgment: "Yeh, I'd say McDonald's fries are the best. They're just a tiny bit crisper than anybody else's. But not that much better. Most people couldn't tell the difference."

If most people can't tell the difference, then what makes the difference for McDonald's? At the drop of a spatula, Ray Kroc will cite his formula for success—"Quality, Service, Cleanliness"—and other McDonald's officials reverentially invoke it, too—usually in shortened form as "Q.S.C." But, when questioned, most concede that any good company tries to practice "Q.S.C." Burger Chef, McDonald's main competitor in the hamburger field, has its "Four Pillars of the Burger Chef Way: Quality, Service, Cleanliness and Courtesy."

After two weeks of observing the company's operations, I concluded that what makes the difference for McDonald's is that McDonald's people take the hamburger business just a little more seriously than anybody else. They take it very seriously indeed.

Above many executives' desks in McDonald's sleek new headquarters at Oak Brook, Illinois, is an embossed scroll bearing Ray Kroc's favorite homily, "Press On":

Nothing in the world can take the place of persistence. Talent will not; nothing is more common than unsuccessful men with talent.

Genius will not; unrewarded genius is almost a proverb.
Education will not; the world is full of educated dere-
  licts.
Persistence and determination alone are omnipotent.

Perhaps nowhere does one sense this deadly seriousness
better than at what McDonald's calls its "Hamburger University" in Elk Grove, Illinois. Other franchise operations
have their training courses and seminars, but only McDonald's
has a "university" with a 19-day course leading to a "Bachelor
of Hamburgerology, with a minor in french fries."

In early May I attended several days of classes at old HU,
a sleek white concrete-and-tinted-glass building surrounded
by shade trees and a reflecting pool. Each course is divided
into two sections—Basic Operations (attended by all new
owner-operators) and Advanced Operations (in which the
owners are joined by managers, assistant managers and sometimes a few veteran owners back for a "refresher").

The first day, I was ushered into a classroom where Basic
Operation Class 120 (the 120th in the university's ten-year
history) was about to get under way. Nine new owners sat in
three rows under rectangular fluorescent ceiling panels as a
young man in a green blazer with the McDonald's Golden
Arches emblazoned on the pocket introduced himself as
"Jerry Gorman, your instructor for Basic Operations." Leading his middle-aged students through a complicated registra-
tion form and the affixing of plastic name tags, he had the
genial informality of all McDonald's junior executives, but
beneath the smile was a firm no-nonsense air. "All classes do
require your attendance," he told them. "Personal conduct
both in and out of class is of utmost importance. We are
representing McDonald's. Keep your manuals and notebooks
with you at all times, and watch your conversation in public
places. Our competition can pick things up that way, too."

That afternoon the class convened at a McDonald's restaurant several hundred feet down the road, which the university
uses as a training ground. There, in a basement classroom,
the students got their first lecture on "The Burger." Assistant
instructor Paul Robillard told them how to tell when a burger
is done ("It starts turning brown around the edge"), how to
flip one ("Go with the natural action of your wrist") and how
to scrape the grill ("Get your hip into it").

We moved on to Production Control. Jerry Gorman explained that McDonald's is dedicated to speed—turning out a hamburger, french fries and a shake in 50 seconds. But, he said, they are also dedicated to freshness; so any cooked burger unsold for more than ten minutes must be thrown away. Thus, the most difficult job in the restaurant is knowing how to regulate production so no customer has to wait much more than 50 seconds but the restaurant doesn't get stuck with a lot of stale food. This vital function is performed by the production-control man, stationed near the middle of the counter, who yells instructions to the grill man, the shake man or the fry man. The most complex instructions are for the grill man, who has to be told how many hamburgers, double hamburgers, cheeseburgers and double cheeseburgers to make.

"Our basic run of burgers is twelve," Gorman explained. "But to that the production man must add enough burgers for the doubles he thinks he'll need. So let's say he thinks he'll need six doubles. He yells, 'twelve and six,' and the grill man lays 18 burgers down. The next thing the grill man needs to know is how many of those burgers should have cheese on them. So the grill man will yell, 'cheese on six and six,' which means of the six doubles and six regulars I've got, how many do you want cheesed? Now, let's say the production man wants two cheeseburgers and two double cheeseburgers. He'll yell back, 'two and two,' which tells the grill man what he needs to know, unless you get some 'grills'—that is, orders for burgers without some of our normal ingredients. The grills come in on slips from the countermen, and the grill man has to deduct the grills from the other totals. Got that?"

Most of the class looked blank. But a big black man in the front row nodded.

"OK," Gorman said, looking a bit skeptical. "Let's see. If the calls go this way—'twelve and four,' 'cheese on four and eight,' 'two and two,' and you get two 'catsup only' grills, what do you make?"

Most of his students still looked completely bewildered. So was I. But the big black guy shot back calmly, "Two double cheeseburgers, two double hamburgers, two cheeseburgers, four hamburgers and two hamburgers with catsup only."

Gorman nodded. "You got it."

For several more hours we practiced the calls. After class I asked Gorman who the big guy was. "Oh, didn't you know?" he said. "That's Brad Hubbert, who used to play full-back for the San Diego Chargers."

Suddenly it all fell into place. I realized what the Mc-Donald's operation reminded me of: pro football. All those signals, set plays in the huddle, audibles on the line. The mathematical precision. The sheer technology of it all. Even those bulky operations manuals the students carried around like the football "play books" rookies had to memorize at the start of a season. I remembered that Bob Jennings had told me he liked to hire high-school athletes for his crew because "they work best as a team." Of course. The production-control man was the quarterback; the grill man, the fullback; the fry man and shake man, the running backs; the counter-men, the line; and the customers storming the windows, the opposing team. No wonder Brad Hubbert understood it all.

The next evening, I attended graduation ceremonies for Class 119 at Fritzel's restaurant in downtown Chicago. The evening proceeded with typical McDonald's efficiency: 30 minutes for cocktails; 45 minutes for dinner; then a 15-minute ceremony in which Rob Doran, the 24-year-old dean of HU, handed out the 41 parchment diplomas and several awards: the coveted "Archie" for the top man in the class (a plastic disk symbolizing the hamburger nestling in an ebony base shaped like a McDonald's restaurant) and the "Seminar Awards" (black Parker pens with little Plexiglas windows that flash "Quality," "Service," "Cleanliness," "McDonald's" when you push the plunger). Promptly at 8:30 P.M. Doran gave the class his parting words—"Be effective"—then announced, "Gentlemen, the bus is waiting." I had looked forward to celebrating with them in the bars and discothèques that line Rush Street, a few blocks away, but the new graduates obediently trooped into the bus for the ride back to their suburban motel.

Even after the new owners get home to their restaurants, McDonald's keeps them on a tight rein. The company allows little experimentation with menu or decor. Fred L. Turner, its president since 1968, says, "In an age when so many Americans are on the move, one of our main assets is our consistency and uniformity. It's very important that a man who's used to eating at a McDonald's in Hempstead, Long Island, know he can get the same food and service when he walks into one in Albuquerque or Omaha. We've found a formula that works, and we stick with it."

To see that units stick with it, the company maintains a staff of "field consultants" ("We don't like to call them inspectors," an official explains). Each consultant is responsible for 30 units on which he pays regular visits—some announced, some unannounced. Occasionally several consultants get together and "blitz" a unit—buying hamburgers, shakes and fries by the hundreds and then confronting an owner with the facts ("Look, Gene, two hundred of the burgers were cold"). Most owners comply quickly with the consultants' reports; only rarely has the company been forced to cancel a recalcitrant owner's franchise. (This doesn't include the 35 to 40 owners in the company's history who have forfeited their franchises because they didn't keep up with their monthly payments or just "walked away from the business." In such cases, an owner receives his $15,000 security deposit and the depreciated value of his equipment—minus, of course, what he owes the company). The most notable cases in which owners were forced to give up their franchises involved two Californians. One refused to serve the fish fillet when it was added to the menu, and the other was not making hamburgers according to specifications and refused to let his field consultant into the restaurant.

A few small variations are permitted to suit regional tastes: On Long Island no mustard is served on regular hamburgers; in Memphis more mustard is served and less catsup; in Texas, even more mustard and less catsup. In parts of New England a coffee milk shake is added to the regular lineup of chocolate, vanilla and strawberry. In parts of the South Dr. Pepper is served as a fourth soft drink.

Over the years the company has expanded the original burger-shake-and-fries menu, but only after exhaustive testing in its own labs and in the field. The double hamburger and double cheeseburger were added in 1963, the fish sandwich in 1964, apple pie in 1967, and in 1968, after months of secret experiments, came the "Big Mac" (two hamburger patties, interspersed with three sesame-bun sections and covered with shredded lettuce, cheese, pickle slices and a "special sauce"). The company is testing fried chicken in Dayton and a big quarter-pound hamburger on the West Coast. When a test fails, McDonald's is quick to admit it. A roast-beef sandwich and fish 'n' chips have recently been abandoned, as have a chain of Jane Dobbins pie shops (named after Mrs. Kroc) and Raymond's, a luxury hamburger chain named after the chairman himself.

McDonald's also sets strict standards for the grooming, dress and behavior of its employees. The manual decrees, "Your windowmen and outside order takers must impress customers as being 'all-American' boys. They must display such desirable traits as sincerity, enthusiasm, confidence and a sense of humor. . . . At McDonald's personal appearance is something we watch every day. A man should shave every day, clean his fingernails every day, keep his teeth and breath fresh and clean all the time, bathe often to prevent underarm and other body odors and use a deodorant. He should have dark pants, black shining shoes, a neat haircut and a clear complexion. Personnel with bad teeth, severe skin blemishes or tattoos should not be stationed at service windows."

These standards, framed in the Fifties, have created some problems of late. McDonald's relies heavily on teenage boys for its crews because they are available for part-time work after school or on weekends and because they will work for the minimum wage (keeping labor costs low is one of the keys to McDonald's success). For years McDonald's refused to hire females, particularly teen-age girls, because as Ray Kroc put it, "they attract the wrong kind of boys." But federal legislation forced the company to drop any discrimination by sex. Now the youth culture is slowly forcing it to relax some of its hair and dress codes.

Ray Kroc still insists the company "will not tolerate moustaches, beards, goatees or sideburns below the ear." But at McDonald's stands in several college towns and black communities I noticed that this rule was not infrequently violated. One official explained, "Look, Ray is out of another era on this thing. He just doesn't understand today's young people. And he'd be prepared to go down with the ship on the hair issue. I don't think Fred Turner and some of the others see it that way. They're trying to be a little more 'with it.' "

Fred Turner does try. The onetime grill man of Ray Kroc's first McDonald's is only 38, wears faintly Mod suits with patch pockets and has recently let his hair grow down to graze his collar. He is largely responsible for the new "think tank" at McDonald's Oak Brook headquarters, which boasts as its centerpiece a circular water bed with burgundy suede headrests.

Under Turner's leadership the company has recently put out a brochure telling owners in college towns how to deal with today's youth. "Talk to the students in a direct manner," it says. "They call it 'talking straight.' Don't attempt to imitate what you think is their language and don't 'put them on.' They would say, 'Tell it like it is.' Be aware of local problems, especially campus problems, but avoid taking sides and steer clear of controversial areas. Don't jeopardize your restaurant's position as 'neutral ground.' "

This is often a hard line to tread. The day after the killings at Kent State, students from Southern Illinois University marched into the McDonald's in Carbondale, Illinois, and demanded that the flag flying above the restaurant be lowered to half-staff. The operator complied, but a neighbor who happened to know Ray Kroc called him and complained. Kroc—a superpatriot who insists that McDonald's outlets fly the flag 24 hours a day if possible—called Carbondale and ordered the flag up again. This brought the students back, now threatening to burn the restaurant down unless the flag was lowered. This time the operator called Fred Turner. McDonald's president thought a moment and said, "Tell you what you do. The next delivery truck that arrives, have him back into the flag pole and knock it down." That's just what happened.

But McDonald's new drive for a youthful clientele has its limits. It stops well short of the dreaded "teen-ager." In the Fifties fast-food operations were largely drive-ins catering to teen-agers who wheeled up in their hot rods to ogle the short-skirted carhops, trade gossip and lounge for hours in the parking lot necking or listening to the radio.

From the start McDonald's has sought to discourage the teen-age crowd. The manual states unequivocally, "McDonald's units shall not have jukeboxes, pinball machines, newspaper racks, gambling devices, phone booths, nor shall they dispense cigarettes, candy, gum, etc."—all regarded as attractions for teen-agers.

But even such precautions have not prevented teen-agers from claiming some McDonald's stands as their own. A notorious case was Vero Beach, Florida, where young people, banned by police from a favorite park, virtually took over the

McDonald's every night. In a recent class on "the teen-age problem" at Hamburger University, Professor Doug Moreland distributed a case history of the Vero Beach situation and then warned, "Watch out for teen-agers. They can definitely affect your profit picture by driving away adults. They are extremely noisy and messy. They'll use profanity, and that can never be allowed at any McDonald's. They'll neck on your lot—and you better nip necking right in the bud. Be particularly careful on the night of a sporting event. The losing team always wants to come to McDonald's and prove they're better than the winner. It can be a really terrifying experience if you have three or four hundred people descend on you for a rumble. We've had managers injured, many of them badly, although I don't recall any being killed."

The teen-ager is a particular threat to McDonald's because the company strives so hard for the family trade. Executives like to say that when they pick a new McDonald's site "we count church steeples, not cars." This is hyperbole, of course; McDonald's makes a careful traffic analysis of any prospective site. But it also looks carefully for signs of substantial family life—churches, schools, playgrounds, shopping centers, tree-lined residential streets. One official explains, "You could say our prime target is a family in which the father is twenty-seven, the mother twenty-five, with two children and another on the way, making over ten thousand dollars and living in the suburb of a major city."

McDonald's advertising—a massive campaign that cost $14,500,000 in 1969—is aimed largely at such families. Under Fred Turner the company's ads have become somewhat more sophisticated. Last year it got rid of its old agency, D'Arcy, because—as Turner put it—"they thought every kid in a McDonald's ad had to have freckles and a space between his two incisors."

The new agency—Needham Harper and Steers—has almost completely redesigned the campaign this season. Starting with a recent study, which showed that in three out of four cases children decide where a family will eat out, the agency had devoted much of its energy to an imaginative new series of TV commercials aimed at children and set in a lush fantasy world called "McDonaldland." The central figure is Ronald McDonald, the clown figure who has long been a fixture on TV (the Fourth Annual Ronald McDonald

Awareness Study showed recently that 96 percent of American children can identify him by name, making Ronald a close second to Santa Claus in recognizability). But there is also a whole range of new characters, including Captain Crook (who lives on fillet-of-fish sandwiches), the Goblins (who gobble french fries), the Hamburglar (who steals you know what), Mayor McCheese and Big Mac, the police chief.

Needham has also scrapped McDonald's old slogan, "Your kind of Place," and come up with a new one, "You Deserve a Break." Peter Nelson, the senior account supervisor, says the new slogan is designed to stress "the McDonald's experience" rather than the food. "The message we're trying to get across," he says, "is that going to McDonald's can be a fun experience for an American family. For the housewife it is a minibreak in the day's routine. For dad it is an opportunity to be a hero to the kids, but in a way that won't cost much money. For the children it's just plain fun. For all of them it's a family-oriented thing."

The payoff from mass family-oriented eating can be staggering. A prime example is the McDonald's at 8040 Nicollet Avenue, Bloomington, Minnesota. Last year the unit, which is owned and operated by the company, grossed $1,100,000; it was the first time any unit had gone over one million dollars. Of course, the Bloomington location is ideal. It is less than a mile from the sports complex in which the Minnesota Twins, the Vikings and the North Stars play baseball, football and hockey, and sports fans are proved McDonald's eaters. Moreover, it is just off a major freeway, near several drive-in theaters, two large shopping centers and several major industries.

But, according to Jim Duval, its manager, the bulk of the unit's customers are the young, prolific, relatively affluent families who live in the rapidly growing suburb of Bloomington. "These people are so loyal it's hard to believe," he says. "Look at it this way: We're number one in the country not only averaged over the year but just about every month, including the winter months, when it gets cold as hell up here. Even when it's five below and a foot of snow on the ground, we get families lined up here for food to take back to their cars and eat huddled up over the heaters."

To build loyalty like that, McDonald's outlets throughout

the country spend a lot of time, energy and money showing that they are "part of the community." This is the major theme in McDonald's public-relations campaign. The means—most of them devised by Cooper and Golin—are varied and imaginative. In Saratoga, California, one McDonald's donated free refreshments to women participating in a "Ladies Litter Pick-Up." In Johnson City, Tennessee, Rick Fulton won a free meal at McDonald's when he was selected as a "safe and courteous driver" by the local police. In Brea, California, McDonald's supplied free hamburgers and soft drinks to men fighting a forest fire. In Fort Worth McDonald's donated a free hamburger to each child who put free reflective tape on his bicycle under the "Lite-A-Bike" program sponsored by the Veterans of Foreign Wars. In Frederick, Maryland, Ronald McDonald—or one of several hundred actors and drama students who impersonate him around the country—led the annual Halloween parade.

McDonald's is not beloved in every community. In Braintree, Massachusetts, civic groups protested plans to erect the giant Golden Arches over the restaurant's new location on Pearl Street. Other towns around the country have complained that the arches, towering signs and red-and-white tile are garish and ill suited to their aesthetic standards. In some cases architectural review boards have forced major changes in design. Fred Turner dismisses many of these critics as "a bunch of old ladies who don't know what they're doing." But McDonald's has recently adopted a muted new design and remodeled some of its old outlets accordingly. The new design had a double mansard roof accented by metal beams, plate-glass windows set in a brick facing, a small McDonald's logo on the wall—all in currently fashionable brown, olive and beige tones.

McDonald's has also had its troubles in black communities, reaching a crisis in Cleveland late in 1969, when blacks boycotted four restaurants in their neighborhoods. The boycott grew out of demands by activists for the sale of the restaurants to Negroes. Ultimately the sale was arranged, but only after bitter recriminations and the conviction of two boycott leaders for blackmail. The Cleveland uproar badly shook McDonald's, raising fears of a nationwide black boycott. At the time only five McDonald's franchises were owned by blacks, all of them in Chicago. Since then the company has taken the initiative in arranging sales of white-owned outlets in predominantly black areas to blacks. Today about 50 restaurants are black-owned, and 15 black owners have been approved and are waiting for units. Special financing arrangements have been worked out through the Small Business Administration, reducing the cash requirement for minority-group members to $25,000.

And McDonald's may soon face a new wave of criticism. As the consumer movement continues to burgeon, some activists have begun to examine the fast-food industry from a nutritional standpoint. There is little serious question about the purity of McDonald's meat. New York City's commissioner of consumer affairs, Bess Myerson, says McDonald's came out well during a recent crackdown on excess fat in hamburger. (McDonald's specifications call for a fat content between 16 and 18.9 percent. The specifications also require that the patties be made from only two cuts of beef—chuck and steer short plates—and that there be no hearts, lungs, tripe, cheek or head meat, suet, flavor boosters, preservatives, protein additives, fillers or cereals.)

But how much nourishment do you get from a meal at McDonald's? Jean Mayer, professor of nutrition at Harvard University's School of Public Health, answers this way: "The typical McDonald's meal—hamburgers, french fries and a malted—doesn't give you much nutrition. It's very low in vitamins B and C but very high in saturated fats. It's typical of the diet that raises the cholesterol count and leads to heart disease. Don't make me sound like a fanatic. Once in a while I like to have a meal of hamburgers and french fries myself. But not as a steady diet."

Fred Turner replies that nobody eats McDonald's food as a regular diet. But Professor Mayer recounts what he heard from a dietitian at a veterans' hospital at Martinez, California. "She told me World War One vets are strictly meat-and-potatoes men. World War Two and Korean vets like a more balanced, varied diet—vegetables, fruits and milk. But Vietnam veterans don't eat meals at all. They don't eat breakfast, just pull the blankets up over their heads and go back to sleep. Then, late in the morning, they start getting hungry and begin munching hamburgers, hot dogs, french fries and soft drinks. They'd probably eat every meal at McDonald's if they could."

The same point is borne out in a strange batch of letters piling up in a drawer at McDonald's headquarters. If this mail is to be believed, the young men fighting in Vietnam are not dreaming of home-cooked meals as their predecessors did. What they are dreaming of is well illustrated by this plaintive appeal, which McDonald's unfortunately was not able to satisfy:

"Dear sirs:

"We are the 1st Platoon of Bravo Company, 4th Battalion, 21st Brigade, Americal Division. We are the infantry. They call us grunts, and we hump in the jungles and rice paddies. Eating C rations is no treat, and grunts are always hungry for some good Stateside food. While thumbing through *Look* magazine, we found a picture of a 'Big Mac' hamburger. First Platoon would like to order 50 Big Macs. We know this is a weird request, but we're so awfully hungry for a good hamburger that we do desperate things like this. When we get back to the world, that will be our first act—going to McDonald's for a burger and a shake. If you could fill our request, we would be forever grateful."

22

The Mostly
Late Bloomers

A popular sport among high school and college students is that of assessing each other's potential for future success. Almost every class yearbook ever published contains a nomination of the student deemed "Most Likely to Succeed." The Most Likely student is usually one who has combined academic excellence with a whirl of extracurricular activity. He's the kid who organizes dances, raises funds, gets elected to high posts in the student government. The big man on campus. The busybody. His fellow students don't necessarily like him to any great degree and may even consider him a damned nuisance. He seldom wins the title of Most Popular or Most Sexy or Most anything else. He is simply the student who, at this early age, most visibly exhibits the traits—the go-get-'em drive, the frantic pace—that are felt to lead to success in the adult world.

Somewhere, however, something is wrong. Of all the immoderately successful men we've studied in this gallery, only one—Benton—was clearly a Most Likely type of kid. One or two others—Paulucci, perhaps the Levitt brothers—might have been voted Next Most Likely if the competition wasn't too formidable. The rest were clearly out of the running, and many, indeed, might have claimed the title of Least Likely or even Absolutely Impossible.

It turns out, as a general rule, that highly successful men tend to be late bloomers. The success drive, whatever it may be, may exist in them during their school days but somehow doesn't find expression in the school society. They tend to be quiet kids at best, academic flops at worst. Not until the third decade of their lives—the decade between age 20 and age 30—do most of them begin to show signs of being more than ordinary men. Some even remain semidormant until the fourth decade.

Let's briefly recapitulate the academic achievements and early careers of the men we've studied:

Benton. Most Likely type. Brilliant scholastic record. Graduated from college and progressed evenly, smoothly upward from there. At age 25 held a salaried job; at 30 was running his own company; at 35 had so much money that he was ready to retire.

Stone. Distinctly Unlikely. Undistinguished school record. Didn't get along with teachers. Dropped out of high school. But by age 25 owned a successful small company, and by 30 was a millionaire.

Hirshhorn. School dropout. Millionaire by age 30.

Cornfeld. Graduated from college with a good school record but few other claims to Most Likelihood. Gloomy, social-protesting type. Began career as social worker. Didn't find his stock-market career until his late 20s; began to grow rich in his early 30s.

Hughes. Mediocre academic record. Other kids in school hardly noticed he was there. Had money and leisure to attend college but refused. But by 25 had multiplied his patrimony into the multimillions.

Getty. Graduated from college without unusual distinction. Quiet kid. Thought he wanted to be a diplomat or writer. But drifted into the oil business and by 25 had made his first killings.

Lear. School dropout. Millionaire by age 30.

Land. Studious intellectual but lacked the Most Likely kind of drive. Finished high school but dropped out of college. Millionaire by age 30.

Ludwig. School dropout. Spotty early career. Was broke much of the time until around age 40.

Ling. School dropout and teen-age bum. But had a prosperous small company going by age 25 and was a millionaire by 30.

Hilton. Ordinary, undistinguished school career. Dropped out of college with thoughts of being a small businessman in a small New Mexico town. Only moderately well off at age 30, but a multimillionaire by age 35.

Levitt brothers. Graduated from college without knowing

exactly where they were going. Small-time builders in their 20s; millionaires in their 30s.

Turner. School dropout. Bounced around with discouraging results in his 20s. Hit the big time in his 30s.

Paulucci. Busy kind of kid, junior promoter; succeeded socially and academically in school. Dropped out of college. Made a good income most of his life but didn't approach millionairehood until his late 30s.

Kroc. School dropout. Knocked about for years, a conspicuous failure. Didn't find his career until age 35 and didn't become rich until after 40.

It seems significant that half these fabulously wealthy men are high-school dropouts and fewer than a third bothered to finish college. But significant in what way? What does it mean?

One possibility, which we've poked at before (chapter 5), may be that American schools teach little or nothing that directly prepares kids to become capitalists. Many people seem to think so, at any rate, for after school they seek fortune teachers to give them the missing lessons.

A second possibility may be that the school social environment is wrong for the kind of youngster who will become a capital gatherer. Something in his psyche makes him a misfit; the environment is set up in such a way that he can't succeed in it. Maybe he doesn't like sitting and passively absorbing lessons taught by adults. Maybe he can't get interested in the work because his emotional makeup demands immediate, tangible rewards such as money—rewards that are handed out only in the adult world, not in schools. Maybe he is troubled by the tightly organized school society. He wants to control his own destiny, but other people have been granted the power to tell him where to sit, what to read, when to arrive and depart.

A third possibility is that the capital-accumulating type of mind (if there is such a thing) may simply take longer to mature or turn on or gain oomph than other kinds of minds. Or—what amounts to the same thing—this slow-developing kind of individual for one reason or another tends to be attracted to the capital-gathering idea after he is pushed out into the adult world.

There is some scholarly evidence—though admittedly not

much—to support the observation that the rich are late bloomers. Some years ago a New Jersey school psychologist, Dr. Paul Feldman, attended the tenth-anniversary reunion of his own college class and was saddened to learn two odd facts. The man voted Most Likely to Succeed had mismanaged his affairs so badly in the intervening ten years that he had run out on a large debt, deserted his family and disappeared. The woman voted Most Likely had been divorced twice and had become an alcoholic.

Feldman wasn't observing anything startlingly new. At thousands of other class reunions down through history, before and since, returning wanderers have noted that not every classmate turned out as predicted in the rosy dawn of youth. The typical reaction to such a discovery is to shrug, utter a few philosophical banalities and pour another drink. Feldman, however, decided to pursue the matter a little further. He went through a bundle of back-issue yearbooks from several high schools and colleges, then tracked down the Most Likely students to find out what had actually become of them.

It turned out that the Most Likely were, on average, among the least successful in actual postschool performance. "It is a peculiar fact, often noted," he wrote, "that the most successful adults, at least in terms of our current money-oriented standards of success, are often men and women who, as students, made the least favorable impressions on their classmates. These are the classroom's social misfits, the shy and the awkward, the 'oddballs' and the 'weirdos.' By contrast, those students who shine the most brightly in the school's firmament, the ones who impress their peers as being destined for great success, do not in fact reliably go on to fulfill their apparent promise."

Why not? Dr. Feldman speculated that the Most Likely type may, in effect, burn himself out early, while the oddballs and weirdos and other misfits gather momentum slowly and explode to prominence later in life. Feldman also speculated that the school environment may be so unlike the adult world that it takes entirely different personality types to succeed in each. A personality that succeeds in one environment will not, for that very reason, find it easy to succeed in the other.

Men such as William Benton—absolute conquerors of both environments—are rare. It might even be argued that

Benton doesn't belong in our gallery, for he is not a true capital gatherer. Of all the men we've studied, Benton is the only one who didn't really want to be very, very rich and didn't try to be—and still volubly insists that he isn't. He got rich by accident. On this basis it could be argued that he is no exception to the rule: The great captial collectors don't shine when they're young.

What does all this mean to you and me? Perhaps that we still have much to hope for.

Our lives may not have started off with a bang. We may have shambled through school with so little distinction that, at the next reunion, nobody will remember who the hell we are. The comments beneath our yearbook pictures may reflect more politeness than enthusiasm. We may be humble wage or salary earners, doomed, it might seem, to oblivion.

But no matter. It is possible to bloom at any age. And if great wealth is what we seek, evidently it is better to bloom late than early.

23

Advice from the Rich

It was December 1970. Times were tough. The stock market had just come through one of the worst slumps in its history. The nation was in the grip of a severe and stubborn recession. To many who were without work, it was even worse than that; it was a plain, old-fashioned depression. The golden years of the 1960s were over, and nobody knew how long it would be till we saw the next glint of gold in the distance.

In the midst of all this gloom the editors of the *Chicago Tribune Magazine* sent reporter Richard Gosswiller out into their city's cold and windy streets with an engagingly cheery question. It was a question that assumed the return of golden years at some undetermined time in the future, and no doubt it encouraged some of the *Tribune's* readers to think about those years instead of brooding about the flat, bleak present. Gosswiller's assignment was to seek out some of Chicago's wealthy men and ask each, "If you were a young man today and you had five thousand dollars to invest, what would you do with it?"

Their answers were diverse. Instructive, too, perhaps. Obviously, as we've noted before, it doesn't necessarily follow that a man can teach a thing simply because he has done it. Not all Gosswiller's rich men may be wise counselors. Some of their advice could lead students to bankruptcy or (what may be nearly as bad) the unhappy state of standing still while everybody else is making killings. Still, it's probably safe to assume that rich men's advice on getting rich is better, on average, than advice from the unrich.

The first man Gosswiller talked to was our old friend Clement Stone, who needs no introduction. The others are introduced as they step onstage. Each man began by answering the *Tribune*'s basic question, and Gosswiller then followed up with further questions for clarification.

Here is what nine rich men of Chicago think you should do with your seed capital.

*How to Get Rich on $5000** by Richard Gosswiller

1. Betting on One Stock

W. CLEMENT STONE,
CHAIRMAN OF THE BOARD,
COMBINED INSURANCE COMPANY OF AMERICA

If you know me and my operation, you know what my answer will be. If you want to sleep and grow rich, you'll own Combined Insurance Company shares. When you stop to consider that a $10,000 investment back in, oh, '51, would have a market value of close to ten million dollars today, that's not a bad deal.

Do you mean that if you were a young man with $5000, you'd plunk down all of it into shares of one company?

If I knew about this company's management and about where the company is going, I would. Other companies are showing less gross income right now, wheras we're showing greater gross income, greater profits.

You mean, if you were a young man reading about companies and you came across Combined . . . ?

Boy, I'd jump at it.

You'd jump at it?

Oh, my, yes.

The whole thing?

Absolutely. And I'll tell you why. I'm a salesman, and as a salesman I can make an income. If I were investing now, and that was your question, I would invest in what I feel would be a sure thing, by virtue of experience, by virtue of management, by virtue of where the company is, by virtue of where apparently it's going.

*Reprinted with permission from the December 6, 1970, issue of the *Chicago Tribune Magazine*. Copyright © 1970 by the *Chicago Tribune* and Richard Gosswiller.

Your stock is at 39 or 40 today. . . .

We've just declared a stock dividend. We've been declaring stock distribution every year for many years.

How much has it gone down in the past year and a half?

I would say between 20 and 25 percent. So it's a real buy at this time.

Despite the decrease?

I would say that for the investor—that was the word you used, not *speculator*—even at the 1968 high, it would have been a good buy, because the investor doesn't buy today and sell tomorrow. Stocks go in cycles, and anyone thinking in terms of three or four years will do well. I'm chairman of the Foundation for the Study of Cycles, and I'm buying many shares of various stocks for our company and others.

But you'd plunk the whole amount in one company?

Well, when you stop to consider the number of millionaires in the United States who own Combined Insurance shares and who had very little money back a few years ago. . . . Check with some broker on the history of Combined. I think you'll see the point.

But supposing you had to choose a company other than Combined?

Let me give you a basic concept. One way to make a fortune is to get involved with a company whose product is needed by a large market. [It's not important that the product is actually needed, only that people *feel* they need it.] The product should be expendable and sold at low cost, enabling the company to sell repeatedly to the same customers and in large volume. In addition, the man who runs the company should be dedicated and should have a shareholder's interest in the company's growth.

Can you recommend a company that meets all of those qualifications?

I happen to be on the board of directors of Alberto-Culver. I'm one of the large shareholders there. Thirteen years ago I helped finance the company with $450,000, for which I received 25 percent of the shares. Today those shares are worth something like $25 million.

And you feel Alberto-Culver is still a good buy.

I think it has a great future. But, then again, I'm definitely prejudiced.

2. Controlling a Business

DONALD O'TOOLE, SR.,
PRESIDENT,
FINANCIAL MANAGEMENT ASSOCIATES

While banks are giving advice to individuals, Donald O'Toole is giving advice to banks. O'Toole, a Notre Dame grad, worked in real estate and banking, then began organizing banks himself. Financial Management Associates, his most recent creation, advises small community banks on how to achieve lower costs, higher profits and greater growth.

If I were starting out today, I would get into a business I could see and understand and over which I could have an effective voice. In other words, I'd put my $5000 in a company only on the assurance that I could have an effective voice in company affairs or would be able to get that voice in time.

Wouldn't this be rather difficult for the average young man?

Well, I'm a lifelong executive myself. When I got out of college, I went directly into managing my own real-estate office. It was my father's business, but six months later he had to step out, and from there on in I had to carve out my own destiny. That was in 1931.

How would you go about selecting a business if you didn't inherit one?

It would depend, first of all, on the man's own capabilities —his knowledge, interests and background. Second, it would require investigation. He might have worked part time in the company during school. Or he might select a company, work a year or two for it and get to know it—meanwhile keeping his $5000 dry. Then, when he was assured that both his talents and his money could be used to affect the progress of the company, he could invest.

You feel this is a better solution than, say, playing the market?

General Robert Wood of Sears, Roebuck once told me— and Sears, of course, is well known for its profit sharing— that when employees have everything they own invested in the business, then they can be motivated to use the last ounce of capability when the situation demands it. Sure, you can have a nicely balanced portfolio of U.S. Steel and Standard

Oil and that sort of thing. You've got yourself on safe ground, but you've also anesthetized yourself. You are literally turning your money over to people to spend. You don't have the challenge to perform yourself. I've told even workingmen who have come to ask about investing much the same thing. They'll say, "I think I ought to own some stocks." I ask, "Where do you work?" They say, "I work for Sherwin-Williams." "What do you think of the company?" "It's a fine company." "Then, buy their stock. It will help the company and make you a better employee."

3. The Service Industries

GEORGE DOVENMUEHLE, CHAIRMAN OF THE BOARD, DOVENMUEHLE, INC.

In Chicago, Dovenmuehle money is old money. The firm was founded by three Chicago families in 1844 and has been loaning money to build the city ever since. In the process, the company and the families have taken a profit—to put it mildly.

I'd use the $5000 to enter a business, and the business I'd choose would be a service industry. If I had mechanical skills, repairing automobiles, for example.

You'd buy into a business?

Or start one of my own. In either case it takes a long while before you begin to make money.

And if you were going to merely invest the money?

If I were a young man, I'd probably put it in the stock market, with all its ups and downs, and I would diversify to some extent.

Any particular area?

Service industry is one. But I would also look to those industries that employ comparatively little labor. For example, the gas industry. Gas is a scarce commodity that requires very little labor for its production compared to manufactured products.

The service field requires labor, doesn't it?

Yes, but there are several services that are in great demand and will be in greater demand. The nursing-homes industry, for example. We've made a number of loans on them. Well, if you know anything about that, that can be a bonanza, because more and more of us are going to need them.

Would you care to mention any specific stocks?

Some might be mining stocks. One example is American Metal Climax. They produce all kinds of metals, including aluminum, which is growing in popularity. But, also, they produce oil, copper, gas—all kinds of things and in many parts of the world.

Why do you emphasize the service industries?

The service business is growing much faster than manufactured products. In our affluence, we are buying more and more services.

How far ahead would you plan for in terms of return on your investment?

I'd be shooting for the long pull, but I'd like to see something materialize within five years.

And what should be a fair appreciation of that $5000 after five years?

Well, I'd certainly be disappointed if it didn't double.

You wouldn't invest in one single company that looked good to you?

A young man can even take that risk if he is convinced, whereas an older man can't.

4. Six Blue Chips

JOSEPH BLOCK,
FORMER CHAIRMAN
OF THE BOARD, INLAND STEEL COMPANY

Block joined Inland in 1922 in the sales department and moved resolutely up the corporate ladder. Now he is off the ladder—and on the roof. He remains a director and is chairman of Inland's executive committee. He still keeps an office and regular hours at company headquarters on Monroe Street.

I would buy a diversified list of well-seasoned American corporate stocks and have faith in the future. With $5000 you can't diversify much, but if a young investor bought six well-seasoned American companies with good records, he wouldn't regret it.

How would he select them?

I think he'd have to get advice where he banks or from investment counselors.

Do any specific companies come to mind?

Right off the top of my head I'd say Sears, Roebuck and General Motors.

Would you look for short-term gains?

I'd think of it as a long-term proposition that had to be watched.

5. Cash and Mutual Funds

E. STANLEY ENLUND,
PRESIDENT,
FIRST FEDERAL SAVINGS AND LOAN

Enlund graduated from Schurz High School and the De Paul University College of Law, but he's been with banks or savings and loans ever since, first at Continental and later at Sears Bank. The company he now heads has assets of $778 million.

I think there's always a value in a guy having a cash cushion, and that probably ought to be somewhere in the range of a thousand bucks. We find in our business that some financial liquidity is vital. Then I think he should look at the dynamic business structure of our country in terms of how does he participate in this growing economy that is going to have some inflation, but hopefully controlled inflation, in the coming years. With the remaining $4000 I would strongly urge that he take a hard look at some of the better growth mutual funds that have had good track records, recognizing that this market's had a lot of squeeze on it—it's had a 30-percent wring-out or better. I think with a mutual fund he'd have a balance, and this would be a fine base from which to build a total program as his career potential develops.

Didn't the growth funds suffer badly in the recent slide?

They took an awful ramming, it's true. They're off just a shade under 30 percent on the average. Some performed better than others, however. And that's something you have to recognize. A fellow might need some help in terms of selection, but there are a solid group of well-managed mutuals operated by men of experience—and that's really what you're doing, hitchhiking on their ability and their judgment.

All we're doing with this money, really, is building the foundation.

How does a fellow choose between the several mutual funds that look attractive?

In my own case I've been developing an educational fund. I've got a little guy—well, he's not so little anymore; he's 14. I've been buying T. Rowe Price for him for years. Well, this has performed real well, except, with all mutuals, it did suffer from the slugging of the market. I'm involved a little bit with Allstate; so I know that performance pattern. I think if he's looking for counsel, then he might go to his local financial institution—either the bank or savings and loan.

Will banks and savings and loans give investment advice?

If a guy comes in here, we obviously can't give him basic recommendations, but we can give him suggestions as to responsible and ethical brokerage houses that can counsel him. And we probably wouldn't recommend just one; we'd recommend three or four.

The other alternative is no-load mutuals, where no broker is involved. What about those?

T. Rowe Price is a no-load. There you go around the mulberry bush. You've got to compare the two. When I look at them, I look at the performance pattern—the bottom line—but I also assess the capability of management. Because when you go into mutuals, you're buying two things— a spread on your risk because you're going to be an investor in a group of securities but, equally important, you're looking for expertise and capability in the group that's doing the investing.

How does one determine which managements are most capable?

By performance. *Investment Companies,* a book published annually by Wiesenberger Financial Services, evaluates mutual funds over a period of time. This is one of the values a guy gets out of making the selection of the fund, as opposed to picking a half-dozen small companies.

What value?

If he's doing the research, he begins to find out that every fund doesn't perform the same way. One fund will be buying and one will be selling. What he's going to learn is that the marketplace isn't a controlled environment, but that it reflects the judgment of investors large and small. This research will broaden his knowledge in terms of how the whole system functions. And he's going to be a part of it.

You think he'll learn more by studying mutual funds than individual firms?

Well, we could develop a brief on both sides. I think, though, with the size of the amount he'd have to spend—$4000—he couldn't get the kind of mix he should have. So I'd be inclined to go to mutual funds. If he had $50,000, he could spread it himself.

What would you expect to accrue from that mutual-fund investment, say, in five years?

Well, if you go into mutual fund, you're not looking for current income. And under SEC regulations they have to define their investment objective. Some funds are geared to a specific income and growth of 10 to 15 percent a year. Now, if I were a young man, I'd be looking for a fund that would be prospering 10, 20, 30 years from now.

But you describe this investment as the foundation?

Yes, but that doesn't mean I'd distribute it. I'd have other income and at some point along the way would become an investor on an individual basis.

6. Real Estate: Buildings

ARTHUR W. RUBLOFF,
PRESIDENT,
ARTHUR W. RUBLOFF AND COMPANY

> *Rubloff has been in real estate since he came to Chicago from Minnesota in 1919. He pioneered Chicago's Magnificent Mile and Sandburg Village projects, then went on to develop Bayshore Properties in San Francisco and to create the Grand Bahama Port Authority in the British West Indies.*

If I had $5000 and I were a young man, I'd go out and buy a small building of some kind, preferably a residential piece of property such as a two-flat or a three-flat or a brownstone or whatever, that I could buy for, say, $15,000 with $5000 down and the balance over a period of time.

An old building or a new building?

An old building. You couldn't very well touch a new building. But I'd buy it in a promising neighborhood, like the Near North Side of Chicago or the Northwest Side.

Aren't old buildings risky?

Well, of course, there's a risk in everything; there's a risk in walking down the street. But if you look at it from a practical point of view, you have to have a little expertise, and it takes great courage and imagination, too. It's easier said than done, but it's been done on countless occasions. I've read countless stories about how young fellows get started in buying a two-flat or a brownstone for a little money against a mortgage and putting it in condition and renting it and building up the income, then selling it and making a small profit, then taking that with his original investment and buying another piece of property.

Can you find that kind of property for $15,000?

Oh, yes. It depends on the neighborhood and the seller and a lot of factors. I don't mean that it's easy to go out in the market and buy $15,000 of good property for $5000 down, but it's done. You have to work at it. I know one man in particular, a junior executive with one of the major insurance companies. He's a man of limited means, but he's bought four little properties on the Near North Side, all on his own initiative. He didn't ask anyone; he didn't seek any advice. And he's doing well with them. He collects his own rent. They're converted properties.

You said a "promising" neighborhood. Does that mean a decent neighborhood?

Not necessarily. The neighborhood may or may not be so decent. I'm talking about a neighborhood where you have real-estate activity, where there's a demand for living quarters. Of course, there's a tremendous demand for older apartments today, anyway. I never saw the demand for older apartments that exists today.

More so than new apartments?

More so by far, because people need larger areas and they can't afford to pay the rents of new buildings because of the high costs of money and construction, and so they have no alternative if they want a roof over their heads. So they take an older apartment and make some of the repairs themselves. You take the North Avenue and Sedgwick area. You can pick up small flat buildings for $15,000 to $20,000, and the guy that wants to sell might take $5000 down. There's a tremendous demand for that kind of space.

And that's the way you'd do it if you were starting now?

That's the way I started. I didn't know any more about the real-estate business than my grandmother. I got a small interest directly in a piece of property, and I pyramided that, and I put the capital into something else. And as I went along, I had several pieces of property, and then I had many more pieces of property over the years.

What could a person using your formula expect to realize in, say, ten years?

It depends, of course, entirely on the leverage [money borrowed]. If you bought a piece of property for $15,000 with $5000 down, you'd have a mortgage of $10,000. Say that the money and amortization cost you 12 percent—that's a lot. That's $1200 a year. And maybe your operating costs would be $300, for a total of $1500 a year. Suppose rents amounted to $200 a month, or $2400 a year. You'd have a profit of $900, and $900 represents almost a 20-percent profit on an investment of $5000. Well, it doesn't take too long on that kind of profit, and with residential property you can take accelerated depreciation—so that your $900 might come back mostly tax-free. Of course, there are some other problems today, because they've changed the tax laws. Now, if you sell the property before ten years have elapsed, you have to give back the depreciation. But, even so, it isn't bad.

And then you reinvest the profits in other properties?

With time and a little patience and ingenuity, you can do it. And as you get more property, you get a little bank credit. And if you get bank credit, you move in on something that's a little larger. And if you get money at 9 and 10 percent and you can make 12, 14 or 15 percent, then you're making profit on your money, aren't you? The point is that the bank will look at the man as a part of the security, at what kind of a person he is. And banks are willing to take some risks on small people. If you talk to investment bankers, they'll tell you how good it is to buy 8½-percent bonds or buy the market. I don't know anything about that. I know I've lost my money in the market, but I didn't lose it in real estate.

7. Real Estate: Land

GEORGE HARRIS,
PRESIDENT,
METROPOLITAN MUTUAL ASSURANCE COMPANY

Harris grew up in Chicago, working first for the city, then taking an interest in real estate. During the Twenties and Thirties he specialized in vacant-land acquisition, financing, planning new construction and mortgage counseling. In 1940 he became president and general manager of the Parkway Amusement Corporation. He joined Metropolitan in 1956. Harris served as president of the National Association of Real Estate Brokers from 1953 to 1959.

If I had some special talent or interest in a specific business, I'd go into business. If not, I'd buy land in a developing area. With $5000 there's very little you could buy in improved property; so I'd look for land on the periphery of the city. I might even be able to make a down payment on a tract of land.

You mean an acre or two?

Maybe more. The owner might be willing to sell on contract.

How would you determine which land to buy?

Simply by looking over areas and by following real-estate ads in the newspapers. I'd also keep an eye open for future developments, such as new highways or changes in highway locations.

So you'd prefer that method to, say, the stock market?

Well, it would depend on the person, of course. Land investment is long-range, but if I were a young man, I could afford to wait for its value to rise. On the other hand, if I wanted immediate return on my investment, I wouldn't go into the stock market. I would buy bonds or debentures, which are now paying in the area of nine percent.

But don't such bonds lock you in?

You can't redeem them for five years, but every year you're going to get that nine percent. So a man with $5000 could buy five $1000 bonds and would get $450 a year for his investment. This could go on for quite a long time. Some bonds being issued now mature in the year 2000 or 2010.

And that nine percent is guaranteed until that time.

Where do you buy such bonds?

Any of the bonding houses [listed under Bonds—Special Investment in the Yellow Pages]. They publish ads in the newspapers all the time listing new issues coming out. Consolidated Edison, for example, is just putting out a new issue of bonds that will pay from 9¼ to 9½ percent. If I wanted immediate return on my money, I'd buy them.

8. Plunging in Commodities

LEO MELAMED,
CHAIRMAN OF THE BOARD,
CHICAGO MERCANTILE EXCHANGE

Melamed graduated from the John Marshall Law School in 1955 but began trading in commodity futures "with a very little money" while still in school. Now he's the principal partner in a law firm, partner in an investment company and is serving his second term as chairman on the Chicago Mercantile Exchange. The exchange is a marketplace for the buying and selling of future contracts in pork bellies (uncured bacon), live cattle, hogs, potatoes, eggs, turkeys, lumber and hams.

First a person has to determine in his mind whether he's looking for security by way of an income. But $5000 is so small and insignificant a figure to start building a base on that it almost rules out any kind of investment that would give you income security—either via bonds or stock market or anything like that.

Supposing, instead, he's looking for quicker results?

Even then, let's face it, $5000 is not a dramatically big figure to start with. But, certainly, commodities could produce some good results. However, I would immediately hasten to advise the young man—or whoever—that before he takes a dive into commodities, he should very carefully research the subject, do some self-educating on it, talk to some people in the industry and find himself a reliable brokerage firm. After he's done that and after he realizes that his venture into the commodities may lose him the $5000, after he's done all that and he's willing to take the risk, then I would say, certainly, commodities can offer the opportunity for a very good return.

What kind of a return?

A person can look forward over a year, if he's done very well, to making 50 to 100 percent on his money.

That's very well, indeed.

Well, let's say in a year or two. Please understand, this is a very, very difficult area. You just can't go blind into it, merely relying on somebody's opinion. If he wants to be involved in what he's doing, he should consider commodities. If he wants to invest $5000 into something where he can just forget about it and be sure that it's going to make him some money in years to come, that's not commodities. In commodities you're involved, you have to keep abreast of trends, you have to be interested. You just can't invest in commodities and turn around and let your broker worry about it. It isn't good enough. The successful people in commodities worry about it themselves and pay attention and learn as they go along. And they do well.

All of them?

They *can* do well. Naturally, there is a multitude that don't do well. It doesn't turn merely on paying attention, obviously. If that were the only criterion, then everybody would pay attention. It requires an ability to analyze and learn statistics and to discuss it with a broker. Naturally, he's going to rely heavily on a broker's advice, but in order to understand the broker's advice, he has to first educate himself.

How would he begin this education?

There are a number of good books and pamphlets on commodity trading that would give him a base. The exchanges themselves offer much information that's free—historical facts about what commodities do, seasonal trends, and so forth. After he has the basic education, then he should get in touch with a reputable broker.

Are some commodities better than others for the neophyte to begin with?

There are various guidelines he'll learn, and one is to begin with a commodity that isn't too volatile. Something like cattle or a grain that rises and falls, but not dynamically overnight. Trading in pork bellies or eggs, let's say, which are affected by various factors daily should be done only after the trader has some experience—though it should be an objective. Pork bellies is the number-one trader at this time. Another rule would be not to go into too many commodities at one time, even if he were successful. You've got to pay attention, as I said before. And you can't pay attention to all of them at one time. One or two markets are sufficient at the start. He'll have to do that, and he'll have to learn how to cut his loss when he's wrong and to admit an error so that he can fight again.

He's got to learn when to sell.

Yes, as quickly as possible he must accept his loss. In the area of commodities that is perhaps the most salient rule of all. Learn to take your loss quickly; profit will come. Chance dictates that you'll be right some of the time. The question is, how much will you lose when you're wrong versus how much will you make when you're right? And you've got to learn to limit your losses. But you said something about "when to sell." That's human nature. We always think of buying first and selling later. In commodities that isn't necessarily the case, because they travel in both directions and it's not like stock. You can invest in a sale first. The short side of commodities is potentially as good as the long side. The public is hard pressed to learn that.

It's a hard concept to understand—selling something you don't have.

It's a promise, so to speak. But, nonetheless, it's got to be part of the good commodity trader's repertoire. And for that reason good stock firms have done well with commodities, because even in these hard times in the stock market, profits from commodities have continued pretty good. Good brokers have learned that there are two sides to the commodity market, and they've learned to tell their customers.

Isn't trading in commodities really just gambling?

The rules of gambling and the rules of chance and probabilities do not apply to commodities, and people who think that are not going to make money in it. It's not gambling. It's supply and demand and economics.

9. Savings and . . .

PHILIP M. KLUTZNICK,
CHAIRMAN OF THE BOARD,
URBAN INVESTMENT AND DEVELOPMENT COMPANY

Klutznick is best known as the developer of Park Forest and three of the Chicago area's major shopping

*centers, Old Orchard, Oakbrook Center and River Oaks.
He served as U.S. representative to the Economic and
Social Council of the United Nations under President
Kennedy and as a member of several delegations to the
General Assembly of the UN. Recently his company an-
nounced with Sears and Marshall Field and Company
a quarter-billion-dollar community to be developed in
Lake County. Urban Investment will also build a $60-
million complex on North Michigan Avenue.*

What kind of person are you talking about? Is he married?
Does he have children? Is his education completed?

Let's assume you were beginning your career.

If I were beginning my career again as a professional man
and I had $5000 and a young family, I'd put it in either a
savings account or a savings-and-loan association, or I'd buy
something that is extremely secure, such as a U.S. government bond or municipal bond. If I were going into business,
I'd invest it in my business. I would not gamble with $5000
if I were beginning my career. I would learn the habit of
saving.

*Supposing you were single and didn't have quite all those
responsibilities?*

The first thing I would do with the first money that I had,
if I were young and starting, is to save it and not gamble with
it. I'd gamble only when I'd accumulated enough that I could
afford to gamble by buying equities and common stocks. I'm
a conservative man.

How much would "enough" be?

Enough to carry myself if I lost my job.

After the $5000 doubled, for example?

After it doubled or tripled, depending upon what the dollar was worth at the time.

How many years would it be before you began investing?

Depends on how much money I was making. I think the
most important habit that a young man starting out must learn
is to save, and, having saved to the point where he has a
measure of transient security, then he should invest in the
equities of this country, which I consider to be great. I'm
sorry, but that is the way I would live my life.

And is that what you did?

No. When I was in college in 1929, I invested in the stock
market.

24

Fortune Makers of the Future

Business, like horse betting, is largely a game of predictions. You bet money or time or work, or all three, on some outcome that you hope or believe will occur in the future.

Most businessmen would argue tearfully that business is less of a gamble than horse betting. They would be right, of course. Once you've placed your bet at a racetrack, you are a totally helpless victim of the events that follow. You have no control over the outcome. In business, having placed your bet, you retain a degree of control over the future events that will cause you to win or lose. But you don't have complete control, and if your predictions are too far wrong, you lose no matter what you do.

No matter how smart an operator a man might have been, if he had predicted early in the 1900s that automobiles were a passing fad and if he had then sunk his money into the buggy-whip business, he would have lost. In more recent times some very clever businessmen predicted in 1950 that nuclear energy would be a big civilian business by 1970. They lost.

Thus, prediction is undeniably a key part of the game. If you harbor a dream of getting very, very rich sometime in the decades ahead, one thing you absolutely must do is look into the future and arrive at some estimate of that future's shape. Where and how will the next big fortunes be made?

You can be certain that thousands of other men right now are attempting to make a forecast. Some will be wrong. Some will be right and, it must surely follow, rich.

Let's look briefly at some of the long-range forecasts that are now being made. There is, of course, no guarantee that they are correct. What can be said, however, is that they represent the thinking of organizations and men who enjoy a respectable reputation for having been right in the past.

One such organization is the National Industrial Conference Board, which periodically makes detailed studies of current trends and projects them into the future—with great accuracy thus far. Another is the Economic Unit of *U.S. News and World Report*, a magazine that doesn't seem to mind climbing out on a limb. (In the late 1950s *U.S. News* looked ahead to the next decade, the 1960s, and predicted that air and water pollution would become a major national concern. This forecast sounded crazy in the self-satisfied 1950s, when only a few college professors knew what the word *ecology* meant.)

On the basis of predictions made by such future gazers as these, we can look ahead and guess that the great rich of the coming decades may make their fortunes out of situations like these:

Empty places. Most forecasters expect the U.S. population will increase by roughly ten percent during the 1970s, to about 225 or 230 million by 1980. The forecasters also believe, optimistically, that all these people will be richer than they are now. The average American household is expected to enjoy a 30- to 40-percent increase in real income during this decade and perhaps another 40 percent during the 1980s.

Where will they all live and work? Anybody who answers this question correctly today and who has enough faith in his forecast to act on it (see chapter 13, on the trick of not listening to scoffers) stands to become one of the very, very rich.

Today's cities and city-suburb complexes appear to be facing obsolescence. They don't work well anymore. It is a fairly safe bet that new kinds of metropolitan centers will be developed sometime between now and the year 2000. Real-estate giants such as William Levitt (chapter 17) are talking about going out into the vast, empty wilderness areas that still exist in this country and building whole new citylike complexes from the ground up.

It is wholly conceivable that some men are going to grow ridiculously rich by buying land for $50 an acre in empty areas of New Mexico, Kansas and Vermont, then selling it for thousands of dollars an acre when some new population center springs up nearby. Others may make it by being the

organizers of, or stockholders in, companies that play a role
in the pulling apart of old cities and the building of new ones.

Dark-horse countries. A little over 20 years ago Japan
and Germany were so nearly dead as economic entities that
their financial pulses could barely be heard at all. While
they lay gasping in bed with their tongues lolling out, some
fabulous fools invested in them—bought their real estate, their
industrial stocks. Those fools have since multiplied their
money by factors of 1000 and more.

There are undoubtedly similar dark-horse countries in the
world today. As of now, in the 1970s, these countries seem
unlikely to get very far economically in our lifetimes. Only
fools are investing in them. The fools are picking up stocks
and real estate and other properties at bargain prices. Maybe
they will live to see their money disappear down the drain.
On the other hand. . . .

South Africa is an interesting country from this point of
view. So are some northern African nations. So is Australia—
vast, empty, developed only around the coastal fringes. South
America contains a number of huge, potentially rich countries such as Brazil and Argentina. Sometime between now
and 2000, one or more of these sleeping giants will probably
wake up and go.

The "third industrial revolution." As *U.S. News* sees it,
there have been two distinct industrial revolutions so far:
the first arising from the development of steam power, the
second from electrical energy. The third, which the magazine's economists believe will be recognizably here by 1980,
will arise from a massive and sweeping application of electronics and nuclear energy dwarfing anything we've seen
so far.

Nuclear energy will come into general use when the nation
runs out of other forms of energy. People have been making
grandiose nuclear-energy predictions for 20 years, and so far
the predictions haven't come true except in a very limited
sense. But the error seems to have been in timing, not in
basic fact. If the country's population and its use of energy
continue to grow as projected, a time is bound to come
eventually when we've got to turn to the atom as a source of
power on a big scale. There's no other power source left.

Electronics will be needed in the clerical and information-
juggling work of keeping this huge, staggeringly complicated

society glued together. The society's structure is already starting to fall apart in many places. There aren't enough clerks in Wall Street, for instance, to keep the stock market running smoothly anymore. The U.S. postal system is being crushed under the weight of increasing loads of mail. The nation's telephone system is badly overloaded. The daily flow of checks in and out of banks is already so enormous that another few percentage points of increase could bring the whole system down in a ghastly collapse. In these areas and hundreds more, electronic data processing seems to offer man his only hope of not drowning in his own seething sea of paper.

Somebody will make money out of both nuclear energy and information systems. Exactly how that money will be made, or when, is by no means clear. But the time for placing bets seems to be drawing near.

Transportation. It has been obvious for some time now that older means of transportation, perfectly satisfactory 20 years ago, are becoming less and less useful as the population grows and society changes. Fortunes will be made by men who solve the world's transport problems—and, at second hand, by men who invest in those solutions, whatever they turn out to be.

The conventional automobile is now reaching the point of being killed by its own outrageous success. There are too many cars on the roads, creating too much air pollution. Air travel is up against similar congestion. Many city airports are overcrowded. Attempts to build badly needed new airports always meet opposition from residents of surrounding areas, and the proposed new airports are seldom ideal solutions, anyway, because the land is either too costly or too far from the city being served.

Radically new approaches may be necessary—and this is where a lot of money will quite probably be made in years ahead. The U.S. Department of Transportation believes some answers may lie in high-speed trains running between neighboring cities and from suburbs to downtown areas. Hundred-mile-an-hour trains or other fast, convenient innovations in mass transit would not only reduce the numbers of cars on the roads but would also cut down the need for shorthaul air traffic. Thus the long-depressed railroad industry might spring to new life by 1980 or 1990. Whole new transportation industries may be born.

New kinds of nonpolluting automobiles may also be scuttling along the roads by then. Inventors such as Bill Lear (chapter 11) are tinkering with electric engines, turbines, steam power and other means of propulsion for private vehicles. So far no system has been developed that clearly beats the dirty old gasoline engine's three-way combination of high power, low operating cost and all-around convenience. But Lear and others think such a system may be only a few steps away.

It is pleasant to dream of being a stockholder in the company that gets there first.

Food technology and the oceans. Like nuclear energy, ocean farming has been talked of as a business of the future for many years. The future has always turned out to be farther away than the crystal balls seemed to indicate, and it hasn't arrived yet. But an ocean-based business boom seems almost bound to occur sooner or later.

With ever more people trying to live off the produce of ever fewer arable land acres, land-grown foods will almost certainly grow more costly as this century progresses. The more costly these foods grow, the larger and hungrier will grow the potential market for ocean foods. The first companies and men who find a way to exploit that market will sail away rich.

The U.S. Agriculture Department and companies such as General Foods have been experimenting with ocean farming for years: fenced-in fish pastures, plots of cultivated sea vegetables. But one large problem has always frustrated the seafaring farmers—the human palate. For reasons that aren't at all clear, mankind in general tends to shy away from fish whenever meat is available. In every nation where there is an open choice, people prefer beef to mackerel. And the preference is even more stark when it comes to vegetable products. Several common sea plants are perfectly edible and highly nutritious—but, no matter how delicately they're seasoned, they still taste like wet newspaper.

This frustrates the sea farmers, for the ocean offers enormous promise in terms of yield per acre—and, as a corollary, profit per acre. It may take a promoter like Jeno Paulucci to sell new ocean foods on a large scale. It may take an intuitive flavoring genius like Ray Kroc, who made a fish sandwich palatable with a surprising slice of cheese.

One way or another, somebody will someday start to pump money out of the oceans.

It's great fun to speculate about future businesses such as these, and it's fun to dream of getting aboard on the ground floor just before the elevator starts to rise. But listen. Don't ever forget old Clement Stone. He invented no dazzling new industry. He began his long climb in a business that had existed for centuries. The only predictions he made were that it would continue to exist and that he would grow in it. He can claim very little in the way of innovation. He didn't change the shape of the industry very much. Working within a framework that other men had engineered long before, he made his fortune mainly by applying the force of his own tough, aggressive, optimistic personality.

Innovation isn't a necessary prerequisite for becoming very, very rich. Nor is it necessary to make far-out predictions. You don't have to be Edwin Land. There are probably hundreds of businesses in existence today in which men whose names we don't yet know—men not yet born, perhaps—will grow monumentally wealthy.

Accurate crystal gazing helps a man grow rich, but it isn't the whole story. The main parts of the story are tangled up in the man's own character.

If our visit to this golden gallery has taught us any lessons, the most important one is surely this: Character is the king-pin of self-made wealth. To get rich, you need a pinch of prediction and a dash of luck and perhaps little bits of many other things. But the one thing you need in great quantity is internal strength.

In a word: guts.

Bibliography and Supplemental Reading

Most of this book's chapters are based on firsthand rather than published sources—that is, on interviews with the man whose life and thoughts are being discussed or on interviews with his business associates, friends, enemies and others who have drifted in and out of his life. However, the editor and the authors of the various chapters are indebted to many published sources for general background information and for shadings of opinion.

For the reader who may want to pursue his studies of wealth further than this book has been able to take him, the sources and supplemental reading suggestions are listed below by chapter.

CHAPTERS 1 AND 2. GENERAL AND HISTORICAL BACKGROUND

Alsop, Stewart. "America's New Big Rich." *Saturday Evening Post,* July 17, 1965.

Brooks, John. *Once in Golconda.* New York: Harper & Row, 1969.

Holbrook, Stewart. *The Age of the Moguls.* Garden City, N.Y.: Doubleday & Co., 1953.

Hoyt, Edwin P., Jr. *The House of Morgan.* New York: Dodd, Mead & Co., 1966.

Kirstein, George. *The Rich, Are They Different?* Boston: Houghton, Mifflin & Co., 1968.

Lamott, Kenneth. *The Moneymakers.* Boston: Little, Brown & Co., 1969.

Louis, Arthur. "America's Centimillionaires." *Fortune,* May 1968.

Lundberg, Ferdinand. *The Rich and the Super-Rich.* New York: Lyle Stuart, 1968.

Myers, Gustavus. *The Ending of Hereditary American Fortunes*. New York: Julian Messner, 1939.

Rees, Goronwy. *The Multimillionaires*. New York: Macmillan, 1961.

Schafer, R. C. *How Millionaires Made Their Fortunes and How You Can Make Yours*. New York: Pyramid Books, 1970.

Tebbel, John. *The Inheritors*. New York: G. P. Putnam's Sons, 1962.

Thomas, Dana. *The Plungers and the Peacocks*. New York: G. P. Putnam's Sons, 1967.

Wall Street Journal, eds. *The New Millionaires and How They Made Their Fortunes*. New York: Bernard Geis Associates, 1960.

3. BENTON

Benton, William. "Young Man, Be Your Own Boss." *Reader's Digest*, May 1957.

Commonweal. "No Doom, No Gloom." February 28, 1958.

Forbes. "The Marvelous Encyclopedia Business." February 15, 1965.

Hoyt, Edwin P., Jr. *The Supersalesmen*. New York: World Publishing Co., 1962.

Hyman, Sidney. *The Lives of William Benton*. Chicago: Chicago University Press, 1969.

New Republic. "Benton Versus McCarthy." September 17, 1951.

Time. "Busy Man." October 8, 1951.

———. "Benton v. Bowles." March 17, 1958.

4. STONE

Barron's National Business and Financial Weekly. "Combined Insurance Co.: A Formula for Growth." January, 18, 1971.

Braden, William. "My Ambitions Are Very Humble . . ." *Chicago Sun-Times*, January 19, 1969.

Business Administration. "A Millionaire in Your Mirror." March 1970.

Business Week. "How to Grow Wealthy with Positive Thought." July 13, 1968.

Cole, Robert. " 'Think, Act,' He Says—He Must Be Right."

New York Times, May 2, 1971.

Garino, David. "It's All Mental." *Wall Street Journal,* February 27, 1969.

Model, Peter. "W. Clement Stone: Social Capitalist." *Finance,* April 1971.

Nation's Business. "How to Motivate Yourself and Others." July 1968.

Stone, W. Clement. *The Success System That Never Fails.* Englewood Cliffs, N.J.: Prentice-Hall, 1962.

5. FORTUNE SCHOOLING

Burger, Chester. *Suvival in the Executive Jungle.* New York: Collier Books, 1964.

Carnegie, Dale. *How to Win Friends and Influence People.* New York: Simon & Schuster, 1947.

Fortune, eds. *The Executive Life.* Garden City, N.Y.: Doubleday & Co., 1956.

Hill, Napoleon, and Stone, W. Clement. *Success Through a Positive Mental Attitude.* Englewood Cliffs, N.J.: Prentice-Hall, 1960.

Mayes, Herbert. *Alger.* New York: Banner Press, 1928.

Meyer, Paul. *How to Become Financially Independent.* Waco, Tex.: Success Motivation Institute, 1970.

New York Tribune. Horatio Alger obituary. July 19, 1899.

Peale, Norman Vincent. *The Power of Positive Thinking.* Englewood Cliffs, N.J.: Prentice-Hall, 1948.

Strohschein, Carol. "The New Breed: Paul J. Meyer." *Texas Business & Industry,* November 1969.

Wright, Louis. "Franklin's Legacy to the Gilded Age." *Virginia Quarterly Review,* Spring 1946.

6. HIRSHHORN

Business Week. "Making an Industry in the North." January 7, 1956.

Jacobs, J. "Collector." *Art in America,* July 1969.

Time. "Big Spender." July 25, 1955.

———. "Billion-Dollar Empire." August 1, 1955.

7. CORNFELD

Ball, R. "The Salesman Who Believed Himself." *Fortune,*

September 1970.

Business Week. "Lavish Hand with Too Little Control." May 16, 1970.

Cowan, Edward. "IOS Dissidents." *New York Times,* July 1, 1971.

Forbes. "Croesus, American Style." September 15, 1967.

Hodgson, Godfrey; Page, Bruce; and Raw, Charles. *Do You Sincerely Want to Be Rich?* New York: Viking Press, 1971.

Mayer, M. "Bernie Cornfeld's First Billion." *Fortune,* March 1968.

Newsweek. "Crisis for Cornfeld." May 18, 1970.

Time. "Midas of Mutual Funds." January 12, 1970.

———. "Comedown for Cornfeld." May 4, 1970.

8. HUGHES

Business Week. "Duel of Aces in Las Vegas." July 12, 1969.

———. "Howard Hughes Meets Tight Money." December 12, 1970.

Demaris, O. "You and I Are Very Different from Howard Hughes." *Esquire,* March 1969.

Fortune. "Invisible Hand of Howard Hughes." November 1968.

Gerber, Albert. *The Bashful Billionaire.* New York: Lyle Stuart, 1967.

Keats, John. *Howard Hughes.* New York: Random House, 1966.

Newsweek. "Case of the Invisible Billionaire." December 21, 1970.

Time. "Money at Work." July 12, 1968.

———. "Shootout at the Hughes Corral." December 21, 1970.

9. GETTY

Getty, J. Paul. *How to Be Rich.* Chicago: Playboy Press, 1965.

———. "Milestones of Success." *Playboy,* August 1965.

———. "Business Is Business." *Playboy,* June 1967.

Hewins, Ralph. *The Richest American.* New York: Dutton, 1960.

10. LUCK

Carr, A. H. Z. *How to Attract Good Luck*. New York: Simon & Schuster, 1952.

Gardner, Martin. "It's More Probable Than You Think." *Reader's Digest*, November 1967.

Getty, J. Paul. "Wall Street Is Not Monte Carlo." *Playboy*, December 1961.

Klein, Frederick. "Ph.D. of the Turf." *Wall Street Journal*, January 31, 1968.

Knebel, Fletcher. "Las Vegas." *Look*, December 27, 1966.

Kobler, John. "ESP." *Saturday Evening Post*, June 28, 1968.

Machirella, Henry. "Bank Steno Hits 250-G Jackpot." *New York Daily News*, March 29, 1968.

Mazza, Frank. "Lottery's Big Little Winner Bucks Odds Third Time." *New York Daily News*, May 22, 1968.

11. LEAR

Business Week. "Lear Trades Steam for Gas Turbine." November 22, 1969.

Garrison, P. "King Lear." *Flying*, February 1970.

Newsweek. "Lear Steams Back." September 21, 1970.

Wells, D. "Lear's Steam Dream." *Motor Trend*, June 1969.

12. LAND

Bigart, H. "Men Who Made the World Move." *Saturday Review*, April 22, 1967.

Business Week. "Black and White Issue Faces Polaroid." November 14, 1970.

Forbes. "Polaroid." June 15, 1969.

14. LUDWIG

Business Week. "Tanker King Who Shuns the Crown." March 16, 1957.

Life. "Mighty Shipping Magnates." December 21, 1962.

Newsweek. "On the Crest of the Seas." October 14, 1957.

Saunders, Dero. "The Wide Oceans of D. K. Ludwig." *Fortune*, May 1957.

Time. "New Argonauts." August 6, 1956.

————. "Twilight of a Tycoon." November 30, 1970.

15. LING

Altwegg, Al. "A Falcon Under Fire." *Dallas Morning News,* March 30, 1969.

Brown, Stanley. "Jimmy Ling's Wonderful Growth Machine." *Fortune,* January 1967.

Dallas Times Herald. "Man of the Year." January 5, 1969.

Forbes. "Jim Ling's Instant Conglomerate." November 1, 1967.

Gould, Susan. "Man on the Move." *Signature,* March 1968.

Metalworking News. "Daylight at the End of the Tunnel?" April 20, 1970.

Newsweek. "Ling the Merger King." October 9, 1967.

Time. "The Conglomerates' War to Reshape Industry." March 7, 1969.

Weiner, Sam. "How to Turn a $3,000 Stake into Millions." *Houston Post,* February 12, 1961.

16. HILTON

Bigart, H. "Men Who Made the World Move." *Saturday Review,* April 22, 1967.

Dabney, Thomas E. *The Man Who Bought the Waldorf.* New York: Duell, Sloan & Pearce, 1950.

Time. "Widening Father's Footsteps." August 29, 1969.

17. LEVITT

Business Week. "Levitt's Secret Is Change." July 29, 1967.

———. "Housing Enters the Era of the Superbuilder." December 26, 1970.

Fortune. "Levitt's Progress." October 1952.

Langewiesche, W. "Bill Levitt, Big Answer Man." *Reader's Digest,* March 1968.

Nation's Business. "Revolutionizing an Industry." February 1967.

Newsweek. "Where Are They Now?" October 6, 1969.

Time. "Profits v. Shortage." July 26, 1954.

———. "After the Levittowns." May 19, 1967.

18. PSYCHOLOGY

Alexander, Franz. *Our Age of Unreason.* Philadelphia: Lippincott, 1942.

Allen, Vernon, ed. *Psychological Factors in Poverty.* Chicago: University of Chicago Press, 1970.

Bergler, Edmund. *Money and Emotional Conflicts.* Garden City, N.Y.: Doubleday, 1951.

Cuber, John F., and Harroff, P. B. *The Significant Americans: A Study of Sexual Behavior Among the Affluent.* New York: Appleton-Century-Crofts, 1965.

Fenichel, Otto. "The Drive to Amass Wealth." *Psychoanalytic Quarterly,* vol. 7, 1938.

McClelland, David. *Studies in Motivation.* New York: Appleton-Century-Crofts, 1955.

Rosen, Bernard. "The Psychosocial Origins of Achievement Motivation." *Sociometry,* September 1959.

Sorokin, Pitirim. "American Millionaires and Multimillionaires: A Comparative Statistical Study." *Journal of Social Forces,* May 1925.

Wyllie, Irving. *The Self-made Man in America.* New York: Free Press, 1954.

20. PAULUCCI

Nation's Business. "Dynamic Growth Companies." March 1970.

Paulucci, Jeno. *How It Was to Make $100,000,000 in a Hurry.* New York: Grosset & Dunlap, 1969.

21. KROC

Business Week. "McDonald's Makes Franchising Sizzle." June 15, 1968.

Forbes. "Mirror, Mirror on the Wall." November 1, 1970.

Nation's Business. "Appealing to a Mass Market." July 1968.

24. FORECASTING

Bright, J. R. "Evaluating Signals of Technological Change." *Harvard Business Review,* January 1970.

Business Week. "1970's: Bumpy Decade with a Social Sense." December 6, 1969.

Mechanics Illustrated. "A Look into the 1970's." January 1970.

Monthly Labor Review. "The U.S. Economy in 1980."

April 1970.

Science News. "Toward the Year 2000." September 19, 1970.

Seaborg, G. "Our Nuclear Future." *Bulletin of the Atomic Scientists,* June 1970.

Time. "The Sizzling '70s." May 23, 1969.

U.S. News & World Report. "The Spectacular '70s." June 23, 1969.

―――. "Official Preview of the U.S. in 1980." April 27, 1970.

MAX GUNTHER, born in England, came to the United States when he was 11 years old, attended schools in New Jersey and received his B.A. from Princeton University in 1949. He served in the U.S. Army in 1950 and 1951 and was a staff member of *Business Week* from 1951 to 1955. Mr. Gunther then served as a contributing editor of *Time* for two years. Since 1956 he has published articles in several magazines, including PLAYBOY. Among his other books are *The Split-Level Trap* and *Wall Street and Witchcraft*.

Mr. Gunther lives in Ridgefield, Connecticut, where his wife is a real-estate broker. They have three children. The author says that his diversions include surfing and skating, carving chess sets and playing chess, and painting.

PLAYBOY PRESS PAPERBACKS BUSINESS BOOKS

ONE OF THE FINEST, MOST AUTHORITATIVE SELECTIONS OF BUSINESS BOOKS AVAILABLE ANYWHERE

_____ 16501 **CONFESSIONS OF A WALL STREET INSIDER**   **$1.95**
C. C. Hazard
What really goes on in the brokerage houses.

_____ 16452 **THE FUNNY MONEY GAME**   **$1.95**
Andrew Tobias
The inside story of the explosive rise and fall of a $100-million conglomerate.

_____ 16488 **GUIDEPOSTS FOR EFFECTIVE SALESMANSHIP**   **$1.95**
Robert R. Blake & Jane S. Mouton
The widely acclaimed grid approach to achieve sales excellence.

_____ 16617 **HOW TO BE A SUCCESSFUL EXECUTIVE**   **$2.25**
J. Paul Getty
Twelve articles full of "must" reading for young men and women on the way up—by one of the world's richest men.

_____ 16613 **HOW TO BE RICH**   **$2.25**
J. Paul Getty
The biggest businessman of them all gives away the formulas for his fabulous success in business, real estate, the stock market and fine art.

_____ 16614 **HOW TO MAKE MEETINGS WORK**   **$2.50**
Michael Doyle and David Straus
An explanation of the new Interaction Method that's already worked for more than 10,000 people in such businesses as IBM, Xerox and Bank of America.

___ 16615 **HOW TO SELL YOUR HOUSE**
FOR MORE THAN IT'S WORTH $1.95
Jerry Pennington and Fred G. Schultz
Authoritative, comprehensive, easy-to-read, step-by-step
advice from a vice-president of the largest home-building
company in the U.S.

___ 16616 **MASTERY OF MANAGEMENT** $2.25
Auren Uris
How to avoid obsolescence by preparing for tomorrow's
management today.

___ 16647 **100 SUREFIRE BUSINESSES YOU CAN**
START WITH LITTLE OR NO INVESTMENT $2.25
Jeffrey Feinman
A guide to starting your own business. Tells how to enter
each field and succeed.

___ 16645 **THE VERY, VERY RICH AND HOW THEY**
GOT THAT WAY $2.50
Max Gunther
Success stories of 15 men who made it to the top.

___ 16465 **YOU CAN STILL MAKE IT IN THE STOCK MARKET** $1.95
Nicolas Darvas
A breakthrough system for charting the stock market by
the author of *How I Made $2,000,000 in the Stock Market*.

PLAYBOY PRESS PAPERBACKS, Dept. SCS
747 Third Avenue, New York, New York 10017

NAME _____

ADDRESS _____

CITY _____ STATE _____ ZIP _____

Please enclose 50¢ for postage and handling if one book is ordered;
75¢ if two to five are ordered. If six or more are ordered, postage is
free. No cash, CODs or stamps. Send check or money order.
Total amount enclosed: $ _____

THE BEST
PAPERBACK BAR GUIDE
AVAILABLE

PLAYBOY'S
BAR GUIDE
BY THOMAS MARIO

A perennial best seller, _Playboy's Bar Guide_ is the authority on every kind of drink from aperitifs to after-dinner concoctions. Complete with more than 700 recipes for the most exciting potations, _Playboy's Bar Guide_ is a perfect party companion for every festive occasion.

16449 $1.95

PLAYBOY PRESS PAPERBACKS, Dept. SCS
747 Third Avenue, New York, New York 10017

NAME _____

ADDRESS _____

CITY _____ STATE _____ ZIP _____

Please enclose 50¢ for postage and handling if one book is ordered; 75¢ if two to five are ordered. If six or more are ordered, postage is free. No cash, CODs or stamps. Send check or money order.
Total amount enclosed: $ _____